Teaching the New English

Published in association with the English Subject Centre
Director: **Ben Knights**

Teaching the New English is an innovative series concerned with the teaching of the English degree in universities in the UK and elsewhere. The series addresses new and developing areas of the curriculum as well as more traditional areas that are reforming in new contexts. Although the series is grounded in intellectual and theoretical concepts of the curriculum, it is concerned with the practicalities of classroom teaching. The volumes will be invaluable for new and more experienced teachers alike.

Titles include:

Charles Butler (*editor*)
TEACHING CHILDREN'S FICTION

Michael Hanrahan and Deborah L. Madsen (*editors*)
TEACHING, TECHNOLOGY, TEXTUALITY
Approaches to New Media

Anna Powell and Andrew Smith (*editors*)
TEACHING THE GOTHIC

Forthcoming titles:

Gail Ashton and Louise Sylvester (*editors*)
TEACHING CHAUCER IN THE CLASSROOM

Lisa Hopkins and Andrew Hiscock (*editors*)
TEACHING SHAKESPEARE AND EARLY MODERN DRAMATISTS

Gina Wisker (*editor*)
TEACHING AFRICAN-AMERICAN WOMEN'S WRITING

Teaching the New English
Series Standing Order ISBN 1-4039-4441-5 Hardback 1-4039-4442-3 Paperback
(*outside North America only*)

You can receive future titles in this series as they are published by placing a standing order. Please contact your bookseller or, in case of difficulty, write to us at the address below with your name and address, the title of the series and the ISBN quoted above.

Customer Services Department, Macmillan Distribution Ltd, Houndmills, Basingstoke, Hampshire RG21 6XS, England

---

Also by Charles Butler

FOUR BRITISH FANTASISTS: Place and Culture in the Children's Fantasies of Penelope Lively, Alan Garner, Diana Wynne Jones, and Susan Cooper

Teaching Children's Fiction

Edited by

Charles Butler
Senior Lecturer, University of the West of England, Bristol

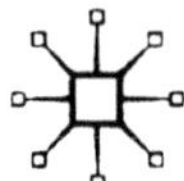

First published in 2006 by
PALGRAVE MACMILLAN
Houndmills, Basingstoke, Hampshire RG21 6XS and
175 Fifth Avenue, New York, N.Y. 10010
Companies and representatives throughout the world.

PALGRAVE MACMILLAN is the global academic imprint of the Palgrave Macmillan division of St. Martin's Press, LLC and of Palgrave Macmillan Ltd. Macmillan® is a registered trademark in the United States, United Kingdom and other countries. Palgrave is a registered trademark in the European Union and other countries.

ISBN-13: 978–1–4039–4494–8 hardback

ISBN-13: 978–1–4039–4495–5 paperback

This book is printed on paper suitable for recycling and made from fully managed and sustained forest sources.

A catalogue record for this book is available from the British Library.

Library of Congress Cataloging-in-Publication Data

Teaching children's fiction / edited by Charles Butler.
p. cm. – (Teaching the new English)
Includes bibliographical references and index.
ISBN 1–4039–4494–6 (cloth) – ISBN 1–4039–4495–4 (pbk.)
1. Children's literature – Study and teaching (Higher) 2. Children's stories – Study and teaching (Higher) I. Butler, Charles, 1963– II. Series.

PN1008.8.T43 2006
809′.892820711—dc22 2005055280

10 9 8 7 6 5 4 3 2 1
15 14 13 12 11 10 09 08 07 06

Transferred to Digital Printing in 2011

For my daughter, Charlotte

Contents

List of Figures

All figures are taken from Anthony Browne's *The Tunnel* (London: Julia MacRae, 1989).

Acknowledgements

Thanks are due to Anthony Browne for permission to reproduce pages from *The Tunnel*.

Series Preface

One of many exciting achievements of the early years of the English Subject Centre was the agreement with Palgrave Macmillan to initiate the series "Teaching the New English." The intention of the then Director, Professor Philip Martin, was to create a series of short and accessible books which would take widely-taught curriculum fields (or, as in the case of learning technologies, approaches to the whole curriculum) and articulate the connections between scholarly knowledge and the demands of teaching.

Since its inception, "English" has been committed to what we know by the portmanteau phrase "learning and teaching." Yet, by and large, university teachers of English—in Britain at all events—find it hard to make their tacit pedagogic knowledge conscious, or to raise it to a level where it might be critiqued, shared, or developed. In the experience of the English Subject Centre, colleagues find it relatively easy to talk about curriculum and resources, but far harder to talk about the success or failure of seminars, how to vary forms of assessment, or to make imaginative use of Virtual Learning Environments. Too often this reticence means falling back on received assumptions about student learning, about teaching, or about forms of assessment. At the same time, colleagues are often suspicious of the insights and methods arising from generic educational research. The challenge for the English group of disciplines is therefore to articulate ways in which our own subject knowledge and ways of talking might themselves refresh debates about pedagogy. The implicit invitation of this series to take fields of knowledge and survey them through a pedagogic lens. Research and scholarship, and teaching and learning are part of the same process, not two separate domains.

"Teachers," people used to say, "are born not made." There may, after all, be some tenuous truth in this: there may be generosities of spirit (or, alternatively, drives for didactic control) laid down in earliest childhood. But why should we assume that even "born" teachers (or novelists, or nurses, or veterinary surgeons) do not need to learn the skills of their trade? Amateurishness about teaching has far more to do with university claims to status, than with evidence about how people learn. There is a craft to shaping and promoting learning. This series of books is dedicated to the development of the craft of teaching within English Studies.

Ben Knights
Teaching the New English *Series Editor*
Director, English Subject Centre
Higher Education Academy

The English Subject Centre

Founded in 2000, the English Subject Centre (which is based at Royal Holloway, University of London) is part of the subject network of the Higher Education Academy. Its purpose is to develop learning and teaching across the English disciplines in UK Higher Education. To this end it engages in research and publication (web and print), hosts events and conferences, sponsors projects, and engages in day-to-day dialogue with its subject communities.

http://www.english.heacademy.ac.uk

Notes on the Contributors

Charles Butler is Senior Lecturer in English at the University of the West of England, Bristol, where he specializes in children's and Renaissance literature. He is also the author of five children's novels, the latest of which is *Death of a Ghost* (2006). His monograph, *Four British Fantasists: Place and Culture in the Children's Fantasies of Penelope Lively, Alan Garner, Diana Wynne Jones, and Susan Cooper*, is due to be published in 2006.

Professor Judith Elkin is Vice-Principal of University College Worcester. She has published widely in the fields of library and information studies, specializing in the study of literacy and reader development. Her books include *Reading and Reader Development: the Pleasures of Reading* (2003), written with Briony Train and Debbie Denham. Among her many activities she is a member of the Herefordshire Learning Partnership Strategic Board, and the British Council Knowledge and Information Advisory Committee, and chair of MLA West Midlands: the Council of Museums, Libraries, and Archives.

Richard Flynn is Professor of Literature at Georgia Southern University in Statesboro, Georgia, and the editor of the *Children's Literature Association Quarterly*. He is presently working on the Norton Critical Edition of *The Wizard of Oz*.

Roderick McGillis is a Professor of English at the University of Calgary. In 2004, he was the first Scholar in Residence at Hollins University, Virginia. His novel, *Les Pieds Devant*, was published in 2005.

Maria Nikolajeva is Professor of Comparative Literature at Stockholm University, Sweden, and Associate Professor of Comparative Literature at Åbo Akademi University, Finland. Her books include *Children's Literature Comes of Age: Toward a New Aesthetic* (1996), *How Picturebooks Work* (with Carole Scott, 2001), *The Rhetoric of Character in Children's Literature* (2002), and *The Aesthetic Approach to Children's Literature* (2005). Professor Nikolajeva is a former President of the International Research Society for Children's Literature (IRSCL), a member of the International Committee of the Children's Literature Association, and a coordinator of the Nordic Network for Children's Literature Research. Amongst her numerous awards is the International Brothers Grimm Award 2005 from the Osaka Institute for Children's Literature, given for a life-time's achievement in children's literature research.

Pat Pinsent, for many years a Principal Lecturer in the English Department, is currently a Senior Research Fellow at the University of

Roehampton. She has been responsible for the production of Distance Learning materials for the MA in Children's Literature and has a tutorial responsibility for a number of Ph.D. and MA students. Her books include *The Power of the Page: Children's Books and Their Readers* (1993) and *Children's Literature and the Politics of Equality* (1997), together with a number of edited compilations of conference proceedings. She has also written numerous articles on both children's literature and her other main research interest, seventeenth-century poetry. Her main current interest is in the relationship between children's literature and spirituality/ religion. She edits the journal of the British Section of the International Board on Books for Young People, *IBBYLink*, and also edits a journal devoted to feminist spirituality and theology.

Kimberley Reynolds is Professor of Children's Literature at the University of Newcastle in the UK, where she runs undergraduate and postgraduate programmes in Children's Literature. She has published widely on aspects of children's literature, and works nationally to develop children's literature in British culture. She was elected IRSCL President in 2003 and 2005. Recent publications include *Children's Literature Global and Local: Social and Aesthetic Perspectives* (co-editor with Emer O'Sullivan and Rolf Romoren, 2005); *Modern Children's Literature: An Introduction* (editor, 2004); *Children's Literature and Childhood in Performance* (editor, 2003); *Childhood Remembered* (editor, 2003, first published 1997); *Frightening Fiction* (with Geraldine Brennan and Kevin McCarron, 2001).

David Rudd teaches Children's Literature in the Department of Cultural and Creative Studies at the University of Bolton, England. He has published some eighty articles on the subject and two books: one on Roald Dahl, *A Communication Studies Approach to Children's Literature* (1992) and one on Enid Blyton, *Enid Blyton and the Mystery of Children's Literature* (2000) though both are more widely concerned with how adults deal with children's literature. Most recently he has written a chapter about "The Conditions of Possibility of Children's Literature" for the new *International Companion Encyclopedia of Children's Literature* (ed. Peter Hunt, 2004), and articles on Peter Pan and E. Nesbit.

Professor Jean Webb is Director of the International Centre for Research in Primary English and Children's Literature at University College Worcester. Amongst other publications she has edited *Text, Culture and National Identity in Children's Literature* (2000); contributed to Roderick McGillis (ed.) *Voices of the Other* (2000); with Dr Debby Thacker written *Introducing Children's Literature: Romanticism to Postmodernism* (2002) and is editor of *The Sunny Side of Darkness: Children's Literature in Totalitarian and Post-Totalitarian Eastern Europe* (2005). She was the founding Chair of the British Association for Lecturers in Children's Literature, and a founding executive member of the NorChilNet Nordic network for postgraduate and postdoctoral training programmes in children's Literature.

Introduction

Charles Butler

The last decade has seen an unprecedented growth in the attention given to children's literature, both within the academy and beyond it. Following from such spectacular individual successes as those of Philip Pullman and J. K. Rowling, children's books in general have assumed an increasingly high profile, topping best-seller lists and contending for major literary prizes from which they would not long ago have been excluded by definition. This shift in cultural attitudes towards children's literature is a phenomenon that has attracted attention in itself, highlighting the dual readership of children's literature, and the different motives, perspectives, and values that adult and child readers may bring to it. For these and other reasons, the status of children's literature as an academic field has been dramatically enhanced, with a growing number of scholars, books, journals, conferences, and research centres being devoted to the subject. It is now a vigorous and diverse area taught throughout the English-speaking world at undergraduate, postgraduate, and doctoral level, in English departments and in centres for the study of childhood, besides its longstanding role as a component of degrees in Education, Library, and Information Studies.

The differing aims and origins of these programmes, and the complex definition of their subject matter, mean that the teaching of children's literature within Higher Education today draws on many disciplines. The familiar approaches available from literary criticism and theory have been supplemented by others derived from cultural studies, childhood studies, developmental psychology, visual design, and educational and literacy theory. This multiple heritage is one of the subject's strengths. Children's literature, long considered a marginal area of English studies, can rightly claim to be a paradigmatic example of the profession's new commitment to context and interdisciplinarity. Moreover, many considerations that have only relatively recently come to prominence within the wider academy (the reception of texts; ideology and censorship; the ethics of writing; the problematic relationship between critics and readers; the status of books as commodities and cultural artefacts) have been fundamental to the study of children's literature from the beginning.

To study children's literature today is thus to be involved in an exciting and rapidly-changing area, in which no one set of texts or critical approaches has achieved clear dominance and which is, to a greater extent than most areas of English studies, "up for grabs." Like all revolutions, however, this one has the potential to be chaotic. In a stock-taking article in 2000 Susan Gannon asked a telling series of questions:

> Is "Children's Literature" a discipline? Does it have a distinctive methodology? An accepted theoretical framework? A body of systematically classified knowledge? A recognized course of study? Is its relationship to other disciplines clear to everyone? Do its exponents agree on an approach to "their" subject? (Gannon 2000, 26)

Even when applied to English studies as a whole most of these broad questions would probably have to be answered negatively, but the case of children's literature is especially acute: partly because of its multidisciplinary inheritance; partly because its canons are less fixed than those of older and traditionally more culturally-prestigious literary forms; partly because terms such as "child" and "childhood" are themselves notoriously resistant to definition; and partly because the formal range of texts that comes within the remit of "children's literature" is so wide. It is hard to imagine a single critical methodology that could be equally satisfactorily applied to short (possibly textless) picture books, to series about boarding-school life in the 1920s, and to sophisticated, theologically-provocative fantasies, for example. Gannon herself opts for a language that discards altogether the quasi-geographical metaphor of a staked-out piece of "territory," preferring to follow Margaret Meek and Richard Flynn in conceiving of the discipline as "a network of related scholarly, pedagogical, and practical studies, all equal in status, their immediate importance depending on their usefulness in answering whatever question needs to be addressed at a particular point" (Gannon 2000, 38).

Whether this flexible and pragmatic approach is sustainable, or will be understood in retrospect as an evolutionary stage in the development of a more distinctive and clearly-defined set of tools for the study of children's literature, remains to be seen. In the meantime, the pedagogical implications of this diversity of critical practice, as of the multidisciplinary background of the subject, are a potential source of confusion for both teachers and their students. Teachers coming from one or other of the field's contributary disciplines may find the aims, methodologies, and bodies of knowledge assumed by their colleagues unfamiliar and opaque; the opportunity to make innovative and fruitful connections may be lost; and the design and delivery of courses may lack direction and intellectual coherence. Here again, the situation of children's literature can be seen as an extreme version of that facing English Studies as a whole, a fact that makes its representation within the *Teaching the New English* series particularly appropriate.

The aims of this volume are threefold: first, to provide an account of some of the intellectual and educational traditions within which children's literature has been studied and taught, and to give some historical context for the current state of the discipline; second, to discuss and disseminate ideas for developing teaching practice; and third, to provide a convenient point of access to resources and information that will be useful to existing and prospective teachers of children's literature within Higher Education.

The essays in this book are written by a group of experienced teachers and scholars. Each focuses on a different aspect of children's literature studies, and blends expository information with a consideration of practical classroom applications. In her chapter on "Historical Studies," Pat Pinsent provides an overview of the development of historical studies of children's literature in the early days of the discipline, and their role in winning it academic respectability. Drawing on her experience at Roehampton University she advises as to the practical considerations involved in setting up and running a course in the history of children's literature, taking into account such problems as the limited availability of historical texts.

David Rudd's chapter on "Cultural Studies" introduces a suite of ideas and methodologies that has assumed increasing importance within English studies as a whole, but nowhere more so than in the field of children's literature, with its commitment to consider the wider field of cultural meaning within which the production, consumption, and interpretation of texts take place. Rudd draws a map of the ways in which the cultural studies approach—or rather, approaches—have transformed our understanding of children's books by treating them as subject to the same forces as other cultural objects, rather than as privileged denizens of a sequestered literary realm subject to different rules.

Jean Webb, in her discussion of "Genre and Convention," draws on some of the historical concerns addressed by Pinsent and places them in part of that wider cultural context. Children's literature does not have, or is only now in the process of acquiring, a canon. Webb considers the pressures that militate towards the construction of a canon, not least from within the academy, where a recognized body of canonical works has traditionally been seen as a *sine qua non* for serious study. One of the necessary elements of such a consideration is the question of genre. How do genres evolve within children's literature? How can we describe the relationship between the genres used in children's and adult fiction? What is the role of genre in shaping the practices of readers and writers? What kind of awareness of generic conventions and constraints can we expect from an inexperienced (though not necessarily unsophisticated) child readership?

Questions of self-awareness are central to Roderick McGillis's essay "Looking in the Mirror: Pedagogy, Theory, and Children's Literature." In explaining the ways in which concepts drawn from literary theory may be introduced into pedagogic practice, McGillis emphasizes their utility as a means of causing students and other readers to be reflective about their own readings, methods, and assumptions, and problematizing such apparently-simple concepts as "reading" and "childhood."

In "Word and Picture" Maria Nikolajeva, like McGillis, develops her theoretical and pedagogic ideas by way of a detailed exemplary discussion, in her case of Anthony Browne's picturebook *The Tunnel*. Nikolajeva suggests ways in which to overcome the common initial assumption of students that picturebooks are too "simple" to warrant serious discussion. She draws attention to the multiple interactions of text and picture, to the book's status as a physical artefact, and to questions of sequence, omission, perspective, ellipsis, and focalization. More generally, Nikolajeva argues for the development of a critical vocabulary specific to picturebooks as a genre, rather than one that simply borrows existing terms from literary and visual criticism.

Finally, Judith Elkin's essay on "Children as Readers" considers the experience of children and the value of reading for childhood development. In order to approach the subject of what children's reading is and does, Elkin draws on many different sources, ranging from adult reminiscence to empirical observation, and the accumulated experience of educators and librarians in dealing with child readers professionally. She then turns to the question of how children's literature might be effectively taught to undergraduates in the light of the insights gained from such an exercise.

As I hope will have become clear from the description above, these essays are written from many different points of view, not always easily compatible. There are radical differences in terminology and approach between, say, the essays of McGillis and Elkin; and rather than artificially disguise or smooth them over I would wish these to be left visible. Children's literature criticism is, in Francis Bacon's phase, "knowledge broken"—a discipline undergoing such a rapid process of development, and drawing its ideas and methods from so many disparate fields, that a fairly wide range of approaches is not only inevitable but even (I would argue) desirable. Also desirable, however, is that these points of view, though far from respresenting the unanimity of a new orthodoxy, engage in fruitful conversation with each other. The discussions that comprise the bulk of this book are not intended to be either presciptive or mutually exclusive, but we hope they will provide fertile ground for thought, discussion, and the development of exciting and innovative teaching.

These central essays are supplemented by chapters on the particular issues associated with the teaching of children's literature at postgraduate level in the United Kingdom (contributed by Pat Pinsent and Kimberley Reynolds) and the United States (contributed by Richard Flynn), and by a set of resources, contained in the Appendices, which are intended to be of use to those planning syllabi and individual classes, as well as to children's literature scholars at large.

Work Cited

Gannon, Susan. 2000. "Children's Literature Studies in a New Century," *Signal* 91 (January): 25–40.

1 Historical Studies

Pat Pinsent

The history of children's literature resembles its theory, in that it is being reshaped before it has been properly researched.

(Hunt 2001a, 10)

Historical studies of children's literature as an academic discipline

It was by no means self-evident to the dignatories of the nineteenth-century universities that the study of modern literature was a worthwhile intellectual pursuit. The evolution of historical studies of English literature as such took some time to be "rescued" from gentleman-amateurs who presented lists of books and writers they enjoyed to a somewhat dilettante audience.[1] Even when scholarly histories of English literature began to appear, there was little place in them for books aimed at a child audience, apart from their inevitable mention of the trio of books with implied adult audiences which had subsequently become significant in the development of children's literature: Bunyan's *Pilgrim's Progress*, Swift's *Gulliver's Travels*, and Defoe's *Robinson Crusoe*. It is unsurprising therefore that the study of the history of children's literature as such should be a discipline still more recent in its evolution.

It is impossible to disentangle the undergraduate and postgraduate study of the history of children's literature from on the one hand the scholarly sources which provide secondary texts for students, and on the other, the provision of accessible primary texts. In this chapter I propose therefore to look at both the history and the historiography of children's literature and the interplay between these and the more recent development of academic studies of this history.

The story of the writing of the history of children's books, much later than that of "adult" English literature, has, like it, been fraught with vicissitudes and the need to establish its respectability. The title and the register of Roger Lancelyn Green's *Tellers of Tales* betray how he envisaged his task and his audience. His introduction begins:

> We are all collectors in one way or another: some of us collect stamps, others birds' eggs, and others again cigarette cards; but at some time all of us have surely collected books. And among all the "crazes" in which we have delighted from time to time, what can be more fascinating and enthralling than that for a "favourite author"? (Green 1946, 7)

It is tempting to deconstruct this in terms of its white male middle-class assumptions, but even apart from these, it reveals much about how he, as a prominent children's author of the period, saw the development of children's literature. Green's "collection," ranging from Catherine Sinclair to Beatrix Potter, is not a "history" as such, but there had at that date been relatively few attempts at the history of the genre. His approach affords an effective contrast with that implied by the opening words of the much more recent *Cambridge Guide to Children's Books in English*, edited by Victor Watson, who describes the book as:

> a reference work providing a critical and appreciative overview of children's books written in English across the world. It gives due weight to the history of children's books from pre-Norman times as well as acknowledging recent and current developments in publishing practices and in children's own reading. (Watson 2001, vi)

Perceptions of the history of children's literature, as can be deduced from my epigraph, are far from being univocal, so perhaps it is scarcely surprising that its historiography should also be somewhat clouded. This situation, in both instances, results from problems of definition. It is notoriously difficult to define children's literature. As Hunt notes:

> The definition of children's literature is an immensely complex and variable one, and generally rests upon authorial intention (however deduced), or the reader implied in the text (however deduced), rather than a factual examination of which books were or are marketed for, adopted by, or imposed upon children. (Hunt 2001b, xvi)

In effect, the issue comes down to the questions: What is a child, what is literature, and what is history? Much of the dissent about what children's literature is, and when it is held to have begun, arises from different answers to these questions, and while it is impossible to provide definitive answers to them, they surely need to be addressed as an essential preliminary to discussing the evolution of the history of children's literature.

The history of literature for children is inextricably bound up with the history of childhood, and the attitude taken towards the young. John Rowe Townsend begins his much-reprinted *Written for Children* with the words:

> Before there could be children's books, there had to be children—children, that is, who were accepted as beings with their own particular needs and interests, not merely as miniature men and women. (Townsend 1976, 17)

Townsend appears to be implicitly drawing on the contested claim of Philippe Ariès (Ariès 1962) that it was not until the evolution of the relatively modern idea of the family that childhood could be recognized as a state, and that the consequence of this situation was that only then could such a thing as a special literature *for* children be formulated.[2] Another landmark in the writing of the history of childhood is the publication of Peter Coveney's *The Image of Childhood* (first published in 1957 as *Poor Monkey*, and revised in 1966, with an Introduction by the influential critic F. R. Leavis). Although his book is not directly concerned with children's literature, Coveney's "study of childhood as it has been presented in literature written for adults in . . . the nineteenth and early twentieth centuries" (Coveney 1967, 11) has had the effect of foregrounding the depiction of childhood and making it a respectable academic pursuit.

A further, related, question appertains to the blurred boundary line between childhood and adulthood, a line somewhat dependent on period and class—in the nineteenth century the children of the middle classes could be described, as often in for instance the work of L. T. Meade, as "little girls," at an age when their working-class counterparts would be seen as young adults as they entered into positions as domestic servants. Thus books addressing the latter group might well appear on an "adult" list while "children" were the audience of those addressing the former.[3] The phenomenon of the family reading of books, such as the Victorian classics, which have a universal address, also complicates the issue; subsequently many such books, notably Dickens' *Oliver Twist* and George Eliot's *Silas Marner*, also figured significantly on school literature curricula, thus making it difficult to determine whether or not they should be seen as part of the "corpus" of children's literature. While such books generally find no place in histories of children's fiction, understandably given their authors' prominence in adult histories, to ignore their existence is to falsify the understanding of what was familiar to young people during the nineteenth century, and indeed later. More recently, the increasing use of the term "young adult" for books which address more mature young people creates further debate. Even though it did not exist at the time when texts under discussion were published, it certainly now applies to some of their subject matter.

What is literature?

Much of the debate about the origins of children's literature, and hence its history, relates to the question of whether "literature" is confined to what appears in the form of a book. That children were part of the audience for oral narrative is apparent from the words of Sir Philip Sidney when he claimed that the poet (in which category he includes the story-teller) "cometh to you with a tale which holdeth children from play and old men from the chimney corner" (Sidney 1966, 40). But should the material enjoyed by this mixed audience be termed literature? There were also many non-literary texts around from the sixteenth to the nineteenth century, such as the broadsheet ballads, which attracted child readers as much as adults. Other functional material certainly directed towards children, from the poems instructing them about good manners to the alphabet books and the rhymed versions of the Bible that they were expected to learn, also defies categorization.

An indication of ambivalence towards such material is to be found in F. J. Harvey Darton's history of children's literature, which starts fairly dogmatically with the claim that

> Children's books did not stand out by themselves as a clear but subordinate branch of English literature until the middle of the eighteenth century . . . commencement took place in 1744, when John Newbery . . . published his first children's book. (Darton 1932, 1)

Despite his conviction about dating, Darton goes on to devote chapters to the Fables and Romances of the Middle Ages, to rhymes from peddlars' packs, to the edifying tracts of the Puritans, and to the legacy of fairy tale and nursery rhyme, before he at last catches up with his original date, nearly half-way through the book in chapter VIII. A more recent historian of material for children, Nicholas Orme, Professor of History at Exeter University, has a different understanding of the term "literature" and has consequently located the beginnings of the genre as early as the seventh century (Orme 1998).

As well as the question of whether or not texts are written, children's literature by its nature has become involved in the question of whether "popular" material is worth academic study. This has applied not only to ephemeral publications such as magazines and comics, but also to well-known authors. In an article in *Children's Literature in Education,* Peter Hunt describes the experience of writing at the same time a book on Kenneth Grahame and an article on Enid Blyton. On the former he found any amount of secondary material, but on the latter, relatively little, because as he says ironically: "Grahame is a Classic: Blyton merely popular trash" (Hunt 1995b, 232).[4]

What is history?

A further question relevant to the historiography of children's literature is that of determining whether its history comprises for instance the early single volume all-embracing studies or allows for the wide range of more specialist studies which have succeeded them. While the history of children's literature has not perhaps yet arrived at a stage kindred to that of the Oxford, Pelican and Sphere histories of English Literature, which recognize that few academics have the expertise to write about the many centuries involved, there is by now a realization that different kinds of specialisms are needed by those exploring gender aspects, or sociological trends related to publishing, or illustration, or culture, or the interplay between literature, religion, and philosophy.

Initially the period regarded as "historical" as far as children's literature was concerned tended to be largely nineteenth century, with brief reference to earlier texts such as Sarah Fielding's *The Governess* (1749) and Thomas Day's *Sandford and Merton* (1783–9), but recent research has led to the extension of this further into the past. The realization too that the twentieth century is now an historical period is particularly acute in relation to children's literature because children have no personal memories of the past of more than a few years.

In a chapter entitled "Matters of History," Peter Hunt raises a number of issues relevant to this debate. He suggests that "there is much to be gained by an historicist approach (broadly, placing books in a complex context and trying to understand what they meant in that context)" (Hunt 2001a, 9). I would suggest that those histories of children's literature which remain the most relevant today have in most instances arisen, albeit often intuitively rather than intentionally, out of such an approach.

Histories of children's literature

Before any discipline can be studied within higher education, there is an acute need for respectable texts: primary sources which are both available and relatively inexpensive (a subject which I shall look at later) and secondary writings ranging from critical and theoretical material to reference books. There is an almost inevitable symbiosis between the research of academics writing about aspects of a subject, and undergraduate study of the same area.

The acknowledged pioneer in writing the scholarly history of children's literature was F. J. Harvey Darton, whose *Children's* Books *in England* (1932) bears the revealing subtitle *Five Centuries of Social Life*. Darton's work had been preceded by Mrs E. M. Field's *The Child and his Book: Some Account of the History and Progress of Children's Literature in England* (1892), which was published by his own firm, but her work, as Darton indicates, "has no sustained argument . . . and virtually stops short with the accession of Victoria" (Darton 1932, v). Field's study is by no means negligible however, and involved her in research "at the British Museum, Bodleian, and South Kensington Libraries" (Field 1892, vi). It is however frequently speculative, as when she conjectures that in the early days the child's "first teacher was probably the Druid" (Field 1892, 10); ultimately the book has sunk into oblivion as better-informed works have replaced it.

In an Introduction to the second edition of Darton's history, Kathleen Lines observes that it was initially slow to sell, but eventually "found its way into libraries, schools, and training schools for librarians" (Darton 1958, x) before it fell out of print in 1945. The second edition made few textual changes, but added a brief supplement on books about children's literature published between 1932 and 1958. The consequence of Darton's monumental work was that for some time, relatively few other writers recognized a need to enter on to the same territory. When they did, not only was his work an essential source for them, but they also felt that they needed a different kind of approach to justify their exploration of the area.

The first sentence of Percy Muir's history provides ample evidence of this situation: "Some temerity is needed to embark on a history of English children's books because F. J. H. Darton covered the ground so adequately . . . I have leaned heavily on Darton throughout" (Muir 1954,

15). Muir goes on, however, to make clear his own predisposition towards a different emphasis, one very relevant to the early development of the study of the history of children's literature: the collection of early books, reflected in his claim that "all such matters as this should be approached from a bibliographical angle" (Muir 1954, 15). Muir's appreciation of the "bibliophile" interest in children's books guided his approach to writing the history, and his book, more lavishly illustrated than that of Darton (even in its 1982 edition), together with his selection of "certain noble or outstanding specimens" and his grouping other examples around them, makes his intentions appear far more characteristic of his period than was Darton's plan to tell "the story of English Children's Books . . . as a continuous whole" (Darton 1932, v) of his.

The effect of the collector-driven passion for attractive little books which generate a sense of the remoteness of past childhoods, or for material evoking a sense of nostalgia for the collector's own childhood, has been that some areas of children's literature have been more fully documented than others. An instance of this is in the history of school stories; as Rosemary Auchmuty observes: "It is amateur booklovers who have made the most substantial contribution to knowledge about both boys' and girls' school stories, setting up networks and journals to exchange information and ideas about the books and their authors" (Auchmuty 2000, viii); many of these networks and journals existed well before histories included this kind of material.

Another landmark in the writing of the history of children's books was *A Critical History of Children's Literature* (1953) by American author Cornelia Meigs and her three collaborators. Her aim is clear from her title, though it must be admitted that, despite the proclaimed interest in literature rather than social history or bibliography, there is relatively little that would be seen as "critical" by the more rigid scrutiny of the twenty-first-century reader. The inclusion of American children's literature, and the recognition that none of the four authors alone would have been expert enough to take on a timespan which culminated in the actual date of publication, also mark developments from the approaches of Darton and of Muir. A revised edition, correcting errors and updating the material, appeared in 1969, while Gillian Avery's more specific history of the American children's book did not appear until 1994.

The gradual increase in the attention being given to children's literature frequently did not involve an historical perspective. The first edition in 1962 of the classic collection of essays, *Only Connect: Readings on Children's Literature* did have three articles which provided some historical perspective, but the fact that the book's main emphasis was on twentieth-century texts merely reflected the implicit understanding that "librarians, parents, teachers and students," its primary audience, were more interested in contemporary literature.

In 1963 the Library Association published Mary Thwaite's *From Primer to Pleasure,* a book with the modest aim of introducing librarians, whose knowledge she feared might be limited (just as she describes her own as being when, thirty years previously, she was put in charge of a children's library), to scholarly histories like those of Darton. Like some of the other writers, she does not include the twentieth century within her historical time span, though she does include a chapter on developments abroad, even displaying awareness of children's books in other languages.

J. R. Townsend succeeded in breaking through the barrier that divides the academic text from the popular one. *Written For Children,* his survey of children's books, was first published in 1965; a revised and expanded edition followed it in 1974, but the book only became widely known when this later version was taken over by Pelican Books (an imprint of Penguin) in 1976, at which point its affordable price made it the preferred historical text for the increasing number of students of children's literature. Like the other books mentioned, Townsend's work has also come out in several editions, the one of 1990 (Bodley Head) being proclaimed as "25th anniversary edition". In it Townsend attempts to bring the story up to date.

The 1980s marked a further step in the development of children's literature studies, at the point at which the matchless collection of 20,000 children's books acquired by Iona and Peter Opie was incorporated into the Bodleian Library in 1988. This was significant to the history of children's books in several ways. The history of children's literature had been given the accolade of respectability by the oldest British university. As part of the process, the now-indispensable *Oxford Companion to Children's Books* (Carpenter and Prichard 1984) was produced as a fulfilment of work that the Opies themselves had projected many years before. The Opies' contribution to children's literature was also marked by a volume of essays, largely historical, edited by Gillian Avery and Julia Briggs (Avery and Briggs 1989). Another important aspect was the way in which the process displayed the integration between the approach to children's literature of the bibliophiles who saw it as something to be collected, and that of the academic researchers. An article in Avery's volume by Brian Alderson, who earlier in the decade had produced a revised edition of Darton's magisterial work, is titled: "Collecting Children's Books: Self-indulgence and Scholarship," and indicates the mutual dependence of one sector of interest on the other.

Since 1980, approaches to writing the history of children's literature have tended to be divided between those with the aim of providing an attractive and general introduction—very useful to the general reader and to students beginning their studies of the field—and those which with a more scholarly intent examine a more limited area or period in detail. Books written or edited by Peter Hunt appear in both categories (1994 and 1995a, and 2001a respectively) while those making a closer examination of specific periods (for instance Carpenter 1985; Jackson 1989; Reynolds 1994) have proved of considerable value to undergraduate students of the history of children's literature.

The Opies had also been pioneers in the field of specialized studies of specific areas of children's literature, for instance with their work on nursery rhymes and poetry for children, and their linking of playground rhymes to children's culture. Styles' more systematic history of poetry for children did not however appear until 1998. Goldthwaite's somewhat idiosyncratic approach to the history of fantasy (Goldthwaite 1996) also devotes some attention to poetry for children. Other subgenres attracting the interest of historians include the school story (Cadogan and Craig 1976, and Auchmuty 1992, for girls; Musgrave 1985, and Richards 1988, for boys), the "reward" book (Bratton 1981) and book illustration (Whalley and Chester 1988).

Children's literature, by its nature, demands something of a cross-disciplinary approach, embracing art, sociology, pedagogy, and, because of both the nature of its audience and the sex of many of its authors, women's studies (and more recently gender studies). This area demands scrutiny of those magazines for young people which clearly indicated whether their implied audience was male or female (Reynolds 1990; Nelson 1991; Nelson and Vallone 1994).

It is clear that students of children's literature now have at their disposal a variety of approaches to its history, ranging from comprehensive studies, popular or learned, to detailed scrutinies of specific areas. They also have available a good range of scholarly reference books to supply them with information about the development of subgenres and details about authors from the past.

The academic study of the history of children's literature

The development of the study of children's literature in higher education has inevitably been bound up with training for teaching.[5] Until the last third of the twentieth century, it was frequently assumed that teachers in secondary schools would come into the profession via a degree and a year's course of postgraduate training for teaching. Before the advent of the professionally-orientated Bachelor of Education degree in the late 1960s, primary teachers were frequently nongraduates, who had completed a shorter training (until 1962, usually only two years). The children's literature curriculum, if indeed the subject was studied at all by prospective teachers (which might well not be the case for secondary-trained students), would be likely to consist largely of books they might teach their pupils. This category might include some classic texts, though it would often have been considered probable that students already knew these from their own childhood and did not need any further knowledge in that area. An historical perspective was much less frequent than a pedagogical one, the concern being with *how* books might be used with children, both in developing their own reading and in building up a love of literature. Indicative of this attitude is the popularity on teacher-training courses of the now-classic *The Cool Web* (Meek 1977), a collection of essays initially planned to be published at the same time as the Bullock Report, *A Language for Life* (DES 1975) (a government-sponsored investigation into the teaching of reading and language in English and Welsh schools). The synchronistic rather than diachronistic approach of *The Cool Web* may be deduced from the headings of its sections: "The reader," "What the authors tell us," "Approaches to criticism," and "Ways forward."

It would be too space-consuming and repetitive to provide a broad picture of the development of the studies of the history of children's literature at undergraduate level at all the higher education institutions involved. While details may vary (in some institutions it was impossible to incorporate children's literature into a full English literature Honours degree), similar processes were generally involved, so it may be more illuminating to look in detail at the evolution of the course at one establishment.

Case study: the teaching of children's literature at Roehampton

In 1967, when the University of London instituted the Bachelor of Education degree for students at colleges associated with the London Institute of Education, the only students eligible to take this one-year course were those who had attained a sufficiently high level in the three-year course Certificate in Education which had qualified them as teachers. The assessment in English faced by these hard-pressed students (who also had to take four papers on Education or another subject) comprised four examination papers: on periods of literature, Shakespeare, and an innovatory syllabus on children's development and use of the English language. No room was found for a study of children's literature, and indeed it is probable that to have included it as an option might have been felt to detract from the academic status of the new degree. By 1975, however, a new form of the degree, open to undergraduates as a form of initial training for teaching, was instituted.

At the same period, four Colleges of Education associated with the University of London Institute of Education, Digby Stuart, Froebel, Southlands, and Whitelands, had come together to form the Roehampton Institute. Each of the colleges had a long tradition in the training of teachers and, unlike some institutions, all had, in professional courses, placed a good deal of emphasis on children's books, holding reasonable collections of these in their libraries. With the change in the format of the B.Ed. degree, it became possible to offer a paper in Children's Literature to undergraduates reading English (provided they were also training for teaching). It was not however until Roehampton degrees were validated by the University of Surrey, from 1982 onwards, that the course became available to students of English literature who were not also training to be teachers.

Probably as a reaction against the study of children's literature not having been seen (even by some members of the English department) as sufficiently academic to be available to nonteaching students, the syllabus that was offered from 1975 was particularly slanted towards the history of children's literature. The convener of the course, Gaye Trickett, herself a former teacher, devised an academically rigorous syllabus that culminated in the students being confronted with probably the most demanding examination paper of those they sat, whether in English or Education; it certainly covered a longer period (in effect from 1700 to 1970) than the others, and made very specific demands on knowledge of individual authors. At scrutiny boards, in fact, draft examination papers were often challenged as being more difficult than those for other areas of the English syllabus. An essential aspect of this development towards academic respectability at Roehampton was the fact that several of the librarians had a considerable degree of commitment to children's literature, and worked towards building up a collection which included a good many eighteenth- and nineteenth-century children's books, as well as a substantial number of secondary texts. The study of children's books, both classic and contemporary, also continued to form an essential part of the professional course for teachers, but this remained completely separate from the course which was part of the English Literature Honours degree, which never focused on pedagogical issues other than within an historical context.

The evolution of the children's literature course tends to reflect the gaining of status of the study of the subject in the academic world at large—from being just a part of teacher training to being gradually incorporated into the English literature degree course as such. Subsequent improvements in status have been associated with higher degree courses and, at Roehampton, the establishment of a substantial research ethos in the area, as well as the Queen's Award-winning National Centre for Research in Children's Literature. Inevitably these developments have done a good deal for the undergraduate teaching of children's literature, to the extent that the notion of it being a "soft option" is no longer extant among English Literature staff, or, hopefully, among prospective students.

Children's literature and other subject areas

I have suggested that one of the reasons for the history of children's literature being particularly significant in the Roehampton course from its inception during the 1970s was its role in convincing other staff, both within the validating authority of London University and within the English Department of what was then the Roehampton Institute, of the subject's academic worth.[6] Beverly Lyon Clark's article, "Kiddie Lit in Academe" (1996) documents a very similar process in America during her own academic career. Graduating as an English major in 1970, having taken no courses in children's literature, by 1979 she had the opportunity to teach a university course in the subject, supported by the desire of the college librarian to build a strong collection of cognate material. In the United States, as in Britain, the association of the subject with librarians and teachers has often led to a dismissive attitude among "pure" literature scholars. To have instituted a syllabus that consisted only of contemporary children's books would at that period have been to lay oneself open to the charge of studying literature of an inferior quality. History has often tended (sometimes fallaciously) to be seen as a subject providing "harder" and more objective "facts" than pure literary studies, and thus examination of literature from the past, with its concurrent demands for an understanding of the historical background, conferred some extra academic respectability to what was all too often seen as an easy option—reading all those "easy" books! It was not until the incursion of "Theory" into literary studies, largely during the 1980s, that it became respectable to devote attention to "popular" fiction without having an historical emphasis.

Studies of the history of children's literature have, to a greater extent than in traditional English literature courses, demanded a good deal of interdisciplinary cooperation. While in the early days, its students may have largely been confined to those taking English and Education, often in preparation for teaching, insights were needed from many other fields. The most obvious of these are History and Sociology; to understand the literature, students needed to be aware of the conditions in which it was produced and read. Without an awareness of the relationship between the cultural and social presumptions of the period and the literature produced, books are likely to be read in a decontextualized manner. As well as more pragmatic areas such as those concerned with the market envisaged by publishing houses which produced children's literature, there is a considerable degree of overlap with philosophical and religious perspectives. To get a broad enough picture, there is also a need for an awareness of the situation elsewhere in English speaking world, especially in America.

To a greater extent than for much of the rest of English literature, English language children's literature needs also to be seen within the context of translation. This is not so much because of children's novels being translated from continental languages; relatively few such have made much impact on English children's literature; from the nineteenth-century, *Swiss Family Robinson, Heidi* and *Pinocchio* stand virtually alone. Much more important is the impact on British literature of the fairytales of Perrault from the French, the Grimms from the Germans, and Hans Andersen from the Danish.

The study of the history of children's literature would be impoverished without an awareness of the role within it of illustration. The attraction of the pictures in early editions of Aesop's *Fables*, making more vivid the verses of the Alphabet Books, or accompanying poems in the early Emblem books, not to mention the woodcuts in the chapbooks, were an essential aspect of the development of books for children. Similarly, while the reading of Dickens' novels is enriched by looking at the illustrations, perusal of the work of Beatrix Potter demands an appreciation of the link between text and picture.

More recently, as has been indicated above, the areas of Women's Studies and Gender Studies have formed an indispensable part of studies of the history of children's literature, and there has been a good deal of focus on the images of femininity and masculinity present within books presented to children. Other cognate areas, such as philosophy, religion, and cultural studies, have all offered valuable insights—to the extent that students on combined degrees with some of these or other areas, have found their work on the history of children's literature provided useful cross-fertilization with their other studies. In effect, insights applicable to the aspects of Theory most relevant to historical studies, such as New Historicism, Marxism and Postcolonialism, had been latent in one form or another within historical studies of children's literature for some time before their explicit acknowledgement within literary studies generally.

Children's librarians and the study of the history of children's literature[7]

Ever since the inception of library schools, teaching the history of children's literature has been seen as an important element in the training of children's and school librarians. However, not every library school offered such a course. Loughborough Technical College, which ran professional courses in librarianship, leading to the Library Association final exam for those without a degree, and a postgraduate diploma for those with one, was one pioneer in the field from the 1960s onwards.

The history of children's literature has in most instances been seen as a valued option rather than a core subject. It has been the subject of many MA dissertations and research degrees. Other departments in the United Kingdom, such as Birmingham Polytechnic (now University of Central England), Robert Gordon's, and Leeds Metropolitan have also provided optional courses in children's literature and librarianship/ school librarianship. Loughborough's reputation for involvement in the children's literature field led to the establishment of an international conference which ran for several years, and the setting up of the *International Review of Children's Literature and Librarianship* under Margaret Kinnell as editor, carrying on that Loughborough tradition of research /teaching on children's literature. This is now the *New Review of Children's Literature and Librarianship*.

Without the departments of library and information studies, children's literature in the UK would probably not have been promoted or supported as a serious academic subject. Among the key individuals who supported this work nationally and internationally are Esme Green, Eileen Colwell (librarian, story-teller, writer, honorary graduate of Loughborough) and Brian Alderson. These were some of the real pioneers who took the study of children's books seriously and kept a focus on the significance of children's literature for any real understanding of the relationship between literature for adults and that for children.

Resources: primary texts for undergraduate study

Undergraduate study of the history of any area of literature demands student access to the most significant texts in the best possible editions. The nature of the material concerned, however, means that certain problems arise about the textual provision of historical children's works that do not exist for students studying Shakespeare's plays or the Victorian novel, for instance. Such problems may be linked to several interrelated questions:

- To what extent can any children's books be regarded as canonical texts which must be included in any syllabus?
- How far beyond this canon should students go in order to appreciate the cultural and societal forces related to material presented to students?
- What affordable scholarly editions of the texts exist?
- Are there any, cheap or otherwise, editions of less-known texts?
- Should students be provided with an anthology which includes lesser-known material? Should tutors provide a course-pack of such material?

Designing the syllabus

Certain texts automatically self-select for a reasonably comprehensive undergraduate course on the origins and development of children's literature (terminating for convenience at the onset of the First World War, though admittedly much of the rest of the twentieth century is also history as far as children are concerned): a selection of fairytales by Perrault, the Grimms and Andersen; *Alice in Wonderland; The Water Babies; Tom Brown's Schooldays; Treasure Island; The Wind in the Willows; Peter Pan; The Secret Garden*, to name some of the most obvious ones. To these must be added selected works by MacDonald, Nesbit, Potter, and Kipling, while to omit leading works from other countries, such as *Little Women, What Katy Did, Pinocchio, Heidi*, etc. would give too partial a view.

We can already see that the syllabus is in danger of overloading a single semester's course, though account has yet to be taken of no longer popular, but historically very significant, writers such as Thomas Day, Sarah Trimmer, Maria Edgeworth, Mary Martha Sherwood, Catherine Sinclair, Hesba Stretton, Mary Louisa Molesworth, L. T. Meade, etc.

To confine study to books which have remained relatively popular with children into the twenty-first century is to overlook some vital trends in the development of children's literature, notably the explicit didacticism of much of the early material and the gradual incorporation of more entertaining material. It is scarcely surprising that courses on the history of children's literature tend to have the longest reading lists. A difficult question relates to the fact that the inclusion of less-known material may demand the omission of well-known children's classics, of which it could be claimed no student doing a course on the history of children's literature should be unaware.

It is notable too that even the writers of the texts which may be regarded as canonical among children's books are seldom to the forefront in the adult canon, where Kipling and Stevenson are perhaps the most likely to figure in the study of the comparable period, but generally as minor figures. Since most people who teach children's literature are likely themselves to derive from an English Literature background, there is a danger that they too may be inclined to marginalize the subject because of its foregrounding of writers not part of the adult canon, without taking heed of the fact that they are dealing with a different, rather than an inferior, area of writing, which demands a different set of skills from its practitioners.

Inevitably there is a good deal of subjectivity in the selection of required reading. For the one tutor who prefers boys' school stories there will be another who prefers girls' adventure stories. Creation of a syllabus is in effect a negotiation between the ideal and the pragmatic, efforts to reflect the development of the genre with regard to such aspects as cultural history, the evolution of the concept of childhood, gender, didacticism, religion, etc. being set against presenting a reasonable balance between different literary modes such as realism in the form of the historical or school novel, and fantasy.

Problems of selection from too large a body of material can be tackled by providing broad sweep lectures dealing with certain texts or groups of texts, though this may increase the likelihood of not all texts being read. Students can also be allowed the opportunity to select certain texts for closer group study, with the possibility of plenary discussion of their findings for the benefit of a larger group.

Availability of texts

The books and authors listed in the first paragraph of the section on Syllabus above are in most instances available in fairly cheap editions—itself an important factor when deciding on set texts. Children's literature is generally a popular option in the relatively few institutions that teach it at undergraduate level, and it would be unrealistic to expect university libraries to provide an adequate number of books for all the students. In some instances, for instance *Little Women*, students have the choice between an edition with a scholarly introduction and footnotes, and a range of cheaper versions intended for children. Variations between texts can provide an interesting area for study; *The Water Babies* for instance is often abridged for young readers, while *What Katy Did* often appears without its slightly "precious" framing. Books in print today are much more likely to feature on a syllabus than for instance *Masterman Ready, Eric or Little by Little, The Fifth Form at St Dominic's,* or books by Bessie Marchant

For those books which have not been reprinted in recent years, the main choice (other than assuming that recommending students to read about them in the histories gives sufficient coverage) is between anthologies and the provision of a course pack. Both of these strategies generally imply that students will be reading selections rather than complete works. The students' reading will therefore be determined by either the editor of the anthology or the course tutor, or both. It is evident that a great deal of subjectivity comes in to any selection, and the chances of the subjectivities of anthology compilers and the (usually several) tutors teaching a specific course coinciding are not high. Prescribing an anthology for student purchase tends to impose the necessity of class discussion of a sufficiently large number of the extracts to make students feel happy with their expenditure. Hunt's admirable collection (2001b), for instance, does include material by Edgeworth, Sherwood and Sinclair, but only for the third of these are the selected stories those which I personally would regard as indispensable on a course I was teaching. It also includes on the one hand excerpts from several books which I would want students to read in their entirety, such as *Alice through the Looking Glass* and *What Katy Did*, together with others of more interest to specialists than to undergraduate students. This is in no way to fault the anthologist, whose aim was not to provide a set text for a course I was teaching, but rather to provide "a record of spectacular change" (Hunt 2001b, xiii). As such it is a valuable resource for students who want to go beyond their prescribed reading list.

An alternative approach is used in the *Masterworks of Children's Literature* collection, the seven volumes[8] of which tend to include complete works published between 1550 and 1900, though in some instances, as in the case of Thomas Day's *Sandford and Merton*, these are abridged. Here again those teaching a course are likely to find that works which seem essential to them, such as Sherwood's *History of the Fairchild Family*, are omitted, while, strangely, the readily available Thomas Hughes' *Tom Brown's Schooldays* appears complete. Again, for me, this is a collection for the specialist or the undergraduate student who seeks to go beyond the syllabus.

Additional factors

With the expansion of children's literature teaching, many texts have become more easily available in an electronic form. Complete texts of important but less available writers such as Edgeworth, Sherwood, Sinclair, Stretton, and Meade are now available in this format and can be downloaded as desired. Further digitalization of resources should open up possibilities of widening the syllabus, though again, particularly at an undergraduate level, this raises the potential problem that tutors may be tempted to demand reading of texts which stand outside the canon, to the detriment of the students' reading of significant and influential standard works.

A further factor, probably more important at postgraduate level, is the increasing establishment of collections of historical children's books. Even if undergraduate students may not be required to look closely at these, they do open up perspectives for them and are likely to be a factor in encouraging them to go on to research in the area.

Case study: the evolving content of the coursepack for "Origins and Developments of Children's Literature" at Roehampton

When Gaye Trickett first taught this course in the mid-1970s, her practice was to issue typewritten handouts of all the passages for discussion. This was before photocopying became a cheap and routine practice; the time-consuming labour of producing material on stencils was the only way to provide these texts. It has not been possible totally to reconstruct her choice of material, but it certainly involved a good deal from Mary Sherwood, including the contents page of *History of the Fairchild Family* and several complete stories, notably the Introduction, "Mrs Fairchild's Story," "Man before the Fall," and the almost notorious "Story on the Sixth Commandment," where the children visit the dark wood and see a gibbet with a body hanging on it. Trickett also provided a good deal of background historical and critical material; to a largely unacknowledged extent she performed an important instrumental role in the furtherance of the study of children's literature in higher education, particularly in incorporating a scholarly approach to it.

As photocopying became more easily available, tutors on an historical course had the considerable advantage that provided the library possessed originals of early material, there were no copyright problems about providing copies for the students. Initially such copies were provided at the point in the course when a specific text was to be studied; the flexibility which this involves should however be set against the way in which such loose papers can be easily lost, and lack the authority of a book. So by the mid-1980s there was a policy of providing coursepacks which contained extracts from any works not easily available to students, together with others that it would be unreasonable to expect them to buy because the course focused on them only relatively briefly. None of the "canonical" books listed in the first paragraph of the Syllabus section about resources were included in the coursepack.

Scrutiny of the coursepacks for 1993/4 and 1998/9 reveals a substantial element of continuity in choice of both authors and excerpts from their works: Sarah Fielding's *The Governess* or *The Little Female Academy* (1749); Edgeworth's Introduction to *The Parent's Assistant* and two stories about Rosamund, "The Purple Jar" and "The Birthday Present"; Sherwood's Introduction, "Mrs Fairchild's Story," "Sixth Commandment" and "The Fatal Effects of Disobedience to Parents"; "The Terrible Fire" from Catherine Sinclair's *Holiday House*; together with excerpts from Hesba Stretton's *Jessica's First Prayer* or *Little Meg's Children* and L. T. Meade's *A Sweet Girl Graduate*. Other authors such as Bessie Marchant, Elizabeth Whitaker, and Charlotte Yonge figure in one or other of these coursepacks.

While provision of coursepacks, for which students pay a small sum to cover photocopying, still remains somewhat onerous, and is probably less aesthetic in appearance (and thus less likely to be retained by the student once their course is over) than an anthology, it has several advantages for course tutors. Notable among these is flexibility. Since variations are possible as personnel teaching the course change, specialisms and enthusiasms can more easily be allowed for. It does not rigidify a syllabus, but allows access to vital texts which are otherwise only available in the library, which would be hard put to provide copies for perhaps one hundred students at the same time. Perhaps its very ephemerality can be seen as an advantage too, for it highlights the provisional nature of any choice of texts.

Conclusion

While the last thirty years have seen a substantial increase in the academic study of the history of children's literature, I am not convinced that it is yet regarded as comparable in its demands with the study of books written for adults. Its need for historical, sociological, pedagogical, philosophical, artistic, and cultural background is not yet fully recognized, but perhaps the current increase in the number of adults reading contemporary children's books may lead some academics to realize the wide ramifications that such a study involves.

Notes

1. The history of English literature developed as an academic pursuit during the nineteenth century, through the work of scholars such as Sir Edmund Chambers, Professor George Saintsbury, and the French Émile Legouis, but it was not until the middle of the twentieth century that the allocation of single periods, or even specific topics, to individual experts, as in the *Oxford History of English Literature*, or the *Pelican Guide to English Literature* respectively, superseded the notion of the single omniscient author.
2. The debate about the validity or otherwise of Ariès' understanding of childhood is fully explored in Lesnik-Oberstein (1994, 10–17).
3. The Catholic journal, *The Tablet*, recommended a small book, *Bessy; or the Fatal Consequences of Telling Lies* (1880) as "a very good tale to be put in the hands of young servants" (quoted Drew 1880, endpapers).
4. Hunt's article is discussed by Jean Webb elsewhere in this volume. [*Editor's note*].
5. Training for librarianship, which might include a component on children's literature, also tended to be professionally rather than academically organized.
6. Roehampton attained University status in 2000, as part of the Federal University of Surrey, becoming the autonomous Roehampton University in 2004.
7. Thanks are due to Sally Maynard of Loughborough University, who provided most of the information for this section.
8. An eighth volume consists of historical essays about twentieth-century children's literature.

Works cited

Ariès, Philippe. 1962. *Centuries of Childhood*. Trans. R Baldick. London: Jonathan Cape.

Auchmuty, Rosemary. 1992. *A World of Girls: The Appeal of the Girls' School Story*. London: The Women's Press.

Avery, Gillian. 1965. *Nineteenth Century Children: Heroes and Heroines in English Children's Stories 1780–1900*. London: Hodder and Stoughton.

———. 1994. *Behold the Child: American Children and their Books*. London: Bodley Head.

Avery, Gillian, and Julia Briggs. 1989. *Children and their Books: A Celebration of the Work of Iona and Peter Opie*. Oxford: Clarendon Press.

Bratton, Jacqueline S. 1981. *The Impact of Victorian Children's Fiction*. London: Croom Helm.

Butler, Francelia, Jonathan Cott, Robert Bator, Robert Lee Wolff, William T. Moynihan, and Mary E. Shaner, eds. 1983–86. *Master Works of Children's Literature*, 8 vols. London: Allen Lane, and New York: Stonehill Inc. and Chelsea House Inc.

Cadogan, Mary, and Patricia Craig. 1976. *You're a Brick, Angela! The Girls' Story 1839–1975*. London: Gollancz.

Carpenter, Humphrey. 1985. *Secret Gardens: The Golden Age of Children's Literature*. London: Unwin.

Carpenter, Humphrey, and Mari Prichard. 1984. *The Oxford Companion to Children's Literature*. Oxford: Oxford University Press.

Clark, Beverly Lyon. 1996. "Kiddie lit in Academe." *Profession 1996*. New York: Modern Language Association, 149–57.

Coveney, Peter. 1967. *The Image of Childhood*. Harmondsworth: Penguin.

Darton, F. J. Harvey. 1932. *Children's Books in England: Five Centuries of Social Life*. Cambridge: Cambridge University Press.

———. 1958. *Children's Books in England: Five Centuries of Social Life*, 2nd edn with Introduction by Kathleen Lines. Cambridge: Cambridge University Press.

———. 1982. *Children's Books in England: Five Centuries of Social Life*, 3rd edn, revised by Brian Alderson. Cambridge: Cambridge University Press.

Department of Education and Science. 1975. *A Language for Life*. London: DES.

Drew, F. B. 1880. *Dominus Vobiscum*. London: R & T Washbourne.

Egoff, Sheila, G. T. Stubbs, and L. F. Ashley eds. 1962. *Only Connect: Readings on Children's Literature*. Toronto: Oxford University Press.

Field, E. M. 1892. *The Child and his Book: Some Account of The History and Progress of Children's Literature in England*. London: Wells Gardner, Darton & Co.

Goldthwaite, John. 1996. *The Natural History of Make-Believe*. Oxford: Oxford University Press.

Green, Roger Lancelyn. 1946. *Tellers of Tales*. Leicester: Edmund Ward.

Hunt, Peter. 1994. *An Introduction to Children's Literature*. Oxford: Oxford University Press.

———. 1995a. *Children's Literature: An Illustrated History*. Oxford: Oxford University Press.

———. 1995b. "How not to read a Children's Book." *Children's Literature in Education* 26.4: 231–40.

———. 2001a. *Children's Literature*. Blackwell Guides to Literature. Oxford: Blackwell.

———. 2001b. *Children's Literature: An Anthology 1801–1902*. Oxford: Blackwell.

Jackson, Mary V. 1989. *Engines of Instruction, Mischief, and Magic: Children's Literature in England from its Beginnings to 1839*. Lincoln: University of Nebraska.

Kirkpatrick, Robert J., ed. 2000. *The Encyclopaedia of Boys' School Stories*. Aldershot: Ashgate.

Lesnik-Oberstein, Karín. 1994. *Children's Literature: Criticism and the Fictional Child*. Oxford: Clarendon Press.

Meek, Margaret, Griselda Barton, and Aidan Warlow, eds. 1977. *The Cool Web: The Pattern of Children's Reading*. London: Bodley Head.

Meigs, Cornelia, Anne Thaxter Eaton, Elizabeth Nesbitt, and Ruth Hill Viguers, [1953] 1969. *A Critical History of Children's Literature: A Survey of Children's Books in English, prepared in four parts*. Revised edition. Toronto: Macmillan.

Muir, Percy. 1954. *English Children's Books 1600–1900*. London: B. T. Batsford.

Musgrave, P. W. 1985. *From Brown to Bunter: The Life and Death of the School Story*. London: Routledge & Kegan Paul.

Nelson, Claudia. 1991. *Boys will be Girls: The Feminine Ethic and British Children's Fiction 1857–1917*. New Brunswick and London: Rutgers University Press.

Nelson, Claudia, and Lynne Vallone. 1994. *The Girl's Own: Cultural Histories of the Anglo-American Girl, 1830–1915*. Athens and London: University of Georgia Press.

Opie, Iona, and Peter Opie, eds. 1951. *The Oxford Dictionary of Nursery Rhymes*. Oxford: Oxford University Press.

———. 1977. *The Lore and Language of School Children*. London: Granada.

Orme, Nicholas. 1998. "The Earliest Children's Literature in England." 2–15 in *Childhood Remembered: Proceedings from the 4th Annual IBBY/MA Children's Literature Conference*. Edited by Kimberley Reynolds. NCRCL Papers 3. London: Roehampton Institute.

Reynolds, Kimberley. 1990. *Girls Only?: Gender and Popular Children's Fiction in Britain, 1880–1910*. Hemel Hempstead: HarvesterWheatsheaf.

———. 1994. *Children's Literature in the 1890s and the 1990s*. Plymouth: Northcote House.

Richards, Jeffrey. 1988. *Happiest Days: The Public Schools in English Fiction*. Manchester: Manchester University Press.

Sidney, Sir Philip. 1966. *A Defence of Poetry*. Edited by D. Van Dorsten. Oxford: Oxford University Press.

Sims, Sue, and Hilary Clare, eds. 2000. *The Encyclopaedia of Girls' School Stories*. Aldershot: Ashgate.

Styles, Morag. 1998. *From the Garden to the Street: An Introduction to 300 Years of Poetry for Children*. London: Cassell.

Thwaite, M. F. 1965. *From Primer to Pleasure: An Introduction to the History of Children's Books in England, from the Invention of Printing to 1900. With a Chapter on Some Developments Abroad*. London: The Library Association.

Townsend, John R. 1976. *Written for Children: an Outline of English-Language Children's Literature*. Revised Edition. Harmondsworth: Penguin.

———. 1990. *Written for Children: 25th Anniversary Edition*. London: Bodley Head, 1990.

Watson, Victor, ed. 2001. *The Cambridge Guide to Children's Books in English*. Cambridge: Cambridge University Press.

Whalley, Joyce Irene, and Tessa Rose Chester. 1988. *A History of Children's Book Illustration*. London: John Murray with the Victoria and Albert Museum.

Further reading

Ariès, Philippe. *Centuries of Childhood*. Trans. R. Baldick. London: Jonathan Cape, 1962.

Avery, Gillian, and Julia Briggs. *Children and their Books: A Celebration of the Work of Iona and Peter Opie*. Oxford: Clarendon Press, 1989.

Bratton, Jacqueline S. *The Impact of Victorian Children's Fiction*. London: Croom Helm, 1981.

Cadogan, Mary, and Patricia Craig. *You're a Brick, Angela! The Girls' Story 1839–1975*. London: Gollancz, 1976.

Carpenter, Humphrey. *Secret Gardens: The Golden Age of Children's Literature.* London: Unwin, 1985.

Coveney, Peter. *The Image of Childhood.* Harmondsworth: Penguin, 1967.

Darton, F. J. Harvey. *Children's Books in England: Five Centuries of Social Life.* Cambridge: Cambridge University Press, 1932.

Hunt, Peter. *Children's Literature: An Illustrated History.* Oxford: Oxford University Press, 1995.

Jackson, Mary V. *Engines of Instruction, Mischief, and Magic: Children's Literature in England from its Beginnings to 1839.* Lincoln: University of Nebraska, 1989.

Reynolds, Kimberley. *Girls Only?: Gender and Popular Children's Fiction in Britain, 1880–1910.* Hemel Hempstead: HarvesterWheatsheaf, 1990.

Townsend, John Rowe. *Written for Children: 25th Anniversary Edition.* London: Bodley Head, 1990. [Earlier editions of this book remain of considerable interest in this area.]

Whalley, Joyce Irene, and Tessa Rose Chester. *A History of Children's Book Illustration.* London: John Murray with the Victoria and Albert Museum, 1988.

2
Cultural Studies

David Rudd

The term *cultural studies*, like similar phrases, *women's studies, media studies*, and *communication studies*, immediately announces itself as a recent coinage and, simultaneously, hints at a lack of pedigree (unlike *literature* or *English*). In the UK it has been associated with the newer university sector, and has been seen as an area with dubious credentials. Its development is part of a larger debate about English being subsumed by wider cultural influences, which became headline news over Colin MacCabe teaching modern French literary theory at Cambridge in the 1980s. However, though there have been a number of protests about cultural studies over the years, many of its concerns have now become fairly orthodox in the teaching of English literature. In 1991, for instance, Antony Easthope wrote a provocative book called *Literary into Cultural Studies*, linking the two areas, whereas, by the new century, their yoking had become quite commonplace (e.g. Barry 2002; Davis and Schliefer 1998).

So, what is cultural studies? At its simplest, it is concerned with the way that meanings coalesce and circulate in particular cultural objects or practices (During 1999; Grossberg et al. 1991; Storey 1996). It can therefore be seen to encompass many of literature's concerns, but unlike literature, does not focus on the book as the cultural object *par excellence*. It is also concerned with TV, film, the internet, magazines, food, music, and so on; not only that, it also queries the preeminence of the book as a cultural object and, moreover, the evaluative judgements made about it (why is *Charlotte's Web* valued more highly than the *Teletubbies*, for example?).

A second main difference is that, in certain conceptions of literature, the text itself was seen as central (what the New Critics referred to as "the verbal icon"), contextual matters being very much secondary.

Cultural studies queries this, arguing that texts only ever exist in particular contexts ("there is nothing outside context" as Derrida (1988, 136) puts it), which must, therefore, always be taken into account. In line with this, this chapter has been organized to consider this more extended notion of how meanings coalesce and circulate in cultural objects. Thus it explores the *pre-text*: how texts come to be produced (and *children's literature* in particular); the *con-text*: the discourses out of which the text is woven (e.g. of gender, ethnicity, class, nationhood); and finally, the *post-text*, the way that texts are consumed, valued, and adapted (into different versions, different media).

A third main feature of cultural studies is its emphasis on theory. It uses insights from literature, certainly, but also sociology, linguistics, psychology, psychoanalysis, history, art, film, and other areas to inform its readings. For some, this is seen to be at the expense of the text, whilst for others, it constitutes an enrichment. However, this background has meant that it is hard to pin down cultural studies as a discipline. Courses can be very different, and national differences make these even greater. This can be read in a negative way (anything goes) or more positively, emphasizing that cultural studies is less about content than a certain, reflective way of looking at things—which the word *query* effectively captures (and the less felicitous, *problematize*), as used above. So, as culture is itself dynamic, with ever new cultural objects, plus reevaluations of older ones, cultural studies must be similarly mobile. But beyond this, it should be forever critical and self-reflexive, querying, or *queering* the pitch on which any cultural studies might try to build a permanent base. Nick Lee (1998, 465) provides us with an interesting analogy with childhood here, which he suggests is itself "constitutionally incomplete," "disturbing social ordering practices" and leading us "away from a reified view of conventions."

Children's literature has a number of other connections with cultural studies: its study is also a relatively recent phenomenon, with a somewhat negative image, lacking credibility in high places; secondly, the study of children's literature is itself very much a hybrid area, having diverse histories in literature, librarianship, and education. In this way, one could argue that children's literature has always had to consider the context in which literature operates, that it has always had an awareness of audience, and of its involvement in praxis. Lastly, children's literature is itself a discipline very much in transition, emerging from the three areas above. Courses are thus very different, depending on their institutional home. More recently, some children's literature courses have themselves been subsumed under the wider umbrella of *child studies*, or *childhood studies*, which consider other aspects of children's culture—aspects that I'll consider after looking at the pre-text, the con-text and the post-text.

The pre-text

The key question here is when and how children's literature came into existence. In answer, it is often noted that there could be no children's literature till there were children. But this moves us on little further, for, we might then ask, what is a child? Childhood is obviously far more than a simple biological stage, given the myriad ways that it has been conceived by different societies. In exploring the social construction of children, many courses begin with Philippe Ariès's famous statement that, "In medieval society the idea of childhood did not exist" (Ariès 1973, 125), which, in turn, led to an industry of further work, with studies by, for example, Shulamith Shahar (1989), Linda Pollock (1983) and others detailing the ways that childhood did exist in medieval times. However, Karín Lesnik-Oberstein (1998) has criticized these in turn, making the point that these critics already *presume* the existence of some underlying, *real* child, and read the historical evidence accordingly. This said, when we look at how Ariès arrived at his original thesis, where he disputes childhood's existence (as an idea), he also drew on and interpreted the evidence, later admitting his ignorance of the wealth of material available, as Alexandre-Bidon and Lett note (1999, 1). Certainly, they, and Nicholas Orme (2001), give useful, detailed accounts of books and toys produced over this period for a category they designate non-adult beings. These, together with some of the other sources mentioned above, can certainly provide materials for a lively class debate which moves us beyond the sterile question of childhood's existence to explore its complex configurations over time, across class, gender and ethnicity (for more modern constructions of the child, see Hendrick (1997)). Also, by using literary extracts from different historical periods (e.g. Demers 2003; Hunt 2001; Kline 2003), the way that children's literature is implicated in these constructions can be more concretely demonstrated, and our own, contemporary understanding problematized.

For many, children's literature as a commercial enterprise started properly in the eighteenth century, with John Newbery's work (Darton 1982, 1). By then, growing industrialization led to an increased emphasis on middle-class children as a market for books and toys (Plumb 1975; Leeson 1985; O'Malley 2003). These products themselves helped define and categorize the child in different ways and, over the years, have led to ever finer gradations of age, and gender-specific, class-specific materials. Michel Foucault is a key theoretical figure here. Rather than seeing the child as an essential being about whom our knowledge increases over time (a humanist conception), Foucault argued that knowledge is always tied to power, so that discourses about the child—especially those tied to important state apparatuses, like the church, medicine, and education—have particular truth-effects. In other words, there is no disinterested, universal knowledge of children (or anything else); we simply read children through different discursive lenses.

The human sciences, in particular, have been prolific in categorizing aspects of the normal child and, therefore, delineating the abnormal (e.g. Donzelot 1979; Henriques 1984; Rose 1989). It has, therefore, been *normal* to see girls as more domesticated and passive than boys, and to read book characters in terms of this framework, thus easily identifying the abnormal, unruly child. Similarly, children have been read as asexual beings, a truth which literature about them has generally attested. *Issues* books—the sort recommended as *bibliotherapy* (Pardeck and Pardeck 1993)—are particularly useful for demonstrating the "power of normalization" (Foucault 1977, 184) and its attendant problems (for Foucauldian readings of children's literature, see O'Malley 2003; Trites 2000; Walkerdine 1990, 87–106).

Foucault's *genealogical approach* was very influential in the development of new historicism (Veeser 1989)—or cultural materialism, as it is often called in the UK (Dollimore and Sinfield 1985). This approach attends to "local, discontinuous, disqualified, illegitimate knowledges against the claims of a unitary body of theory that would filter, hierarchise, and order them in the name of some true knowledge" (Foucault 1980, 83). It has enabled scholars to challenge, for example, the standard shift from instruction to amusement, the latter supposedly representing a more *real* children's literature (Darton 1982). Mitzi Myers, for instance, has sought to avoid this *presentist* stance (reading the past in terms of the present), arguing that it plays into the hands of the Romantics' idealized, male child, "predicated on the opposition of child and adult" (Myers 1992, 132). An example of this Romantic child might be seen in Julia Briggs's comment that many early women writers for children were "excluding or repressing the high spirits, free-floating imagination, and anarchic feelings so characteristic of childhood" (Briggs 222). As Myers argues, though, early writers like Maria Edgeworth had a far more nuanced notion of the educational tale, in which both child and adult are affiliatively connected (Myers 1995).

Barbara Wall's rightly-influential study of the development of writing for children is another example of an essentialist approach, where the child is conceived as an ahistorical being to whom we have only recently learned to talk properly. For her, we can identify writing for children by "the way it is said, and to whom" (Wall 1991, 2; see Lesnik-Oberstein 1994; Rudd 1995). For poststructuralist critics, on the other hand, there can be no child preexisting our descriptions of it: no *natural* child that somehow precedes, or evades, linguistic construction. This is Jacqueline Rose's main point, on which she founds her case that children's fiction rests on an impossibility, in that it is always adult constructions of children that act as lures. Which is not to deny the existence of actual *children*; simply to deny an essential child that we can presume to know. Lesnik-Oberstein has taken this further, stating that Rose's argument "closes down the field of children's fiction, and therefore, by implication, children's literature criticism" (Lesnik-Oberstien 1994, 158–59)—although others have argued that this simply indicates a shift in paradigm, to a recognition that the child, like other cultural objects, is socially constructed (Rudd 2004a).

Again, it should be noted that there are many different stances taken on this issue, themselves dependent on different ontological and epistemological grounds. In Foucault, for instance, the subject is rigidly circumscribed, but is less so in the writing of some of those inspired by him (e.g. Butler 1990; Davies 1989; Said 1978; Walkerdine 1990). For Jacques Derrida, too, there is no subject except as an effect of language, yet he, like Foucault (Moss 1998), has sought to articulate positions of resistance (Derrida 1994). Derrida's deconstruction of binary oppositions has proved particularly influential in cultural studies (e.g. Bhabha 1994; Brannigan et al. 1996; Hall 2002). And in the area of children's studies, it has helped, for example, deconstruct the following binaries: adult/child, natural/cultural, didactic/amusing, book people/child people (Lesnik-Oberstein 1995; Rudd 1994; Thomson 1998), besides inspiring a witty reading of recent Disney animations (Byrne and McQuillan 1999). Other critics, however, have tried to hold on to the grand narratives of liberation (e.g. Dorfman 1983; Dorfman and Mattelart 1975; Kohl 1995; Phillips and Wojcik-Andrews 1990; Zipes 1983, 1992, 2000), and many would adduce (discursively, of course) such evils as child abuse, or the general tendency to treat children as adults (Higonnet 2002; Morrison 1997). But once again, such writers are in danger of reinstating the essential child. However, this problematic is not unique to children's literature; as Halliwell and Mousley argue (2003), traces of humanism are hard to avoid, even in avowedly poststructuralist accounts.

In practical terms, it is certainly worthwhile examining why certain texts are considered unsuitable for children. Another useful exercise is to present anonymous extracts from a mix of adult and children's books, asking students to distinguish them, giving reasons (depending on the extract, this can be very difficult). A follow-up exercise requires students to rewrite adult extracts so that they are suitable for children (and vice versa), again to foreground issues of content, address, and tone. Likewise, this can be done with critical statements, seeing what happens when comments like, "children will really like this book," are recast; for example, why does the statement, "adults will really like *Emma*," sound decidedly odd? It is also worth examining our sentimental attachment to certain images of children. The work of James Kincaid (1992) and Anne Higonnet (1998, 2002) is pertinent here, drawing attention to the dangers of perpetuating the Romantic image of the child. As Kincaid puts it, "By insisting so loudly on the innocence, purity, and asexuality of the child, we have created a subversive echo: experience, corruption, eroticism" (Kincaid 1992, 4–5). As Rose says of Peter Pan, he does not grow up, "not because he doesn't want to, but because someone else prefers that he shouldn't"; it is "the adult's desire for the child" which is at stake, "which fixes the child and then holds it in place" (Rose 1984, 3–4). In which case, can we rise to Anne Higonnet's challenge to "make books, pictures, movies, toys that do more for children than cater to adult fantasies of childhood" (Higonnet 2002, 206)—though, once again, the question of essentialism raises its head.

Returning to Foucault's genealogical approach, it should make students more ready to question the official history of children's literature, whereby it emerged from a didactic past into an enlightened present. New research is continually complicating this orthodoxy; for instance, Ruth B. Bottigheimer (1996) has shown the wide impact of children's Bibles on the area's development. However, chapbooks (also containing Bible stories alongside scatological ones), nursery rhymes, and other aspects of a lower-class, popular, more oral culture, also informed children's reading (Lynn and Preston 1995), as did fairy tales, with their more subversive, utopian elements, and, in some cases, their anti-patriarchal stance (Harries 2001; Warner 1994; Zipes 1979, 1983).

It becomes clear that what is regarded as children's literature is to some extent arbitrary, subject to historical circumstance, and that this arbitrariness continues today—although Zohar Shavit (1986), who notes that the educational system is a key element, argues that children's literature develops not arbitrarily, but in the same systematic way across different societies. Though we know that publishers from the eighteenth century onwards identified a separate market in children's books, it seems that many adults and children continued to read the same texts (e.g. Dusinberre 1987, 30). Towards the end of the nineteenth century, however, there were more concerted efforts by Henry James and others to separate out the novel as an art form (Hughes 1978). This process, however, was also underway elsewhere, in children's books, magazines, toys, and games, which were increasingly categorizing their audience according to age, class, and gender (Drotner 1988; Reynolds 1990; Tinkler 1995).

There is still a huge amount of work to do on the role of publishers and other gatekeepers (Taxel 2002). However, works like Reynolds and Tucker (1998) have made a bold start, showing how decisions were made about marketing particular works as *children's*. As we know, there are a number of titles that have been seen to migrate from adult to child lists (e.g. *The Pilgrim's Progress, Gulliver's Travels*), and vice versa (e.g. *Watership Down* (Adams 1973), *Northern Lights/The Golden Compass* (Pullman 1995). The recent emphasis on *crosswriting* (Knoepflmacher and Myers 1997; Beckett 1999)—that is, for a joint audience of adults and children, as with Pullman's "His Dark Materials" trilogy and Rowling's "Harry Potter" books—might then be seen as a return to earlier times, especially when this phenomenon is linked to debates about the death of childhood. These debates are themselves often related to the demise of a print-based culture, which had previously limited children's access to adult knowledge (Postman 1982; Steinberg and Kinchloe 1997; see Buckingham 2000). Whether TV or ICT is the cause of this shift in perceptions of childhood, there are a number of contemporary discourses concerning how "children become 'adultified' and adults become 'childified' " (Aronowitz and Giroux, cited in Kincheloe 1998, 170). Few would deny that increasing globalization through the concentration of capital in multinational conglomerates has contributed to the demise of local versions of childhood in favour of a multiculturally acceptable, generic child (with Disney being seen as one of the main perpetrators).

The con-text

Some of the earliest cultural work in children's literature grew out of the social unrest of the 1960s, concerned with the rights of marginalized groups (women, Blacks, the working-class, and others). But unlike other *others*, children can be seen as doubly marginalized, in that each of the above groups, in its fight for recognition, ignored its younger members (Clark 2003). This is evident in the criticism of the time, much of which seems less concerned with the children *per se*, than with how children's literature might produce sexist or racist adults. In retrospect, this work seems unsophisticated, treating characters in a monolithic, social-realist manner. However, it was a necessary stage of consciousness-raising, showing how the classics, supposedly canonical because of encapsulated universal truths and values, were, in fact, often restricted, partisan, and occasionally insulting (Dixon 1977a, 1977b). In this section I shall discuss these social issues, beginning with gender, before moving on to race and other areas.

Susan Brownmiller's assertion that "*Red Riding Hood* is a parable of rape" (Brownmiller 1976, 310) captures the provocative tone of the early debates around sexism, which are still powerful in generating class discussion. This is particularly the case with the fairy tale, which I shall concentrate on as it presents material that is likely to be well known to all. Marcia Lieberman's work provides a useful starting point, arguing that females in these tales are either "beautiful . . . passive, submissive, and helpless" (Lieberman 1986, 190–1), or old and ugly (good, older women tend to be remote figures). Lieberman's work can be set beside Alison Lurie's, to whom Lieberman was responding, with her claim that "Fairy tales . . . portrayed a society in which women were as competent and active as men" (Lurie 1991, 34). In an attempt to be more objective, Ruth B. Bottigheimer (1987) conducted a content analysis of the entire corpus of the 1857 Brothers Grimm edition (211 tales). However, it might be objected that this itself introduces a bias, for this collection also "includes unusual fables, legends, anecdotes, jokes, and religious tales," besides omitting thirty-two fairy tales that had appeared in earlier editions of their work (Zipes 1992, xxviii). Bottigheimer's detailed analysis appears exemplary, indicating, for instance, how the use of different verbs shows that females were more passive, becoming increasingly silenced and spoken for; but others have queried this, arguing that it is not the verb *per se* that is important (e.g. *sprechen* vs. *sagen*), but how it operates in a particular context (Kamenetsky 1992, 282).

There are other problems with content analysis: first it tends to read texts rather literally and, secondly, has a fairly passive model of the child reader, similar to the "effects" school of media research (Barker 1987; Rudd 2000). Regarding the former criticism, some writers have argued that the dream-like nature of many fairy tales means that the characters can represent different aspects of the protagonist's psyche (Bettelheim 1976; Thomas 1989; Wilson 1983); for example, Carol Heilbrun reads Sleeping Beauty not as passive in relation to a male hero, but as awakening to an active side of herself (Heilbrun 1979; see also Barzilai 1990 on *Snow White*). The second issue will be addressed in the next section, but Lieberman's question, "What is the precise effect that the story of

'Snow-White and the Seven Dwarfs' has upon a child?" (Lieberman 1986, 187) makes the point clear, as though there could ever be a calculable answer.

Poststructuralist critics, in particular, have challenged social realist approaches, arguing that, rather than conceptualizing readers as unitary subjects, we need to see them as constructed through multiple subjectivities which position them in different ways, dependent on their engagement with particular texts (Davies 1989; Walkerdine 1990):

> Feminist analyses of stories, then, need to pay attention not only to the content, but also to the metaphors, the forms of relationship, the patterns of power and desire that are created in the text. (Davies 1989, 45)

There is no notion here of *more realistic* representations of women, as though some essential woman exists beyond the text, which the text should aspire to configure. We only ever have textual constructions of women, children—and of everything else. Therefore we need to look at how such tales operate at a phantasy level, to see how they help girls (in this case) come to accept a more selfless position, in the sure personal knowledge that "Some day my prince will come" (Walkerdine 1990, 87–106).

Davies draws on Julia Kristeva's useful three-tier model of feminist struggle, the first corresponding to liberal feminism, where equality is demanded; the second, radical feminism, where the male order is rejected and the female extolled; and the third, where the whole division between masculine and feminine is seen as artificial (Davies 1989, 70). Thus one might see Blyton's *Famous Five* as engaging with liberal feminism: rather than the books themselves being simply sexist (belittling female readers' enjoyment), they can be seen as exploring sexism, querying why, for instance, it is the norm for boys to avoid domestic tasks (Rudd 2000). As regards the second tier, one might see many schoolgirl series as constructing a female realm beyond patriarchy (Auchmuty 1992; Foster and Simons 1995; Rudd 2000). The third tier, however, depends on a poststructuralist notion of subjectivity, rejecting biological essentialism. This essentialism was the problem that Davies found young children had with modern fairy tales: while the roles might be reversed, with feisty heroines and wimpy heroes (e.g. Munsch and Martchenko 1980), the children's own identity was still premised on a binary model of the sexes. Such notions are far more deeply entrenched than we might realize, as Perry Nodelman's valuable class exercise shows. He had students read *The Tale of Peter Rabbit* with Peter's gender reversed. As Honeysweet (*sic*!), Master P. Rabbit was read differently: her punishment at the end was seen as less acceptable (males, in other words, being read as naturally naughty and antisocial, it being more challenging for a girl to behave in this way); and her nakedness, too, took on a different meaning:

> A naked girl is a sex object, even a naked girl rabbit. She makes us uncomfortable because the revelation of her nakedness implies, not physical aggression and competence, but availability, lack of control or restraint, a dangerously or deliciously unbridled revelation of passion and instinct. (Nodelman 2002, 6)

This comes from an excellent collection of work on masculinities (Stephens 2002), where it is recognized that, even in tales of positive, counter-stereotypical females, patriarchy is still reinscribed because of underlying differential relations of power—in what is sometimes termed the *nor-male* order. Well-known texts such as Gene Kemp's *The Turbulent Term of Tyke Tyler* (1977) and Anne Fine's *Bill's New Frock* (1990)—certainly worthy of class discussion—are still prey to such nor-male reading practices (Pennell 2002). Judith Butler's work is an excellent resource here, showing how multiple and diffuse our gendered identities are, and generally queering our normal reading practices (Butler 1993; Rabinowitz 2004).

Before leaving the issue of gender, two other issues warrant mention: sexual content in children's books, or its lack, which again can usefully be read in terms of Foucault's "repressive hypothesis" (Foucault 1981); and sexual orientation, another area neglected till recently (Burt 1998; Kidd 1998; and see Nelson 1991; Clark 1996).

A more longstanding concern in children's literature, again going back to the 1960s, is with race and ethnicity. To make its study more than an academic discussion, it is well worth using some of the more notorious texts in class, such as *Little Black Sambo* (Bannerman 1899), *The Adventures of Two Dutch Dolls and a Golliwogg* (Upton and Upton 1895), or *Doctor Dolittle* (Lofting 1922). After the initial cries of "racism" the question of why and how they are racist can be asked. The context and history of each of these books might also be explored, and the debate widened a little (see, for instance, Hay (1981) and Susina (1999) on Bannerman; Olson (2000) and Rudd (2004b) on the Uptons; and Steege (2003) on Lofting). There are many issues to probe: definitions of racism (themselves based on rather questionable nineteenth-century constructions of "race"), and questions about the significance of both authorial intention and reader's perception (an incident is racist if it is so perceived by the victim or anyone else, the UK's McPherson Report (1999) recommended as a universal criterion). There are also issues of whether "racist" material from the past should be left intact, thereby fostering historical awareness, or removed (erased from history), or—also contentious—updated. Often, with children's books, updating is done covertly so that it is invisible (Rudd 2000).

Returning to the more general issue of marginalization, however, the important point is that most children's literature, till quite recently, concentrated on the majority culture (usually middle-class, male, and white). Apart from the stereotypes, other ethnicities are simply absent (Bradford 2001; Morrison 1992; MacCann 2000). Given that many of these attitudes grow out of imperialism, postcolonial studies also has much to offer. It seeks to show how colonial structures and meanings still exert a powerful force, whilst simultaneously seeking to make space for the dominated (Ashcroft et al. 1995). Roderick McGillis's title, *Voices of the Other* (1999), states this purpose exactly. And, just as children are linked to women, so they are to other oppressed groups: "Just as colonial subjects were voiceless . . . children are also voiceless," as M. Daphne Kutzer puts it (2000, xvi; see also McGillis 1996a; Rose 1984). Kutzer explores what she sees as children's literature's "highly conservative" nature (Kutzer 2000, xvi), although, sad to say, she engages very little with poststructuralist theory, unlike, say, Low (1996), McGillis (1999) or Phillips (1997).

The reading of children's texts through an imperial lens is certainly worthwhile, whether it be *Alice's Adventures in Wonderland* (Armstrong 1990; Bivona 1990), school and adventure stories (Bratton 1981; Bristow 1991; Richards 1988), Frances Hodgson Burnett (Phillips 1993; McGillis 1996b), or Kipling's work (Bristow 1991; Low 1996; Randall 2000). Kutzer looks at many of these authors, too, plus Nesbit and Milne, who are perhaps less considered in these terms, and some postwar British books. Others have usefully included school textbooks and magazines in their analyses (Castle 1996).

Nationalism is a closely related issue, as is class. Paul Hazard's wishful claim that "the pleasant books of childhood cross all the frontiers; there is no duty to be paid on inspiration" (Hazard 1944, 147) is a provocative starting point, inviting students to examine the processes by which national identities are forged. Kipling's books, *Puck of Pook's Hill* (1906) and *Rewards and Fairies* (1910) in particular, can be seen to construct a sense of Englishness that continues in the landscapes of Kenneth Grahame and Enid Blyton, through to the Ahlbergs (Meek 2001)—a landscape that is more particularly of southern England (Watkins 1992). The Grimms' fairy tales have also been seen as attempts to give the German state a cultural identity (Ellis 1983; Zipes 1988), to which Nazi ideology gave a peculiarly Aryan spin (Kamenetsky 1984). But if we are looking at national and cultural hegemony, English-language books are surely the victors. As Hunt notes, "Whereas as many as 70 per cent of books for children produced in France are translations into French, fewer than 1 per cent of English-language books are translations" (Hunt 1992, 21). Of course, English speakers are really the losers. *Contra* Hazard, cultural imperialism is alive and well (Lawson Lucas 1997; Webb 2000).

Kutzer finishes her book commenting that "the Bastables and Walkers and Blacketts will, their stories suggest, grow into proper middle-class gentlemen and ladies who have bourgeois, if not conservative, values" (Kutzer 2000, 139), making explicit the links between empire and class. Certainly, English children's literature was solidly middle-class till comparatively recently, whilst American fiction has always been more egalitarian in this respect (Avery 1994; Macleod 1994), but the bias is still there. Once again, it is useful to focus students' attention on the silences of earlier texts, and how these have been subsequently addressed; for example, the way in which Jan Needle's *Wild Wood* (1981) reworks Grahame's *The Wind in the Willows* along working-class lines, or, in colonial terms, *Lord of the Flies* (1954) responds to *Coral Island* and Tournier's *Friday and Robinson* (2003) to *Robinson Crusoe*. In a seminal study, Stephens and McCallum consider such "reversions" in detail (Stephens and McCallum 1998, 4). A more imaginative exercise is to have students generate their own reversions (Pope 2002, 276–80).

Of particular note in Grahame's work is the way that issues of gender and class are concealed through the use of animal characters. These are frequently used in children's literature as a way eliding problematic issues—which would also include those of ethnicity, sexuality, and childhood as a dependent state. In her colonial readings, for example, Kutzer makes an interesting argument for Kanga, Tigger, and Heffalump being *foreigners* in the *Pooh* stories. The way that particular animals signify culturally is currently being explored in an excellent series by Reaktion books (e.g. Sax, 2003; see also Baker 1993; Ritvo 1987). There is also the interesting area of animal–human metamorphosis, which has recently received more attention (e.g. Lassén-Seger, 2004; Warner 2002).

The charge of *presentism*, though, needs to be continually borne in mind, whereby we see our current position as enlightened, demystifying earlier ideological obfuscation without realizing that we also are ideologically situated. A growing discourse of concern, for instance, is ecocriticism (Kerridge and Sammells 1998). Taking just one aspect, animal rights, we can now see that what was previously invisible to many has been foregrounded—as, for instance, with all the hunting scenes that were a standard backdrop in school fiction, and against which might be juxtaposed Dahl's *The Magic Finger* (Cadogan and Craig 2003, 13). For a more general argument against an invidious speciesism in literature in general, see John Simons (2002).

A final area to mention, again often invisible, is disability; that is, the state of being differently abled. Lois Keith (2001) has recently explored how disability is used as a trope for the punishment and disciplining of the unruly child—as, most famously, in *What Katy Did*. Here, and in studies that take more literal readings of disabilities (Quicke 1985), Foucault's power/knowledge is again relevant, whereby the medical model of disability constructs it as being a condition of the individual body, rather than a product of wider social practices.

The post-text

Literary studies, with its stress on the "verbal icon," has generally been reluctant to recognize actual readers, with some rare exceptions (e.g. Richards 1929; Holland, 1975). Even Wolfgang Iser's implied reader is very much a hypothetical construct, and one constrained by the text (Iser 1974, 1978). Historically, though, the discipline of children's literature, with its roots in librarianship and education, has always been concerned with the reader, or audience, as has cultural studies (e.g. Ang 1985; Radway 1987; Willis 1990). What children's literature lacked was a theoretical framing of what otherwise amounts to empty empiricism. Small wonder, then, that it adopted Iser's reception theory with such alacrity (Corcoran and Evans 1987; Hayhoe and Parker 1990). Moreover, cultural studies has not generally shirked studies of children, though their marginalization is still an issue; for example, in comics there is the work of Martin Barker (1989), Elizabeth Frazer (1987), Angela McRobbie (1982), and Valerie Walkerdine (1990); in television, David Buckingham (1993) and Bob Hodge and David Tripp (1986)—and others mentioned later. In this section I will, however, concentrate on studies of books (following my earlier practice), before discussing other cultural products.

On children's reading, apart from some useful groundwork surveys (e.g. Hall and Coles, 1996; Reynolds 1996), there have been various qualitative studies; for instance, Cherland (1994), Christian-Smith

(1990), Frith (1985), Fry (1985) and Sarland (1991), the latter being centrally involved with how children actively make sense of culture's texts. Rudd, also stressing this active engagement, considers readers of Dahl (Rudd 1992) and Blyton (Rudd 2000). Such studies as the above should be useful in combating a tendency to overgeneralize about children's likes, while also showing that children can be involved in discussions of taste. However, empirical research should never be seen as granting unmediated access to reality. Studies always operate within particular regimes of truth, in Foucault's terms, and are always discursively constructed.

There have also been some more detailed, ethnographic studies, wherein child reading is set in the context of everyday life. Wolf and Heath (1992) is exemplary, looking at two young siblings' reading practices, which are shown interwoven with other activities—reminiscent of Barthes' notion of a text being a weave of "citations, references, echoes, cultural languages . . . which cut across it through and through in a vast stereophony" (Barthes 1977, 160). As Wolf and Heath put it, a "text that is known to a child does not remain in its original state or even in a steady, stable form; instead, the child rewrites it. Texts become transformative stock to which young readers can return again and again as they figure out their own roles, words, actions, and critiques of their current situations" (Wolf and Heath 1992, 109–10).

Of course, students' own childhood reading experiences can usefully be explored, to make manifest their perceptions of what children's literature involves, and possible differences between child and adult reading. On this, Francis Spufford (2002) and Kate Bernheimer (1998) are useful resources. What often emerges, as Wolf and Heath showed, is that books are entwined with other aspects of the child's world. Blyton's books, for instance, were not seen by my respondents as self-contained objects, but spilled over into games, role-playing, writing, and the like: the books were a vehicle for fantasy engagements around issues of power and agency (Rudd 2000). Carol Steedman, in *Landscape for a Good Woman*, gives an excellent account of how gender and class impacted on her childhood reading, especially of Andersen's "The Snow Queen," where she saw herself as the boy, Kay, with a lump of ice in her own heart (Steedman 1986). For a male viewpoint, Graham Dawson (1994) and David Jackson (1990) give personal testimony on the power of constructions of masculinity.

Issues of storytelling impinge on some of the above studies, and they have also been studied in their own right. Whilst the universality of narrative has often been claimed (Bruner 1986; Hardy 1975), there are huge cultural differences in what counts as a story. Heath's *Ways with Words* (1983) is a key work, contrasting the literal tellings of a white, American, fundamentalist, Christian community with a black one, where stories were far more open-ended, based on everyday life, but also used wild exaggeration and vivid language. Brian Sutton-Smith's study *The Folkstories of Children* (1981) is also revealing; many of the stories he collected have a Beckettian feel which would make them completely unacceptable to most mainstream children's publishers (see also Steedman 1982).

Notions of subjectivity have also been linked to storytelling, particularly using the work of Lacan (where the individual is shaped by the cultural Other; e.g. Walkerdine 1984; Fox 1993, 31–4) and Bakhtin, where the self is formed through a dialogic relation with the discourses of society. While both thinkers have been profoundly influential in cultural studies, it is Bakhtin's work that I shall mention here, as it permits a far more active, ideologically informed model of text–reader relations than reader-response theory. In his notion of *dialogism*, language is seen as comprising numerous different discourses, or speech genres, which are material carriers of ideology (Bakhtin 1981; Vološinov 1973). As the poststructuralists emphasize, it is only through engaging with these different registers that we become social beings. However, he differs from many poststructuralists in seeing these registers as having a particular social provenance, and themselves being answered from a particular sociocultural location. Being positioned as a child therefore has certain ideological consequences. In Bakhtin's model, the reader is always active, engaged in dialogic relation with the discourses of a text (Barker 1989; McCallum 1999; Rudd 2000; 2004a).

An awareness of ideology is frequently missing in discussions of children's literature. Peter Hollindale's (1988) analysis is still a good starting point, distinguishing three categories of ideology, running from overt prejudices to the ideology intrinsic to language. Of course, most ideology is linguistically mediated, as Stephens (1992) indicates in a more sophisticated analysis that draws on Foucault, Bakhtin, and discourse analysis (Fairclough 1989). Stephens (1992) and Stephens and McCallum (1998) give detailed accounts of how ideology operates in texts, both in a bottom-up way, through narratological elements (point of view, focalization, and so forth), and top-down, through metanarrative framing. Their texts provide a number of worked examples which should inspire further classroom work.

Beyond the book

The three different moments of the life of a cultural object have now been covered—its production, consumption, and appropriation/dissemination—in relation to children's literature. However, though the book has been central to literary study, it has probably never been central to any but a few children, and, nowadays, the book is just one of a number of media products, which are often interlinked. It is therefore artificial to see it as distinctive—especially as, for corporate capitalism, it is intellectual property that is central, regardless of its media incarnation; this property is then exploited across books, film, TV, video/DVD, CD-ROM, Internet, and other merchandizing (Mackey 1998; Rudd 2000). However, although this process has recently escalated, it would be naïve to see earlier children's books as somehow immune from the process. It is no coincidence that in the eighteenth century, when the children's book trade was established, toys and games were also being produced in large numbers, or that John Newbery sold his book with a pincushion and ball. Beatrix Potter, too, had no qualms about exploiting her characters through merchandizing (Mackey 1998).

What needs to be borne in mind, however, is the way that these cultural products help shape the child. Thus the middle-class child is conceived as a being with time to play, and has spaces which foster such play (nurseries, walled gardens)—spaces that are themselves modelled in books. Toys might be given to children by loving adults, but the idea is for the child then to go away and play alone (Sutton-Smith 1986, 53). In Foucauldian terms, there is a shift from a disciplinary regime to a child-centred one, wherein the child is seen to develop him/herself (Walkerdine 1984). Toys also introduce the child to the concept of private property (Dixon 1990) and, more often than not, to gender-appropriate behaviour; as Klugman (1999) notes, even boys' action-men figures have more joints than girls' dolls, giving them more active bodies.

Work on dolls is of particular interest, intersecting closely with literature, as, for example, in the more gender-neutral teddy bear and golliwog, which have been fictionalized by countless writers (Blount 1974), and, in the case of the latter, proved controversial as racist icons (Olson 2000; Rudd 2004b). Girls' dolls are also controversial, though they are far more complex than a straight socializing model might suggest; for example, Formanek-Brunell (1998) found that many treated their dolls in a manner similar to Maggie Tulliver's famously abused doll in *The Mill on the Floss*. Erica Rand (1995) also writes intriguingly about people's "queer" usage of Barbie dolls. For a recent, culturally and economically informed study of the toy industry in general, see Cross (1997).

There has been criticism that many books and TV programmes today are simply commercials for particular products, like "My Little Pony" (Kline 1993). While this is certainly a concern, Ellen Seiter (1993) rightly points out (in a comment reminiscent of Myers's critique of the universalization of the male Romantic child, earlier) that this view has a middle-class, male bias, and belittles girls' affiliative enjoyment of these works. It is worth noting a split here, between those studies which see the child as at the mercy of capitalist enterprise (e.g. Steinberg and Kincheloe 1997; Dixon speaks of children being "commercially and ideologically surrounded" (Dixon 1990, 71) and those who tend to celebrate the child as a subversive being, operating like a poacher, to use Michel de Certeau's term (1984; Fiske, 1989), appropriating material for their own devices. This trend is apparent in Henry Jenkins' compilation, *The Children's Culture Reader* (1998; Jenkins also edited a collection on fan-fiction, called *Textual Poachers* (1992)) and, moving on to television, in Bazalgette and Buckingham's comment: "Children have considerable power to determine their own readings and pleasures: they may well refuse to occupy, or even fail to perceive, the positions our adult analysis identifies as being marked out for them" (Bazalgette and Buckingham 1995, 7).

It is a worthwhile point (said in relation to the finding that in the UK, children were then in the minority in watching children's TV, preferring adult programmes; the majority comprised the unemployed and elderly) but tends to downplay the power disparity between producer and consumer, and to neglect the matter of where children's pleasures originate in the first place. This said, the utopian dimension enacted in these engagements should not be dismissed (Bakhtin 1968; Bloch 1988; Dyer 1981), and the fact that children are active in their reading is certainly borne out in research (Hodge and Tripp 1986; Kinder 1999; Rudd 1994). For a recent overview of TV's general impact on childhood, see Oswell (2002).

In film, video, and DVD there is also growing scholarship on a number of relevant topics: children's cinema (Nation 1997), and film (Wojcik-Andrews 2000), and book adaptation—especially of Disney (Bell et al 1995; Byrne and McQuillan 1999; Schickel 1968), but also other works (Street 1983; Wojcik-Andrews 1996). In-class analysis is especially fruitful in works where different versions exist, as of *Little Women* (McCallum 2000), *The Secret Garden* (Mackey 1996; Gillispie 1996), and *Peter Pan* (Hollindale 1993; Pace 1996). Adaptation, of course, takes many forms, as the excellent monograph by Margaret Mackey (1998) on *Peter Rabbit* shows, where some versions—like the notorious Ladybird edition of 1987—have neither Beatrix Potter's original artwork nor her words.

Space precludes discussion of all relevant areas, but let me briefly indicate a few more, which can be drawn upon when discussing particular texts, or when addressing the whole issue of constructions of childhood: photographs and paintings of the child (Higonnet 1998; Brown 2002); the child in film (Büssing 1987; Wilson 2003); the child in fiction (Blum 1995; Pifer 2000); childhood in autobiography (Coe 1984; Gullestad 1996); children's costume (Brooke 2003); children's bodies (Prout 2000); children's environments (James 1993); children and advertising (Kenway and Bullen 2001); the church and childhood (Wood 1994); computing/the Internet and children (e.g. Buckingham 2000; Meyrowitz, 1985; Steinberg and Kincheloe 1997); and finally, the more general use of the child as a trope (Burman 1998; Connell 2001; Eiss 1995; Lesnik-Oberstein 2003).

Some of the above overlaps with children's own cultural concerns, which have been researched by a number of scholars, looking at children's games, playground chants, skipping rhymes, jokes, verbal lore, sweets, and so on (Butler 1989; Grugeon 1988; James 1982; Kehily and Swann 2003; Opie and Opie 1959; Thomas 1989). Once again, it is worth noting a tendency to romanticize children's culture, whereas, as James et al. note, it operates dialectically in relation to learning about the adult world (James et al. 1998, 89).

Conclusion

At the beginning, I noted that cultural studies is always in process. Accordingly, attempts to give comprehensive coverage of its relevance to child studies are not only difficult, but misplaced. I am aware that some areas have only been skated over—as for example, Lacanian psychoanalysis, which has been very influential in cultural studies (e.g. Coats 2004). While it is the theoretical material that alienates some students, I have found that it can be made more palatable, and seemingly relevant, if it is learned through practical analysis; in short, by *doing* theory, examples of which I've tried to provide. There has also been very little discussion of methodological issues, though these are important in the area of reader studies. For recent developments I recommend Mitchell and Reid-Walsh (2002; see also Rudd 2000).

To finish, I'd like to draw attention to the erstwhile neglect of children's literature—itself a topic worthy of analysis—to indicate some ways in which this is changing, as the area becomes increasingly embedded in general studies of cultural issues. The neglect, first, is a well-known issue. Children's literature rarely features in general works on literature and complete editions of an author's *oeuvre* often deliberately exclude their work for children. Beverly Lyon Clark (2003) provocatively entitled her recent monograph, *Kiddie Lit*, in an attempt to revalue the term. It is no coincidence, either, that the area has been closely associated with women. Peter Hunt quotes some research indicating that, in the late 1980s in the US, "92% of teachers of children's literature in higher education are women [but] . . . only 5% of these [are] full professors" (Hunt 1995, 25). This ghettoization, however, is slowly changing, as a result of larger social issues, including moral panics, about the state of childhood and children's reading. There are works like Marjorie Garber's *Vested Interests*, on transvestism, which includes a chapter on *Peter Pan*; there is James Kincaid's (1992) analysis of paedophilia, which discusses Barrie and Lewis Carroll; and, as a last example, Marina Warner's work is always exemplary in drawing on all cultural products, regardless of origin (e.g. Warner 2002). Moreover, those involved in children's literature are also increasingly writing texts that operate in a wider context, such as, for instance, Lynne Vallone's *Disciplines of Virtue: Girls' Culture in the Eighteenth and Nineteenth Centuries* (1995; also Nelson and Vallone 1994). Where course structures permit it, thinking outside traditional disciplinary boxes can only help strengthen a cultural studies approach to children's literature.

Works cited

Adams, Richard. 1973. *Watership Down*. Harmondsworth: Penguin.

Ahlberg, Janet and Allan Ahlberg. 1978. *Each Peach Pear Plum*. Harmondsworth: Kestrel.

Alexandre-Bidon, Daniele and Didier Lett. 1999. *Children in the Middle Ages: fifth–fifteenth centuries*. Notre Dame, IN: University of Notre Dame Press.

Ang, Ien. 1985. *Watching Dallas*. London: Methuen.

Ariès, Philippe. 1973. *Centuries of Childhood*. Harmondsworth: Penguin.

Armstrong, Nancy. 1990. "The Occidental Alice." *differences* 2:3–40.

Ashcroft, Bill, Gareth Griffiths, and Helen Tiffin, eds. 1995. *The Post-Colonial Studies Reader*. London: Routledge.

Atkins, Laura. 2004. "A publisher's dilemma: the place of the child in the publication of children's books." 47–54 in *New Voices in Children's Literature*. Lichfield: Pied Piper Publishing.

Auchmuty, Rosemary. 1992. *The World of Girls*. London: Women's Press.

Avery, Gillian. 1994. *Behold the Child: the development of children's literature in America, 1621–1921*. London: Bodley Head.

Baker, Steven. 1993. *Picturing the Beast: animals, identity and representation*. Manchester: Manchester University Press.

Bakhtin, M. M. 1968. *Rabelais and his World*. Cambridge: Massachussetts Institute of Technology Press.

Bakhtin, M. M. 1981. *The Dialogic Imagination: four essays*. Austin: University of Texas Press.

Bannerman, Helen. 1899. *The Story of Little Black Sambo*. London: Grant Richards.

Barker, Martin. 1987. "Mass media studies and the question of ideology." *Radical Philosophy* 46:27–33.

———. 1989. *Comics: ideology, power and the critics*. Manchester: Manchester University Press.

Barry, Peter. 2002. *Beginning Theory: an introduction to literary and cultural theory*. 2nd edn. Manchester: Manchester University Press.

Barthes, Roland. 1977. *Image, Music, Text: essays*. Selected and translated by Stephen Heath. London: Fontana.

Barzilai, Shuli. 1990. "Reading 'Snow White': the mother's story." *Signs* 15.3:513–54.

Bazalgette, Cary and David Buckingham, eds. 1995. *In Front of the Children: screen entertainment and young audiences*. London: British Film Institute.

Beckett, Sandra L., ed. 1999. *Transcending Boundaries: writing for a dual audience of children and adults*. New York & London: Garland.

Bell, Elizabeth, Lynda Haas, and Laura Sells, eds. 1995. *From Mouse to Mermaid: the politics of film, gender, and culture*. Bloomington & Indianapolis: Indiana University Press.

Benton, Michael. 1996. "Reader-response criticism." 71–88 in *International Companion Encyclopedia of Children's Literature*. Edited by Peter Hunt. London & New York: Routledge.

Bernheimer, Kate, ed. 1998. *Mirror, Mirror on the Wall: women writers explore their favorite fairy tales*. New York & London: Anchor Books.

Bettelheim, Bruno. 1976. *The Uses of Enchantment: the meaning and importance of fairy tales*. London: Thames and Hudson.

Bhabha, Homi K. 1994. *The Location of Culture*. London & New York: Routledge.

Bivona, Daniel. 1990. *Desire and Contradiction: imperial visions and domestic debates in Victorian literature*. Manchester: Manchester University Press.

Bloch, Ernst. 1988. *The Utopian Function of Art and Literature: selected essays*. Translated by Jack Zipes and Frank Mecklenburg. Cambridge, MA and London: MIT Press.

Blount, Margaret. 1974. *Animal Land: the creatures of children's fiction*. London: Hutchinson.

Blum, Virginia L. 1995. *Hide and Seek: the child between psychoanalysis and fiction*. Urbana: University of Illinois Press.

Bottigheimer, Ruth B. 1987. *Grimms' Bad Girls and Bold Boys: the moral and social vision of the tales*. New Haven: Yale University Press.

———. 1996. *The Bible For Children: from the age of Gutenberg to the present*. New Haven: Yale University Press.

Bradford, Clare. 2001. *Reading Race: Aboriginality in Australian children's literature*. Carlton, Vic.: Melbourne University Press.

Brannigan, John, Ruth Robbins, and Julian Wolfreys, eds. 1996. *Applying: to Derrida*. Basingstoke: Macmillan—now Palgrave Macmillan.

Bratton, J. S. 1981. *The Impact of Victorian Children's Fiction*. London: Croom Helm.

Briggs, Julia. 1989. "Women writers and writing for children: from Sarah Fielding to E. Nesbit." 221–50 in *Children and their Books: a celebration of the work of Iona and Peter Opie*. Edited by Gillian Avery and Julia Briggs. Oxford: Clarendon Press.

Bristow, Joseph. 1991. *Empire Boys: adventures in a man's world*. London: HarperCollins.

Brooke, Iris. 2003. *English Children's Costume 1775–1920*. New York: Dover Publications.

Brown, Marilyn R., ed. 2002. *Picturing children: constructions of childhood between Rousseau and Freud*. Aldershot: Ashgate.

Brownmiller, Susan. 1976. *Against our Will: men, women and rape*. Harmondsworth: Penguin.

Bruner, Jerome. 1986. *Actual Minds, Possible Worlds*. Cambridge, MA & London: Harvard University Press.

Buckingham, David, ed. 1993. *Reading Audiences: young people and the media*. Manchester: Manchester University Press.

Buckingham, David. 2000. *After the Death of Childhood: growing up in the age of electronic media*. Cambridge: Polity Press.

Burman, Erica. 1998. "The pedagogics of post-modernity: the address to the child as a political subject and object." 55–88 in *Children in Culture: approaches to childhood*. Editor Karín Lesnik-Oberstein. Basingstoke: Macmillan—now Palgrave Macmillan.

Burt, Richard. 1998. *Unspeakable Shaxxxspeares: queer theory and American kiddie culture*. New York: St. Martin's Press—now Palgrave Macmillian.

Büssing, Sabine. 1987. *Aliens in the Home: the child in horror fiction*. New York/London: Greenwood Press.

Butler, Francelia. 1989. *Skipping Around the World: the ritual nature of folk rhymes*. Hamden, CT: Library Professional Publications.

Butler, Judith. 1990. *Gender Trouble: feminism and the subversion of identity*.

———. 1993. *Bodies that Matter: on the discursive limits of "sex."* New York & London: Routledge.

Byrne, Eleanor and Martin McQuillan. 1999. *Deconstructing Disney*. London: Pluto.

Cadogan, Mary and Patricia Craig. 2003. *You're a Brick, Angela: the girls' story 1839–1985*, 2nd edn. Bath: Girls Gone By Publishers.

Castle, Kathryn. 1996. *Britannia's Children: reading colonialism through children's books and magazines*. Manchester: Manchester University Press.

Cherland, Meredith Rogers. 1994. *Private Practices: girls reading fiction and constructing identity*. London: Taylor & Francis.

Christian-Smith, Linda K. 1990. *Becoming a Woman through Romance*. New York: Routledge.

Clark, Beverly Lyon. 1996. *Regendering the School Story: sassy sissies and tattling tomboys*. New York & London: Garland.

———. 2003. *Kiddie Lit: the cultural construction of children's literature in America*. Baltimore & London: Johns Hopkins University Press.

Coats, Karen. 2004. *Looking Glasses and Neverlands: Lacan, desire, and subjectivity in children's literature*. Iowa: University of Iowa Press.

Coe, Richard. 1984. *When the Grass was Taller: autobiography and the experience of childhood*. New Haven, NJ: Yale University Press.

Cole, Barbara. 1986. *Princess Smartypants*. London: Hamilton.

Connell, Matt F. 2001. "Childhood experiences and the image of utopia: the broken promise of Adorno's Proustian sublimations." *Radical Philosophy* 99:19–30.

Corcoran, Bill and Emrys Evans, eds. 1987. *Readers, Texts, Teachers*. Milton Keynes: Open University Press.
Cross, Gary. 1997. *Kids' Stuff: toys and the changing world of American childhood*. Cambridge, MA: Harvard University Press.
Dahl, Roald. 1966. *The Magic Finger*. New York: Harper & Row.
Darton, F. J. Harvey. 1982. *Children's Books in England: five centuries of social life*, 3rd edn, revised by Brian Alderson. Cambridge: Cambridge University Press.
Davies, Bronwyn. 1989. *Frogs and Snails and Feminist Tales: preschool children and gender*. Sydney: Allen & Unwin.
Davis, Robert Con and Ronald Schleifer, eds. 1988. *Contemporary Literary Criticism: literary and cultural studies*, 4th edn. Harlow: Longman.
Dawson, Graham. 1994. *Soldier Heroes: British adventure, empire and the imagining of masculinities*. London: Routledge.
de Certeau, Michel. 1984. *The Practice of Everyday Life*. Translated by Steven Rendall. Berkeley and London: University of California Press.
Demers, Patricia. 2003. *From Instruction to Delight: an anthology of children's literature to 1850*, 2nd edn. New York: Oxford University Press.
Derrida, Jacques. 1988. *Limited Inc*. Evanston, IL: Northwestern University Press.
———. 1994. *Specters of Marx: the state of debt, the work of mourning, and the New International*. Translated by Peggy Kamuf. London & New York: Routledge.
Dixon, Bob. 1977a. *Catching them Young, Vol. 1: sex, race and class in children's fiction*. London: Pluto Press.
———. 1977b. *Catching them Young, Vol. 2: political ideas in children's fiction*. London: Pluto Press.
———. 1990. *Playing Them False: a study of children's toys, games and puzzles*. Stoke-on-Trent: Trentham Books.
Dollimore, Jonathan and Alan Sinfield, eds. 1985. *Political Shakespeare: new essays in cultural materialism*. Manchester: Manchester University Press.
Donzelot, Jacques. 1979. *The Policing of Families*. London: Hutchinson.
Dorfman, Ariel. 1983. *The Empire's Old Clothes: what the Lone Ranger, Babar, and other innocent heroes do to our minds*. New York: Pantheon.
Dorfman, Ariel and Armand Mattelart. 1975. *How to Read Donald Duck: imperialist ideology in the Disney comic*. London: International General.
Drotner, Kirsten. 1988. *English Children and their Magazines, 1751–1945*. New Haven and London: Yale University Press.
During, Simon, ed. 1999. *The Cultural Studies Reader*, 2nd edn. London: Routledge.
Dusinberre, Juliet. 1987. *Alice to the Lighthouse: children's books and radical experiments in art*. Basingstoke: Macmillan—now Palgrave Macmillan.
Dyer, Richard. 1981. "Entertainment and utopia." 175–89 in *Genre: the musical, a reader*. Edited by Rick Altman. London: Routledge & Kegan Paul.
Easthope, Antony. 1991. *Literary into Cultural Studies*. London & New York: Routledge.
Eiss, Harry. 1995. *Images of the Child*. Bowling Green: Bowling Green State University Popular Press.
Ellis, John Martin. 1983. *One Fairy Tale too Many: the Brothers Grimm and their tales*. Chicago: University of Chicago Press.
Fairclough, Norman L. 1989. *Language and Power*. London & New York: Longman.
Fine, Anne. 1990. *Bill's New Frock*. London: Mammoth.
Fiske, John. 1989. *Understanding Popular Culture*. Boston and London: Unwin Hyman.

Formanek-Brunell, Miriam. 1998. "The Politics of dollhood in nineteenth-century America." 363–81 in *The Children's Culture Reader*. Edited by Henry Jenkins. New York & London: New York University Press.

Foster, Shirley and Judy Simons. 1995. *What Katy Read: feminist re-readings of "classic" stories for girls*. Basingstoke: Macmillan—now Palgrave Macmillan.

Foucault, Michel. 1977. *Discipline and Punish: the birth of the prison*. Translated by Alan Sheridan. London: Allen Lane.

———. 1980. *Power/ Knowledge: selected interviews and other writings, 1972–1977*. London: Harvester Wheatsheaf.

———. 1981. *The History of Sexuality: an introduction*. Translated by R. Hurley. London & New York: Penguin.

Fox, Carol. 1993. *At the Very Edge of the Forest: the influence of literature on storytelling by children*. London: Cassell.

Frazer, Elizabeth. 1987. "Teenage girls reading *Jackie*." *Media, Culture and Society*, 9:407–25.

Frith, Gill. 1985. " 'The time of your life': the meaning of the school story." 113–36 in *Language, Gender and Childhood*. Edited by Carolyn Steedman, Cathy Urwin and Valerie Walkderdine. London: Routledge & Kegan Paul.

Fry, Donald. 1985. *Children Talk about Books*. Milton Keynes: Open University Press.

Garber, Marjorie. 1991. *Vested Interests: cross-dressing and cultural anxiety*. New York: Routledge.

Gillispie, Julaine. 1996. "American film adaptations of *The Secret Garden*: reflections of sociological and historical change." *The Lion and the Unicorn* 20.1:132–52.

Golding, William. 1954. *Lord of the Flies*. London: Faber and Faber.

Grahame, Kenneth. 1908. *The Wind in the Willows*. London: Methuen.

Grossberg, Lawrence, Cary Nelson and Paula A. Treichler. 1991. *Cultural Studies*. New York: Routledge.

Grugeon, Elizabeth. 1988. "Children's oral culture—a transitional experience?" In *Oracy Matters*. Edited by Margaret Maclure, Terry Phillips, and Andrew Wilkinson. Buckingham: Open University Press.

Gullestad, Marianne, ed. 1996. *Imagined Childhoods: self and society in autobiographical accounts*. Oslo: Scandinavian University Press.

Hall, Christine and Martin Coles. 1996. *The Children's Reading Choices Project, at the University of Nottingham sponsored by W. H. Smith plc: summary report*. Nottingham: University of Nottingham.

Hall, Gary. 2002. *Culture in Bits: the monstrous future of theory*. New York: Continuum.

Halliwell, Martin and Andrew Mousley. 2003. *Critical Humanisms: Humanist–anti-humanist debates*. Edinburgh: Edinburgh University Press.

Hardy, Barbara. 1975. *Tellers and Listeners: the narrative imagination*. London: Athlone.

Harries, E. W. 2001. *Twice upon a Time: women writers and the history of the fairy tale*. Woodstock: Princeton University Press.

Hay, Elizabeth. 1981. *Sambo Sahib: the story of Helen Bannerman, author of "Little Black Sambo."* Edinburgh: Paul Harris.

Hayhoe, Mike and Stephen Parker, eds. 1990. *Reading and Response*. Milton Keynes: Open University Press.

Hazard, Paul. 1944. *Books, Children and Men*. Trans. Marguerite Mitchell. Boston: Horn Book.

Heath, Shirley Brice. 1983. *Ways with Words: language, life and work in communities and classrooms*. Cambridge: Cambridge University Press.
Heilbrun, Carolyn G. 1979. *Reinventing Womanhood*. New York: Norton.
Hendrick, Harry. 1997. *Children, Childhood and English Society, 1880–1990*. Cambridge: Cambridge University Press.
Henriques, Julian, Wendy Hollway, Cathy Urwin, Couze Venn and Valerie Walkerdine. 1984. *Changing the Subject: Psychology, social regulation and subjectivity*. London: Methuen.
Higonnet, Anne. 1998. *Pictures of Innocence: the history and crisis of ideal childhood*. London: Thames & Hudson.
———. 2002. "What do you want to know about children?" 200–206 in *Picturing Children: constructions of childhood between Rousseau and Freud*. Edited by Marilyn R. Brown. Aldershot: Ashgate.
Hodge, Robert and David Tripp. 1986. *Children and Television: a semiotic approach*. Cambridge: Polity Press.
Holland, Norman N. 1975. *5 Readers Reading*. London: Yale University Press.
Hollindale, Peter. 1988. "Ideology and the children's book." *Signal* 55:3–22.
———. 1993. "Peter Pan, Captain Hook and the Book of the Video." *Signal* 72:152–75.
Hughes, Felicity A. 1978. "Children's literature: theory and practice." *ELH* 45.3:542–61.
Hunt, Peter, ed. 1992. *Literature for Children: contemporary criticism*. London & New York: Routledge.
———. 1995. "Dragons in the department and academic emperors: why universities are afraid of children's literature." *Compar(a)ison* 2:19–31.
———, ed. 2001. *Children's Literature: an anthology 1801–1902*. Oxford: Blackwell.
Iser, Wolfgang. 1974. *The Implied Reader: patterns of communication in prose fiction from Bunyan to Beckett*. London: Johns Hopkins University Press.
———. 1978. *The Act of Reading: a theory of aesthetic response*. London: Routledge & Kegan Paul.
Jackson, David. 1990. *Unmasking Masculinity: a critical autobiography*. London: Unwin Hyman.
James, Allison. 1982. "Confections, concoctions and conceptions" 294–307 in *Popular Culture: past and present*. Edited by Bernard Waites, Tony Bennett and Graham Martin. London: Croom Helm.
———. 1993. *Childhood Identities: self and social relationships in the experience of the child*. Edinburgh: Edinburgh University Press.
James, Allison, Chris Jenks, and Alan Prout. 1998. *Theorizing Childhood*. Cambridge: Polity Press.
Jenkins, Henry. 1992. *Textual Poachers: television fans and participatory culture*. New York: Routledge.
———, ed. 1998. *The Children's Culture Reader*. New York & London: New York University Press.
Kamenetsky, Christa. 1984. *Children's Literature in Hitler's Germany: the cultural policy of National Socialism*. Athens, OH: Ohio University Press.
———. 1992. *The Brothers Grimm and their Critics: folktales and the quest for meaning*. Athens, OH: Ohio University Press.
Kehily, Mary and Joan Swann, eds. 2003. *Children's Cultural Worlds*. Chichester: John Wiley in association with The Open University Press.

Keith, Lois. 2001. *Take Up thy Bed and Walk*. London: Women's Press.
Kemp, Gene. 1977. *The Turbulent Term of Tyke Tiler*. London: Faber.
Kenway, Jane and Elizabeth Bullen. 2001. *Consuming Children: education, entertainment, advertising*. Maidenhead: Open University Press.
Kerridge, Richard and Neil Sammells, eds. 1998. *Writing the Environment: ecocriticism and literature*. London & New York: Zed Books.
Kidd, Kenneth. 1998. "Gay and Lesbian Children's Literature." *Children's Literature Association Quarterly* 23.3:114–68.
Kincaid, James R. 1992. *Child-Loving: the erotic child and Victorian culture*. London: Routledge.
Kincheloe, Joe L. 1998. "The new childhood: Home alone as a way of life." 159–77 in *The Children's Culture Reader*. Edited by Henry Jenkins. New York and London: New York University Press.
Kinder, Marsha, ed. 1999. *Kids' Media Culture*. Durham & London: Duke University Press.
Kipling, Rudyard. 1906. *Puck of Pook's Hill*. London: Macmillan.
———. 1910. *Rewards and Fairies*. London: Macmillan.
Kline, Daniel T. 2003. *Medieval Literature for Children*. New York: Garland Science.
Kline, Stephen. 1993. *Out of the Garden: toys, TV and children's culture in the age of marketing*. London: Verso.
Klugman, Karen. 1999. "A bad hair day for G. I. Joe." 169–82 in *Girls, Boys, Books, Toys: gender in children's literature and culture*. Edited by Beverly Lyon Clark and Margaret R. Higgonet. London: Johns Hopkins University Press.
Knoepflmacher, U. C. and Mitzi Myers, eds. 1997. " 'Cross-Writing' and the reconceptualizing of children's literature studies." *Children's Literature* 25.
Kohl, Herbert. 1995. *Should we burn Babar? Essays on children's literature and the power of stories*. New York: New Press.
Kutzer, M. Daphne. 2000. *Empire's Children: empire and imperialism in classic British children's books*. New York & London: Garland.
Lassén-Seger, Maria. 2004. "Exploring otherness: changes in the child–animal metamorphosis motif." 35–46 in *Change and Renewal in Children's Literature*. Edited by T. van der Walt. London: Praeger.
Lawson Lucas, Ann, ed. 1997. *Gunpowder and Sealing-wax: nationhood in children's literature*. Market Harborough: Troubador.
Lee, Nick. 1998. "Towards an immature sociology." *Sociological Review* 46.3:458–82.
Leeson, Robert. 1985. *Reading and Righting: the past, present and future of fiction for the young*. London: Collins.
Lesnik-Oberstein, Karín. 1994. *Children's Literature: criticism and the fictional child*. Oxford: Clarendon Press.
———. ed. 1998. *Children in Culture: approaches to childhood*. Basingstoke: Macmillan—now Palgrave Macmillan.
———. 2003. "The '*Philosophical Investigations*' Children." *Educational Philosophy and Theory* 35.4:381–91.
Lieberman, Marcia K. 1986. " 'Some day my prince will come': female acculturation through the fairy tale." 185–200 in *Don't Bet on the Prince: contemporary feminist fairy tales in North America and England*. Edited by Jack Zipes. Aldershot: Gower.
Lofting, Hugh. 1922. *Doctor Dolittle*. London: Jonathan Cape.

Low, Ching-Liang Gail. 1996. *White Skins/Black Masks: representation and colonialism.* London: Routledge.
Lurie, Alison. 1991. *Not in Front of the Grown-Ups: subversive children's literature.* London: Cardinal.
Lynn, Cathy and Michael J. Preston, eds. 1995. *The Other Print Tradition: essays on chapbooks, broadsides, and related ephemera.* New York: Garland.
Kenway, Jane and Elizabeth Bullen. 2001. *Consuming Children: education, entertainment, advertising.* Milton Keynes: Open University Press.
MacCann, Donnarae. 2000. *White Supremacy in Children's Literature: characterizations of African Americans, 1830–1900.* New York: Routledge.
Mackey, Margaret. 1996. "Strip mines in the garden: old stories, new formats, and the challenge of change." *Children's Literature in Education* 27.1:3–15.
———. 1998. *The Case of Peter Rabbit: changing conditions of literature for children.* New York and London: Garland.
Macleod, Anne Scott. 1994. *American Childhood: essays on children's literature of the nineteenth and twentieth centuries.* Athens & London: University of Georgia Press.
McCallum, Robyn. 1999. *Ideologies of Identity in Adolescent Fiction: the dialogic construction of subjectivity.* New York & London: Garland.
———. 2000. "The Past Reshaping the Present: film versions of *Little Women.*" *The Lion and the Unicorn* 24.1:81–96.
McGillis, Roderick. 1996a. *The Nimble Reader: literary theory and children's literature.* New York: Twayne.
———. 1996b. *A Little Princess: gender and empire.* London: Prentice Hall.
———, ed. 1999. *Voices of the Other: children's literature and the postcolonial context.* London: Garland.
McRobbie, Angela. 1982. "Jackie: an ideology of adolescent femininity." 263–83 in *Popular Culture: past and present.* Edited by Bernard Waites, Tony Bennett and Graham Martin. London: Croom Helm/Open University Press.
Meek, Margaret. 2001. "The Englishness of English children's books." 89–100 in *Children's Literature and National Identity.* Edited by Margaret Meek. Stoke on Trent: Trentham Books.
Meyrowitz, Joshua. 1985. *No Sense of Place: the impact of electronic media on social behaviour.* Oxford: Oxford University Press.
Mitchell, Claudia and Jacqueline Reid-Walsh. 2002. *Researching Children's Popular Culture: the cultural spaces of childhood.* London: Routledge.
Morrison, Blake. 1997. *As If.* London: Granta.
Morrison, Toni. 1992. *Playing in the Dark; whiteness and the literary imagination.* Cambridge, MA: Harvard University Press.
Moss, Jeremy, ed. 1998. *The Later Foucault: politics and philosophy.* London: Sage.
Munsch, Robert and Michael Martchenko. 1980. *The Paper Bag Princess.* Toronto: Annick Press.
Myers, Mitzi. 1992. "Little girls lost: rewriting Romantic childhood, righting gender and genre." 131–42 in *Teaching Children's Literature: issues, pedagogy, resources.* Edited by Glenn Edward Sadler. New York: MLA.
———. 1995. "The Erotics of Pedagogy: Historical Intervention, Literary Representation, the 'Gift of Education,' and the Agency of Children." *Children's Literature* 23:1–30.

Nation, Terry. 1997. *All Pals Together: the story of children's cinema*. Edinburgh: Edinburgh University Press.
Needle, Jan. 1981. *Wild Wood*. London: Deutsch.
Nelson, Claudia. 1991. *Boys Will Be Girls: the feminine ethic and British children's fiction, 1857–1917*. New Brunswick, NJ: Rutgers University Press.
Nelson, Claudia and Lynne Vallone. 1994. *The Girl's Own: cultural histories of the Anglo-American girl, 1830–1915*. Athens, GA: University of Georgia Press.
Nodelman, Perry. 1988. "Children's literature as women's writing." *Children's Literature Association Quarterly* 12:31–4.
———. 2002. "Making boys appear: the masculinity of children's fiction." 1–14 in *Ways of Being Male: representing masculinities in children's literature and film*. Edited by John Stephens. London: Routledge.
Olson, Marilynn. 2000. "Turn-of-the-century grotesque: the Uptons' Golliwogg and dolls in context." *Children's Literature* 28:73–94.
O'Malley, Andrew. 2003. *The Making of the Modern Child: children's literature and childhood in the late eighteenth century*. London: Routledge.
Opie, Iona and Peter Opie. 1959. *The Lore and Language of Schoolchildren*. Oxford: Clarendon Press.
Orme, Nicholas. 2001. *Medieval Children*. New York & London: Yale University Press.
Oswell, David. 2002. *Television, Childhood and the Home: a history of the making of the child television audience in Britain*. Oxford: Clarendon Press.
Pace, Patricia. 1996. "Robert Bly does Peter Pan: the inner child as father to the man in Steven Spielberg's *Hook*." *The Lion and the Unicorn* 20.1:113–20.
Pardeck, John T. and Jean A. Pardeck. 1993. *Bibliotherapy: a clinical approach for helping children*. New York: Taylor & Francis.
Paul, Lissa. 1987. "Enigma variations: what feminist theory knows about children's literature." *Signal* 54:186–201.
Pennell, Beverley. 2002. "Redeeming masculinity at the end of the second millennium: narrative reconfigurations of masculinity in children's fiction." 55–77 in *Ways of Being Male: representing masculinities in children's literature and film*. Edited by John Stephens. London: Routledge.
Phillips, Jerry. 1993. "The Mem Sahib, the worthy, the Rajah and his minions: some reflections on the class politics of *The Secret Garden*." *The Lion and the Unicorn* 17:168–94.
Phillips, Jerry and Ian Wojcik-Andrews. 1990. "Notes towards a Marxist critical practice." *Children's Literature* 18:127–30.
Phillips, Richard. 1997. *Mapping Men and Empire: a geography of adventure*. London & New York: Routledge.
Pifer, Ellen. 2000. *Demon or Doll: images of the child in contemporary writing and culture*. Charlottesville: University Press of Virginia.
Plumb, J. H. 1975. "The new world of children in eighteenth-century England." *Past and Present* 67:64–95.
Pollock, Linda. 1983. *Forgotten Children: parent–child relations 1500–1900*. Cambridge: Cambridge University Press.
Pope, Rob. 2002. *The English Studies Book: an introduction to language, literature and culture*, 2nd edn. London: Routledge.
Postman, Neil. 1982. *The Disappearance of Childhood*. New York: Delacorte.
Potter, Beatrix. 1902. *The Tale of Peter Rabbit*. London: Frederick Warne.

Prout, Alan. ed. 2000. *The Body, Childhood and Society*. Basingstoke: Macmillan—now Palgrave Macmillan.

Pullman, Philip. 1995. *Northern Lights*. London: Scholastic.

Quicke, John. 1985. *Disability in Modern Children's Fiction*. London: Croom Helm.

Rabinowitz, Rebecca. 2004. "Messy new freedoms: queer theory and children's literature" 19–28 in *New Voices in Children's Literature*. Edited by Sebastien Chapleau. Lichfield: Pied Piper Publishing.

Radway, Janice A. 1987. *Reading the Romance: women, patriarchy and popular culture*. London: Verso.

Rand, Erica. 1995. *Barbie's Queer Accessories*. Durham: Duke University Press.

Randall, Don. 2000. *Kipling's Imperial Boy: adolescence and cultural hybridity*. Basingstoke: Palgrave—now Palgrave Macmillan.

Reynolds, Kimberley. 1990. *Girls Only: gender and popular children's fiction in Britain, 1880–1910*. London: Harvester Wheatsheaf.

———, ed. 1996. *Young People's Reading at the End of the Century*. London: Book Trust.

Reynolds, Kimberley and Nicholas Tucker, eds. 1998. *Children's Book Publishing in Britain since 1945*. Aldershot: Scolar Press.

Richards, I. A. 1929. *Practical Criticism: a study of literary judgment*. London: Kegan Paul.

Richards, Jeffrey. 1988. *Happiest Days: the public schools in English fiction*. Manchester: Manchester University Press.

———, ed. 1989. *Imperialism and Juvenile Literature*. Manchester: Manchester University Press.

Ritvo, Harriet. 1987. *The Animal Estate*. Cambridge, MA: Harvard University Press.

Rose, Jacqueline. 1984. *The Case of Peter Pan, or the impossibility of children's fiction*. Basingstoke: Macmillan—now Palgrave Macmillan.

Rose, Nikolas. 1989. *Governing the Soul: the shaping of the private self*. London: Routledge.

Rudd, David. 1992. *A Communication Studies Approach to Children's Literature*. Sheffield: Pavic/Sheffield Hallam University Press.

———. 1994. "Children and Television: a critical note on theory and method." *Media, Culture and Society*, 14, 2:313–20.

———. 1995. "Shirley, the bathwater, and definitions of children's literature." *Papers: explorations into children's literature* 5.2–3:88–96.

———. 2000. *Enid Blyton and the Mystery of Children's Literature*. Basingstoke: Palgrave—now Palgrave Macmillan.

———. 2004a. "Theories and Theorising: the Conditions of Possibility of Children's Literature." 29–43 in *International Companion Encyclopedia of Children's Literature*, Vol. 1, edited by Peter Hunt, 2nd edn. London: Routledge.

———. 2004b. "Golliwog: genealogy of a non-PC icon." 70–78 in *Studies in Children's Literature, 1500–2000*. Edited by Celia Keenan and Mary Shine Thompson. Dublin: Four Courts Press.

Said, Edward. 1978. *Orientalism*. London: Penguin.

Sarland, Charles. 1991. *Young People Reading: culture and response*. Milton Keynes: Open University Press.

Sax, Boria. 2003. *Crow*. London: Reaktion Books.

Schickel, Richard. 1968. *The Disney Version*. New York: Simon and Schuster.

Seiter, Ellen. 1993. *Sold Separately: children and parents in consumer culture*. New Brunswick: Rutgers University Press.
Shahar, Shulamith. 1989. *Childhood in the Middle Ages*. London: Routledge.
Shavit, Zohar. 1986. *Poetics of Children's Literature*. Athens, GA: University of Georgia Press.
Simons, John. 2002. *Animal Rights and the Politics of Literary Representation*. Basingstoke: Palgrave—now Palgrave Macmillan.
Spufford, Francis. 2002. *The Child that Books Built*. London: Faber and Faber.
Stainton Rogers, Rex and Wendy Stainton Rogers. 1992. *Stories of Childhood: shifting agendas of child concern*. London: Simon & Schuster.
Steedman, Carolyn. 1982. *The Tidy House: little girls writing*. London: Virago.
———. 1986. *Landscape for a Good Woman: a story of two lives*. London: Virago Press.
Steege, David. 2003. "Doctor Dolittle and the Empire: Hugh Lofting's response to British colonialism." 91–98 in *The Presence of the Past in Children's Literature*. Edited by Ann Lawson-Lucas. London/Westport, CT: Praeger.
Steinberg, Shirley R. and Joe L. Kincheloe. 1997. *Kinderculture: the corporate construction of childhood*. Boulder: Westview.
Stephens, John. 1992. *Language and Ideology in Children's Fiction*. London: Longman.
———. ed. 2002. *Ways of Being Male: representing masculinities in children's literature and film*. New York & London: Routledge.
Stephens, John and Robyn McCallum. 1998. *Retelling Stories, Framing Cultures: traditional story and metanarratives in children's literature*. London: Garland.
Storey, John, ed. 1996. *What is Cultural Studies? A reader*. London: Arnold.
Susina, Jan. 1999. "Reviving or revising Helen Bannerman's *The Story of Little Black Sambo*: postcolonial hero or signifying monkey?" 237–52 in *Voices of the Other: children's literature and the postcolonial context*. Edited by Roderick McGillis. London: Garland.
Sutton-Smith, Brian. 1981. *The Folkstories of Children*. Philadelphia: University of Pennsylvania Press.
———. 1986. *Toys as Culture*. London: Gardner Press.
Sutton-Smith, Brian, and David M. Abrams, eds. 1999. *Children's Folklore: a source book*. Logan: Utah State University Press.
Taxel, Joel. 2002. "Children's literature at the turn of the century: toward a political economy of the publishing industry." *Research in the Teaching of English* 37.2:145–97.
Thomas, Joyce. 1989. *Inside the Wolf's Belly: aspects of the fairy tale*. Sheffield: Sheffield Academic Press.
Thomas, Keith. 1989. "Children in early modern England." 45–77 in *Children and their books: a celebration of the work of Iona and Peter Opie*. Edited by Gillian Avery and Julia Briggs. Oxford: Clarendon Press.
Thomson, Stephen. 1998. "Substitute communities, authentic voices: the organic writing of the child." 248–73 in *Children in Culture: approaches to childhood*. Edited by Karín Lesnik-Oberstein. Basingstoke: Macmillan—now Palgrave Macmillan.
Tinkler, Penny. 1995. *Constructing Girlhood: popular magazines for girls growing up in England, 1920–1950*. London: Taylor & Francis.
Tournier, Michel. 2003. *Friday and Robinson*. London: Walker Books.

Trites, Roberta Seelinger. 2000. *Disturbing the Universe: power and repression in adolescent fiction*. Iowa: University of Iowa Press.

Upton, Florence K. and Bertha Upton. 1895. *The Adventures of two Dutch Dolls and a "Golliwogg."* London and New York: Longmans, Green & Co.

Vallone, Lynne. 1995. *Disciplines of Virtue: girls' culture in the eighteenth and nineteenth centuries*. New Haven: Yale University Press.

Veeser, H. Aram, ed. 1989. *The New Historicism*. London: Routledge.

Vološinov, Valentin. 1973. *Marxism and the Philosophy of Language*. New York: Seminar Press.

Walkerdine, Valerie. 1984. "Developmental psychology and the child-centred pedagogy: the insertion of Piaget into early education." 153–203 in *Changing the Subject: psychology, social regulation and subjectivity*. J. Henriques, Wendy Hollway, Cathy Urwin, Couze Venn and Valerie Walkerdine. London: Methuen.

———. 1990. "Some day my prince will come: young girls and the preparation for adolescent sexuality." *Schoolgirl Fictions*. London: Verso.

Wall, Barbara. 1991. *The Narrator's Voice: the dilemma of children's fiction*. Basingstoke: Macmillan—now Palgrave Macmillan.

Warner, Marina. 1994. *From the Beast to the Blonde: on fairy tales and their tellers*. London: Chatto & Windus.

———. 2002. *Fantastic Metamorphoses, Other Worlds: ways of telling the self*. Oxford: Oxford University Press.

Watkins, Tony. 1992. "Reconstructing the homeland: loss and hope in the English landscape." 165–70 in *Teaching Children's Literature: issues, pedagogy, resources*. Edited by Glenn Edward Sadler. New York: MLA.

Webb, Jean, ed. 2000. *Text, Culture and National Identity in Children's Literature: international seminar on children's literature: pure and applied*. University College Worcester, England, June 14–19, 1999. Helsinki: NORDINFO.

Willis, Paul. 1990. *Common Culture: symbolic work at play in the everyday cultures of the young*. Milton Keynes: Open University Press.

Wilson, Anne. 1983. *Magical Thought in Creative Writing: the distinctive roles of fantasy and imagination in fiction*. Stroud: Thimble Press.

Wilson, Emma. 2003. *Cinema's Missing Children*. London: Wallflower Press.

Wojcik-Andrews, Ian, ed. 1996. "Children's Films" Special issue. *The Lion and the Unicorn* 20.1.

———. 2000. *Children's Films: history, ideology, pedagogy, theory*. New York: Garland.

Wolf, Shelby Anne, and Shirley Brice Heath. 1992. *The Braid of Literature: children's worlds of reading*. Cambridge, MA and London: Harvard University Press.

Wood, Diana, ed. 1994. *The Church and Childhood*. Oxford: Blackwell.

Zipes, Jack. 1979. *Breaking the Magic Spell: radical theories of folk and fairy tales* [reprinted 1992]. New York: Routledge.

———. 1983. *Fairy Tales and the Art of Subversion: the classical genre for children and the process of civilization*. London: Heinemann Educational.

———. 1988. *The Brothers Grimm: from enchanted forests to the modern world*. New York: Routledge, Chapman & Hall.

———, ed. 1993. *The Trials and Tribulations of Little Red Riding Hood*, 2nd edn. London: Routledge.

———. 2000. *Sticks and Stones: the troublesome success of children's literature from Slovenly Peter to Harry Potter*. London: Routledge.

Further reading

Ashcroft, Bill, Gareth Griffiths, and Helen Tiffin, eds. *The Post-Colonial Studies Reader*. London: Routledge, 1995.

Buckingham, David. *After the Death of Childhood: growing up in the age of electronic media*. Cambridge: Polity Press, 2000.

Clark, Beverly Lyon. *Kiddie Lit: the cultural construction of children's literature in America*. Baltimore & London: Johns Hopkins University Press, 2003.

Dusinberre, Juliet. *Alice to the Lighthouse: children's books and radical experiments in art*. Basingstoke: Macmillan—now Palgrave Macmillan, 1987.

James, Allison, Chris Jenks, and Alan Prout. *Theorizing Childhood*. Cambridge: Polity Press, 1998.

Jenkins, Henry, ed. *The Children's Culture Reader*. New York: New York University Press, 1998.

Lesnik-Oberstein, Karín, ed. *Children in Culture: approaches to childhood*. Basingstoke: Macmillan—now Palgrave Macmillan, 1998.

McGillis, Roderick. *The Nimble Reader: literary theory and children's literature*. New York: Twayne, 1996.

Nodelman, Perry and Mavis Reimer. *The Pleasures of Children's Literature*, 3rd edn. London: Longman, 2002.

Rose, Jacqueline. *The Case of Peter Pan; or, the impossibility of children's fiction*. London: Macmillan—now Palgrave Macmillan, 1984.

Stainton Rogers, Rex and Wendy Stainton Rogers. *Stories of Childhood: shifting agendas of child concern*. London: Simon & Schuster, 1992.

Stephens, John. *Language and Ideology in Children's Fiction*. London: Longman, 1992.

Storey, John, ed. *What is Cultural Studies? A reader*. London: Arnold, 1996.

Wolf, Shelby Anne and Shirley Brice Heath. *The Braid of Literature: children's worlds of reading*. Cambridge MA: Harvard University Press, 1992.

Zipes, Jack. *Fairy Tales and the Art of Subversion: the classical genre for children and the process of civilization*. London: Routledge, 1995.

3
Genre and Convention

Jean Webb

Questions of canonicity

In common with other academic disciplines which endeavour to extend the frontiers of knowledge to bring greater understanding, children's literature is a dynamic, questioning, and self-reflexive field of study. Much deliberation, debate, wordage, and intellectual soul-searching has gone into defining, interrogating, and establishing children's literature as an academic discipline, and the process continues. As discussed by colleagues in this book, the establishment of children's literature as an academic discipline has not been an easy task. However, the very fact that a text such as this exists is evidence of the success, security, and dynamism of the field. Two areas central to this discussion of genre and convention underpin the establishment of children's literature as an academic field of study, namely, questions pertaining to the canon and the notion of a classic children's book. Such parameters lead to the consideration of genre and convention in children's literature. From a pragmatic viewpoint one could rephrase these discussions as questions asked by someone formulating a programme in children's literature: "Which books should I choose?" and having selected them, "What should I teach?" and furthermore, "Why?" Reduction to the pragmatic can oversimplify matters somewhat, since those "innocent" questions mask a host of cultural, social, and political complexities.

In order for a subject to become accepted as a field of study in universities and schools, it is necessary to establish a set of validating parameters. Firstly, academics setting up a field have to identify a sufficient body of work which deserves study; and that such a body of work represents standards which can be used to critique and evaluate other work. Secondly, it is essential to prove that such a body is not merely a transient phenomenon, i.e. that a history can be identified and constructed, thereby signifying a sense of evolution. Thirdly, the pioneering body of academics has to demonstrate that, after the stage of identification, the work withstands fruitful interrogation and critical analysis and makes a significant contribution to knowledge and the understanding of how we function, as human subjects and as subjects within social systems, and how those systems themselves function and why. The test, as it were, is the extent and level of debate which is generated within the emergent field and beyond. Diversion, rejection, and reformulation then come into play, as individuals and schools of thought identify and—one hopes—justify and examine their own parameters and criteria for selection. A canon is, therefore, in one way a positive necessity and liberation, in another a possibly stultifying restriction. The key here is to view the identification of a canon as a starting point, a set of benchmarks to be reviewed—or "touchstones" to use Perry Nodelman's phrase (Nodelman 1985)—to be reviewed, then added to and evaluated. The other key point is to recognize that in an area such as children's literature the interested parties are numerous, and will each construct its own designated canon for its own particular purpose. The question which naturally emerges is: "Can a singular canon exist in children's literature?" An answer has to be considered within the context of the debate about the general notion of a canon.

In 1948, when F. R. Leavis published his articles from *Scrutiny* as *The Great Tradition* (Leavis 1948) in order to make a stand as to which texts in his opinion deserved literary study in English universities, the debate regarding the study of English Literature was a great deal simpler. He was speaking from a singular established position of power, that of the dominance of the university system at the top of the pyramid of education, and of the dominance of the white, middle-class, presumably heterosexual male. By contrast, the field of children's literature has been built and formulated and grown by a "bottom-up" approach, with a high proportion of women engaged in the process. Educationalists, teachers, librarians, literary scholars, writers, artists, publishers, and book collectors have all variously been involved, plus academics from other disciplines, such as history, psychology, sociology, media, and cultural studies; not to mention the various ideological and religious parties which straddle the professions. This process has been carried out within national boundaries, and also internationally. As the field has developed and become more complex, one may add to this the differing foci of study such as nineteenth-century children's literature, or gender studies and methodological approaches derived from theoretical positions, such as structuralist criticism, New Historicism, or cultural materialism. What is under consideration in terms of the contemporary study of children's literature is a subject area which both shapes, is shaped by, and reflects, the multiplicity of postmodernity and the construction and reconstruction of cultures. The strength and weakness of any canon, as well as its determining factor is, by definition, that which is excluded: the silenced as well as the articulated. Karen R. Lawrence's statements on the adult canon of English literature in her introduction to the aptly-titled *Decolonizing Tradition: New Views of Twentieth-Century "British" Literary Canons* (1992) are fully pertinent to the implications of canon formation in children's literature:

> If tradition is regarded as a form of cultural imperialism, then these essays seek to decolonize the empire's literary territory. The conflicts that produce the canon occur on the levels of production and reception; they involve writers' confrontations with inherited tradition and evaluation of texts in relation to it. (Lawrence 1992, 2)

In the current context I would rewrite that sentence as follows:

> If tradition is regarded as a form of cultural imperialism, then scholars of children's literature seek to decolonize the empire's literary territory. The conflicts that produce the canon occur on the levels of production and reception; they involve writers' and academics' confrontations with inherited tradition and evaluation of texts in relation to it.

The following brief consideration of the debates surrounding the notion of a canon variously arising over the past thirty years, will serve to illustrate the above discussion, and demonstrate the developing diversity of considerations to be taken into account, moving from a national to an international perspective. At this point I wish to acknowledge the enlightening and helpful conversations with my German colleague, Martina Seifert, and the full and excellent discussion of canon formation by Emer O'Sullivan in her book *Comparative Children's Literature* (O'Sullivan 2005), and in addition Emer's generous access to her work prepublication. I strongly recommend her chapter "World Literature and Children's Classics," both for an overview of the debate concerning a canon, and for her argument for the need for a canon to provide a core of "touchstone" texts for formulating courses of study on children's literature. As she rightly states:

> Since schools and universities, with their need to impart exemplary values, have been and still are the main agencies in canon formation, one can understand why, although some individual works of children's literature have been acknowledged as classics, there is no canon of children's literature based on the authority of carefully cultivated tradition. As it was not regarded as a part of great literature it was not taught as an academic subject, and received hardly any attention in universities. But the need for a canon is now becoming evident in children's literature studies, for the purposes of writing the history of literature and for university teaching. This canon is established by means of consecrating and preserving the most important texts, by the endeavours to make the subject academically respectable. (O'Sullivan 2005, 130)

O'Sullivan's call in 2004 for a canon, in general and in relation to her particular expertise and drive to develop the study of World Literature, echoes the impetus behind the Children's Literature Association project, carried out almost a quarter of a century earlier in 1980, when "readers of the *ChLA Quarterly* were asked to name those books they considered to be most significant in a variety of categories" (Nodelman 1985, 7). At that time children's literature as an academic study was developing at university level. As this was a project instigated by the American-based ChLA it is not surprising that the focus was on critical interest in the field from an Anglo-centric and American perspective. The result was the *Touchstones* series edited by Perry Nodelman. His introduction in the first volume records the process and the criteria used for selection and elimination:

> The committee considered a number of possible "canons." At one point, (they) prepared a list of hundreds and hundreds of "good" books—an interesting guide to a lifetime of reading, but, we soon realised, far too general, far too broad in its definition of value to serve any more particular purpose. A list that might actually help to define excellence had to separate the good from the likeable, and the great from the good . . . (Nodelman 1985, 7)

The *Touchstones* series comprises a wide range of critical discussions made by individual critics who focus on one text which they have selected as being worthy of inclusion in the canon, and demonstrate the reasons for selection in their essay; the series thus builds a suggested canon. One consideration is the relevance of the text to the modern child reader. For example, Ruth K. MacDonald suggests in her chapter on Louisa May Alcott's nineteenth-century novel *Little Women* (1868) that:

> Certainly the multi-cultural, quickly paced urban lives that so many American children lead today would not predispose them to the leisurely, sentimental journey that Alcott offers. Yet that journey still has much to offer them. (Macdonald 1985, 13)

The underlying criterion for selection here is pedagogic in nature, i.e. that the reading of this text will be beneficial for the American child reader in 1985, and that there are values and experiences in the process of reading which are transferable across the boundaries of time. The question of the child as the implied reader and actual reader, plus matters of dual address, (i.e. where the text addresses both the child listener and the adult reader, as in Milne's *Pooh* stories), further complicate the question of canonicity in the field of children's literature, since the range of criteria needs to account for these variables.

Zohar Shavit considers canon formation in *Poetics of Children's Literature* (Shavit 1986) from the viewpoint of children's literature as part of a cultural system. Her predominantly Anglo-centric historical discussion includes, amongst other matters, the notion of childhood, education, and publishing practice:

> . . . it was through the framework of the educational system that a canonized children's literature system began to develop; at the same time, it was the need to combat popular literature from which the stratification of the whole literary system emerged. (Shavit 1986, 134)

Thus the far-reaching influence of educational practice in determining good literature for children is identified as a factor. The National Curriculum for England and Wales currently suggests texts which can be used to develop children's reading, and to enable the study of literature and the understanding of cultures.[1] The imperative for academic courses which teach children's literature to those teachers, who are one of the primary sources of provision of literary experience and knowledge for children, is to make them aware of where the texts they select sit in relation to the wider field: hence the return to the notion of canon.

In the indications I have given thus far—and they are merely indications, since this is a subject which has rightly generated much discussion over many years—the complexities and debates surrounding the questions of a canon for the field of children's literature are becoming evident. The one conclusion of which one can be sure is that there is no fixed canon for the field as yet. Should this situation arise, then fixity would not reflect the development, evolution, and diversity of the field, and reconsideration and updating would be a necessity. Furthermore, since the study of children's literature, *per se,* is an international field then a singular canon, with clearly agreed criteria, would have to incorporate full representation from each country, which returns us to Emer O'Sullivan's point about writing literary history. The establishment of literary histories for children's literature is an important academic and "political" goal for, unlike literature for adults, children's literature is not automatically recognized by academia as being important, academically valid, nor "visible,"—therefore, literary historians and critics who engage in literary history play an important role in identifying texts which contribute to canon formation.

If one is seeking to begin in an area of study, then titles which include words such as "*Introduction to*" or "*Introducing*" are bound to be attractive starting points. Publishers and booksellers are well aware of this search tool, since, for example, of the 2.8-million books in all subject areas in Blackwell's online bookshop, 10,000 have those words in the title. The publishing industry has a powerful and central role in either enabling or hindering the availability of books. With the usual print run of books for children and academic texts being very small, a book may well go out of print before it has had time to circulate, because the pressures of the costs of shelf space for publishers and booksellers are considerable. The availability of out-of-copyright texts in electronic format can ease the situation in some circumstances; however, this alternative publishing depends upon individual enthusiasts, societies, and grant-funding bodies, such as the Arts and Humanities Research Council.

So, as a new student to the field of children's literature, where should one seek this elusive list which delineates the canon, say in English literature? In short, to my knowledge, it does not formally exist. John Rowe Townsend's *Written For Children* (Townsend 1965) was a starting point in identifying a history of writing for children in English, with the inclusion of some chapters on American books. Peter Hunt's pioneering work over the years has taken the historical perspective combined with literary criticism, and has variously included invaluable lists of titles and publication dates, for example in *An Introduction to Children's Literature* (Hunt 1994). He has also published an extremely useful anthology which makes available both the well-known and less so, *Children's Literature: An Anthology*

1801–1902 (Hunt 2001), which adds to the potential range of texts available for study outside library archives and collections. Peter has contributed to the resources of the field by publishing collections of key critical essays, which may also become difficult to access from the range of sources available to the less experienced seeker, who may become somewhat overwhelmed by the diversity of journals and critical collections available. A further initiative was the publication of his *International Companion Encyclopaedia of Children's Literature* (Hunt and Ray 1996), the second edition of which has recently been published. In addition there is a recent move by publishers and academics to produce encyclopaedias which variously take children's literature as their subject. They are being published both in hardcopy and electronic format: for instance, the forthcoming *Encyclopedia of American Children's and Young Adult Literature* edited by Connie Kirk, and the *Continuum Encyclopedia of Children's Literature* edited by Bernice E. Cullinan and Diane G. Person (Cullinan and Person 2001). Children's literature is also being included in other similar publishing projects, such as the online *Literary Encyclopaedia* (http://www.litencyc.com/) and the new *Oxford Dictionary of National Biography* (Matthew et al. 2004). Whereas fiction for children is sufficiently documented in such texts, by comparison drama is considerably under-represented. The history of English poetry for children has now been documented by Morag Styles in her highly-informative, historically-based *From the Garden to the Street* (Styles 1998), however there is still a good deal of critical work and documentation to be done in this area from Styles' sound beginnings.

The problem still remains as to how one might formulate a programme in the study of children's literature when there is so much to choose from, and where there is almost a "confusing" freedom of choice considering the annual output of 7,500 books on average per year in the English-speaking market, plus the other national and world markets. A point to note here is the lack of books translated *into* English, standing at a maximum of eleven annually, not expressed as a percentage, but the total number of texts,[2] compared with say 85% of books for children per annum in the Icelandic market being in translation from a wide range of languages.[3] The reasons for the lack of books in translation available on the English market emanate from the high costs involved and the difficulties perceived (real or otherwise) by publishers with the translation of culture for the child reader (Webb 1993). The situation emphasizes the dominance of Anglo-American culture both in terms of texts and hence in critical appreciation. Turton & Chambers is a publishing house which has sought to redress the imbalance, although it is an almost insurmountable task. Aidan Chambers, the academic, educationalist, acclaimed critic, and author for children was a driving force behind this initiative. The Turton & Chambers website has a number of pertinent and hard-hitting articles and discussions on the subject, including archived newspaper articles. For example, Catherine Lockerbie, Director of the Edinburgh International Book Festival attacked the UK publishing industry in *The Independent* as follows:

> We don't publish nearly enough translated works in this country. We talk about joining Europe as a political entity yet more often than not we don't know what they're reading or what they're writing so we don't know what they're thinking. (Quoted in Kelbie 2003)

Here Catherine Lockerbie is speaking for literature overall, and within that children's literature comes as a secondary consideration. Added to this question of availability of texts from other languages are the barriers raised by publishers to the global marketing of books. It is difficult, for example, to obtain works by smaller publishing companies, from Ireland or Australia. The control by corporate bookselling outlets results in the under-representation, if not the total invisibility, of the more specialist publishers. For example, the excellent work published by the Australian publishers Lothian, who have a speciality in picture books, with authors such as the award-winning Gary Crew, is absent from UK bookshops. Admittedly there is notional availability via the World Wide Web, however this is not always as straightforward as one would suppose, especially when ordering a number of texts for teaching purposes.

The power and influence of the publishing industry is also evident in the definition of the term "classic." A "classic" is defined in publishing terms as a text which has remained in print, which is a denomination regardless of literary considerations. The commercial is considered when assessing the cultural impact of a text, for example the rise of the Harry Potter phenomenon, where sales of J. K. Rowling's books have soared to the top of the adult as well as the children's lists across the world. For the literary scholar questions of, for instance, poetics, quality, and literary value come into consideration (see for example Shavit 1986). However, what "literary quality" really is forms a debate in itself. In his article "How Not to Read a Children's Book" (Hunt 1995) Peter Hunt convincingly argues the difficulty of defining literary quality by comparing Kenneth Grahame's classic children's book *The Wind in the* Willows (Grahame 1908) as a literary text approved of in terms of what would be described as high literary culture, with the work of Enid Blyton, a populist writer.

His conclusion is that literary criteria are very difficult to apply across the board, since Blyton's work demonstrates qualities which could be applied to that of Kenneth Grahame, or any other author whose work is taken seriously by the literary establishment. A classic text could be one which clearly demonstrates, for example, narrative form, or the defining characteristics of a genre. It could also be a text which acts as a cultural and historical reference point. Hunt takes such criteria and applies them to the work of both writers, proving that Blyton's *Five Go Down to the Sea* (Blyton 1953) is as relevant to the construction of an Arcadian English childhood, as that of Kenneth Grahame, whose work is perceived as being central. Furthermore, Hunt argues that on this basis, *Five Go Down to the Sea* can be cited as a valid precursor to the work of children's authors such as Alan Garner and Philippa Pearce who are celebrated for their high-quality literary contribution to writing for children (Hunt 1995, 237). Hunt's position here is for "childist criticism," a critical approach which takes into account that this is literature *for* children, and that reading considerations such as the culture of childhood, which lie beyond obvious matters such as literacy, should also be taken into account:

> those of us who are concerned with children's literature need to beware of the trap laid for us by the very concept of "literature" and literary standards that claim to be (or aspire to be) authoritative but are actually like the emperor's clothes. If we are tapping into this mystery of what meaning children make, and if we value it at all, as we purport to, we have to see them making it within their own culture, as well as in relationship to other cultures (such as that which validates "literature"). (Hunt 1995, 239)

To conclude this section on the canon and the notion of a classic, I wish to return to the question which initiated this discussion: "Which texts are valid choices for formulating a teaching programme in children's literature?" The key to constructing a set of texts for study, as stated above, is defining the purpose of such a composition, taking the notion of cultural and historical reference points, and the concept of the dominance of the classic in the literary imagination as defining an undefined (and possibly indefinable) benchmark in terms of literary quality. The example I wish to cite is that of the work of Sandra Williams, which is available in her unpublished Ph.D. thesis, "An investigation into readings of cultural indicators embedded in English children's literature texts" (Williams 1998). Prior to her Ph.D., Sandra was working for the British Council in the Czech Republic to teach English to Czech student teachers on a fast-track course of English language, literature, and British Studies. The constraining pragmatic considerations were, amongst others, the time factor and availability of texts. Her decisions in formulating the course had to be time-effective and efficient, and based on texts which could be readily obtained. This was before the advent of online book buying and few people had computers then, especially under the circumstances in which Sandra was working in the Czech Republic. An additional, and major, consideration, was the economic differences between the Czech Republic and the UK. As Sandra has pointed out in conversation, "a few books were equivalent to a week's wages" for the Czech students. Again this is a constraint imposed by the publishing industry, and one which has serious implications for the development of programmes. She elected to use texts written for children for two reasons: firstly because her Czech students were going to be teaching English to children; and secondly, most of the texts could match their level of English. Her choice of texts was enlightened and has proven enlightening for those who have both studied with her and read her work. Through her text selection she gave her students the opportunity to study and critique contemporary British culture. An easy option would have been to abstract a "conventional" model of "Britishness" from John Rowe Townsend's work. Instead Sandra combined classics such as Lewis Carroll's *Alice in Wonderland* (Carroll 1865) with Michael Rosen's *Culture Shock* (Rosen 1991). Sandra formulated a programme which ranged across genres, enabling her students to interrogate the breadth of "Britishness." They might otherwise have retained outmoded stereotypical images of royalty and the white cliffs of Dover, as opposed to the richness and complexity of an evolving British multicultural society in debate with itself as presented through her choice of texts.

The essential point underpinning Sandra Williams' ground-breaking work is that, in order to deconstruct the canon and interrogate British culture, she had to have a clear and informed idea of what that canon "was," which she drew from the reference books discussed above, and her considerable experience as a secondary school teacher. The literary and the educational were combined in her thinking and practice. Furthermore she carefully considered the reasons for her programme design, and her own political and pedagogic position. In other words she "used" the canon to fire her creativity as an educator and critic. The importance of a canon is, in conclusion, twofold: in relation to the field as an academic subject, and as a series of "touchstones" to develop new work, and break boundaries, both visible and invisible.

Boundaries and breaking them: genre and convention

A canon is, in itself, as discussed above, a concept and representation which is defined by boundaries. The components are texts, authors, and also genres. Within a canon, however, there are other defined, boundaried elements such as genre. Children's literature shares some generic categorization with adult literature, as well as displaying some which are specific to the field, such as the school story. Comparison of which genres are applicable to adult literature and which to children's literature raises an interesting set of questions germane to the overall subjects of canon, genre, and convention. When colleagues who are not involved with teaching children's literature were asked to nominate genres in adult literature, their answers were convergent: prose, poetry, and drama: then, for example women's writing, classic realism, crime fiction, and historical fiction, with a general reluctance to identify genres. No one, for example, immediately mentioned the nineteenth-century social-problem novel, or sensationalist fiction, since these are specific to the study of nineteenth-century literature, and the question probably prompted a less time-specific response. They felt more comfortable with Romanticism, Modernism, and Postmodernism. In their terms the organization of adult literature as academics is not so determined by genres, but by time periods and literary movements, plus the overt politicization of literature, as in the study of Women's Writing. I then added to this conversation that thus far I had a list of thirty-one genre categories for children's literature, principally taken from the German work of reference by Günter Lange (ed.), *Taschenbuch der Kinder- und Jugendliteratur* [Handbook of Children's and Youth Literature] (thanks again to Martina Seifert for this information). They are as follows, with my additions in italics: fairy tales; myths; sagas; fables; *didactic stories*; *moral stories*; realist(ic) children's literature; *fantasy*; the fantastic (phantastic); animal stories; religious children's literature; adventure stories for *boys*; adventure stories for *girls*; *domestic fiction for girls*; girl's stories; *the school story*; *the island story*; the psychological children's novel; detective stories; science fiction; the novel of adolescence; *the Young Adult novel*; historical fiction; *magic(al) realism*; poetry; drama; picture books; *flap books; paper sculpture; comics; film and media representation.*

Autobiography is a notable absence, whereas it is a genre central to the study of Women's Writing. The identification of the gap makes visible the power relationship in that children's literature is also writing *for* children *by* adults. The diary of Anne Frank (Frank 1997) is an exception in that these are her words, her account of her short life. The other emanation from this brief comparative exercise is that colleagues nominated "crime fiction" as well as detective stories. What is brought into focus here is the sense of moral responsibility embedded in children's literature. "Detective fiction," as included in the list of genre in children's literature, may well deal with crime; however, it is the way of reading which is emphasized: working out clues through the narrative(s); learning about "red herrings;" learning how to "read" actions and people; making projections and predictions; discriminating, putting together information and coming to a solution—becoming and being the detecting reader. The adult nomination "crime fiction" puts the emphasis on the moral and social transgression, whereas "detective fiction" is placing the reader in an active and positive role: on the "right side of the law," as it were.

The question then arises as to why there are so many genres in the categorization of children's literature? The above list is certainly not exhaustive. What it does indicate are the types of work and writing which one is likely to encounter, and the kinds of conventions which will operate. I have arranged the list in a general order which suggests the chronological development of literature for children; however this will not be the same pattern for all countries and cultures. The children's literature of a particular country and/or culture may evolve with the emphasis on some genres and the absence of others. For example, Greek literature for children has traditionally dominantly fallen into the genre of realism, with a strong political determination, and, until very recently, the absence of fantasy (Sandis 2000). In contrast the English tradition has displayed a strong disposition towards fantasy writing for children since the mid-nineteenth century. The school story (as discussed below) is also a clear and strong line through English writing for children, from Thomas Hughes *Tom Brown's Schooldays* (Hughes 1857), for instance, to J. K. Rowling's *Harry Potter* books and beyond, yet this genre is absent in other national and cultural literatures, to take Greece again as a case in point. New and adapted genres develop in response and in relation to cultural and literary circumstances.[4] There is also a point at which form and genre cross. A story may use realism as a stylistic form to produce a narrative which is defined as fantasy in terms of genre, as in the case of Philip Pullman's *Northern Lights* (Pullman 1995). (See below for discussions of Fantasy and Realism.)

Some of the genres are defined in terms of a critical perspective, for example the psychological children's novel, whilst others incorporate divisions to do with the age of the reader, as with Young Adult Fiction, which implies levels of literacy certainly, but rather more importantly, the emotional, intellectual, and social positioning of the subject reader. Furthermore, there is a direct connection with publishing policy, and the placing of a book in the marketplace. The number of categories is also related to concept of the child reader, who as one gaining experience requires indicators for book selection, added to which adults as book buyers for children need guidance and indicators to make their selections. Blackwell's online bookshop has a section on legends, myths, and fables, which is cognate with the list of genres nominated; in addition there is a category of bedtime stories which could possibly arise as a critical genre in the future. The division into genres is possible because there are conventions which enable the interested party to identify and place a text in a particular category, or multiple categories.

The ordering of the list, beginning with fairy tales and myths, situates children's literature in the oral tradition; a literary heritage from the lips of parents and storytellers who for the child listener are those who teach them about story and narrative; morality, good and evil; modes of behaviour and cultural codes; the real and the fantastic; the plausible and the absurd. Morality and didacticism are embedded deeply in literature for children, whether a text is obviously didactic or predominantly for entertainment. Texts written in the early nineteenth century, which mark the beginnings of English literature written specifically for children outside of the purely educational, were stimulated by the following principal factors: an economy which could support the notion of childhood and leisure reading; growing levels of literacy in adults and in children; the emergence of a publishing industry which had perceived a market in books for children; an educational intention, in the widest sense, which moved beyond literacy; and a response to the impact of Romanticism upon English literary culture. Romanticism centrally places childhood and the construction of childhood in the conceptualization of the developing human subject. Wordsworth's famous line, "The Child is Father of the man" ("The Rainbow," 1802) sums up the importance of the child and childhood to this literary, artistic, and intellectual orientation. Many of the conventions of English children's literature are derived from Romanticism: the movement from innocence to experience; the innocent possessing an untarnished—"innate"—sagacity; the relationship between the emotions, the self, and nature; the privileging of the rural over the urban; the concept of the split self, which includes the darker sides, the uncanny; the importance of the imagination as compared with rationalism; and the construction of parallel worlds of the imagination, for example.

George MacDonald's *At the Back of the North Wind* (MacDonald 1871) is one text which demonstrates the dominant aspects of Romanticism, in the character of the protagonist Diamond and the structure of the narrative. Diamond is a pure innocent, a "child of God." His encounters with North Wind take him from the realities of urban working-class life in nineteenth-century England into other worlds of fantasy, including At the Back of the North Wind itself, a place of otherness and the uncanny which not even North Wind herself has ever seen. Diamond can recall but an impression of his experiences at the Back of the North Wind, and recounts these as poems which are circular in the rhythm and content of the rhyming couplets, taking Nature and the sense of interconnectedness and harmony as their subject. This novel encapsulates, for a child, a focal part of George MacDonald's philosophical approach, which also includes the necessity for children to be educated, since one task for his protagonist is to learn to read, albeit outside a system of formal schooling.

Realism, fantasy, and the school story

The intention of this section is twofold: to combine a discussion of the two major forms, Fantasy and Realism, which can also be qualified as genres, with a consideration of the School Story; and to suggest how a line of argument may be developed through a programme of study in children's literature, demonstrating the centrality of children's literature to literary and cultural studies.

The fixing of form and genre is always debatable, and resolves to a series of conventions which produce a "definition." Realism has been described by Kendall L. Walton as "a monster with many heads in need of disentangling" (Walton 1990, 329), whilst Lillian Furst has devoted an erudite text to the subject, aptly entitled *Realism* (Furst 1992). Fantasy is equally difficult to "fix." Rosemary Jackson's *Fantasy: the literature of subversion* (Jackson 1988), which focuses on adult literature, is a key reference point, whilst the work of Maria Nikolajeva in children's literature and theory is central to understanding this form and genre (Nikolajeva 1988, 1995, 1996, 2000). Although realism and fantasy are, as genres, seemingly at opposite ends of a literary spectrum, there is a position of commonality, where forms can be interdependent.

Realism as a genre purports to convince the reader that this is a "real" world, that this is life as it "really" is. Conventions employed are, for example: detailed description; fixed initial positions, say with characterization; the "self" is a more fixed concept, lacking the division of Modernist thinking and the fragmentation evident in Postmodernism. The narrative voice tends to be singular and is typified in early work by the omniscient narrator; plotting and narrative structure are linear. There is an underlying philosophical position and perspective which declares that there is "truth" which can be known. Early didactic moralistic writing for children such as Mrs Sherwood's *History of the Fairchild Family* (1818) employed realism, as evident in the following scene of moral and "scientific" education:

> When they came to the door they smelt a kind of disagreeable smell, such as they had never smelt before; this was the smell of the corpse, which having been dead now nearly two days had begun to corrupt . . . At last Mr. Fairchild said, "My dear children, you now see what death is; this poor body is going fast to corruption. The soul I trust is in God; but such is the taint and corruption of the flesh, by reason of sin, that it must pass through the grave and crumble to dust . . . Remember these things, my children, and pray to God to save you from sin." (Mrs Sherwood, 1818. Cited in Townsend 1987, 30)

The technique can be compared with that employed by writers such as Mrs Gaskell in her writing of nineteenth-century social problem novels for adults. Such direct and unsentimentalized realism is evident in contemporary children's literature, such as Robert Swindells' *Stone Cold* (Swindells 1993), which confronts the reader with the world of teenage runaways who sleep on the streets. *Stone Cold* won the 1994 Carnegie medal for literary achievement, and also, I would suggest, for its strength in drawing attention to its subject. English fiction for children has a leaning towards fantasy, whereas in Sweden, for example, Young Adult fiction is more directly realist.

Fantasy can also deal with social problems producing a critique of society: however, these are approached through the creation of an imagined reality. Fantasy and realism are interconnected in terms of form. Often a fantasy text has a frame of realism which enables the reader to enter and "realize" the fantasy world: it is the movement from the known and the recognizable to the unknown and the previously unimagined. The text itself, however, will be categorized in the genre of fantasy. The imagined world may be embedded in or through a "real" world, as in the Narnia stories by C. S. Lewis (1950–56), where the wardrobe is the entrance to the fantasy state. Time, place, and character can be disrupted and unstable, as in Lewis Carroll's *Alice in Wonderland* (1865), where Alice enters Wonderland via the rabbit hole and experiences a number of shifts in body size during her adventures. Time is dislocated, as is her sense of subjectivity, for she repeatedly wonders who she is, and is also questioned on this matter by the fantastic characters she meets. Magic is also a component of fantasy writing for children. E. Nesbit, for instance, employs a magic amulet to transport her characters into other times and other places (Nesbit 1906). Fantasy as a form encompasses other genres, such as the fairy tale and science fiction. It enables the writer to create and construct worlds of childhood and constructs of the child which stand beyond, and yet in relation to, reality. The Arcadian pastorals of Kenneth Grahame's *The Wind in the Willows* (1908) and A. A. Milne's *Winnie-the-Pooh* stories (1926) create Romantic ideal worlds of protected childhoods, where animals, toys, and children play and "live" in idealized protection from the harshness and corruption of the "outside" worlds: innocence can grow gently and playfully through to experience. Fantasy is, however, not a soft genre. The subversive capacity of such writing enables harsh and hard-hitting critiques of social, political and religious systems—often in ways which would be unacceptable in adult fiction. One wonders whether Philip Pullman's critique of religious systems in his trilogy *His Dark Materials* (1995, 1997, 2000) would have reached publication had he been "aiming" at an adult market. Would he have been "allowed" to blow up God? Interestingly, the forthcoming film version has removed this radical element. Writing for children has been used as a cloak for political satire by writers such as Pushkin in his use of fairy tale, to produce alternative and dangerously subversive texts for adults. Furthermore, texts for children have been "adopted" by adults to critique and find solace under oppressive political systems, hence the popularity of Milne's *Pooh* stories with the Czechs under Soviet power.

The following discussion of the English School Story traces a line from the nineteenth century, which saw the beginning of the genre, to the employment of the conventions of the school story in J. K. Rowling's *Harry Potter and the Philosopher's Stone* (1997). The starting point is the nineteenth-century boys' boarding school, a particularly English conceptualization, which was closely linked with Muscular Christianity. As Clifford Poultney points out:

> The phrase "muscular Christianity" probably first appeared in an 1857 English review of Charles Kingsley's novel *Two Years Ago* (1857). One year later, the same phrase was used to describe *Tom Brown's School Days*, an 1856 novel about life at Rugby by Kingsley's friend, fellow Englishman Thomas Hughes. Soon the press in general was calling both writers muscular Christians and also applying that label

> to the genre they inspired: adventure novels replete with high principles and manly Christian heroes. (Poultney 2003).

The concept of manliness was closely linked with the values and ethos of British imperialism: patriotism, heroism, self-control, self-sacrifice a sense of duty, and what is "morally right." The public school system was preparing the next generation of governors and administrators of the Empire. The circumstances and setting of the public school story presented the ideal microcosm for the dissemination of such values and attitudes. The pupils were extracted from their home circumstances for considerable periods of time. In *Tom Brown's School Days* (Hughes 1857) for example, the early chapters depict Tom before he enters Rugby, and then follow his school career. The novel therefore becomes a *Bildungsroman* as he moves from the home, where he is a carefree individualist enjoying family life and country pursuits, to Rugby, where he has to learn team spirit, duty, responsibility, caring for and protecting the weak, and defeating the bully. He also has to learn how to win with honour and humility, and how to lose with courage, including the courage to deal with the death of a friend. These are not always easy times for Tom: however, he fights through with determination and admirable strength of character. The key word here is "admirable" for that is what the reader is "supposed" to do, to admire the heroic Tom, who takes his values from the headmaster, Dr Arnold. Tom's first sight of his headmaster as he preaches in Rugby Chapel stirs an emotional response which is aligned with militaristic, hero-worship and with imperialist patriotism:

> The tall, gallant form, the kindling eye, the voice, now soft as the low notes of a flute, now clear and stirring as the call of the light infantry bugle. (Hughes 1989, 141)

As Isobel Quigley comments, Arnold was the opposite of the downtrodden poverty-stricken schoolmaster of Dickensian fame, he was "an outstanding example of the large new professional class emerging in England in his day, a class full of enterprise" (Quigley 1982, 29). It was this class that both male pupils and male readers were to enter and create. The boy's school story began as a patriarchal text, which gave precedence to the rational rather than the emotional. The moral and behavioural boundaries are clear. The hero is delineated from the start, as is the villain. The rite of passage is begun and will be admirably fulfilled with the classic elements of descent and then arising to success, having experienced the experiental path of moral learning.

The nineteenth-century school story can be described as a form which demonstrates enterprise in itself, for here is an ideal narrative structure whose conventions produce an enclosed space. The school is bounded from the outside world; parental influence is supplanted by the ethics, moral code, and rules of the school; the social interaction of the pupils and the developing sense of team spirit and comradeship are clearly traced, enduring adversity as the pupils grow towards a "schooled" maturity, emerging as model citizens. The social environment allows for adventure and a "contained" freedom which would not be so readily available in an exterior world. This was an essential model which transferred readily from and to the adventure story, the island story, the girls' boarding school story, and could later be shifted between realism and fantasy.

The technique employed in *Tom Brown's Schooldays* is realism, employing a detailed narrative which convinces the reader that this is a "real" world, although for most readers who had not attended public school, this was "a fantasy." It was also a model which could produce a clear and separate set of social values from the outside world. Whilst this model could be used to instil "positive" values, the form was sufficiently flexible to enable critique of system and values. In *Stalky and Co* (Kipling 1899) Rudyard Kipling presents a strongly critical view of the elitist and growingly socially unacceptable values of the public school system. The boys are seen abusing their freedom and privilege as they destructively run riot in the rural environment.

As the school story evolved over the twentieth century, the critique of public school elitism grew stronger. The 1944 Education Act enabled the working classes to benefit from secondary and then higher education, resulting in writers for children who demonstrated a critical stance towards society and education. Barry Hines' novel *A Kestrel for a Knave* (Hines 1968) emanates from the conflicting value systems represented by traditional and progressive philosophies of education in the 1960s. *A Kestrel for a Knave* is set in a state Secondary Modern School, and as such is recognizable as a "real" world to the majority of readers who were not educated in the public school system. Billy Casper comes from a dysfunctional family where he is bullied by his brother. He is a social isolate, both in and outside school, finding solace and a sense of identity in rearing and training a kestrel. His class teacher is young and progressive, representing the 1960s movement away from the rigidity of middle-class values and systems, into a more child-centred philosophy. Here the teacher is endeavouring to confront the realities and social problems bearing upon the lives of his pupils. Hines' novel brought together two parallel worlds: the interior culture of the school and classroom, and the external culture of family and home—each representing different, and often conflicting, value systems and modes of behaviour. Both teacher and dislocated pupil try to learn to negotiate these barriers, although some are insurmountable. The school story was thus the vehicle for serious and far-reaching social critique; the conventions of power relationships and the questioning of such being central to the impact which this book made, and continues to make—for it is still studied as a recommended text in the National Curriculum. The gateway had, as it were, been opened for the television drama series *Grange Hill* by Phil Redmond (1978 onward), accompanied by a series of books by Robert Leeson for young teenagers. *Grange Hill* confronts and interrogates the contemporary culture of urban childhood in the East End of London, presenting and examining subjects such as bullying, gang warfare, homosexuality, drug abuse, etc. which may have been thought of as taboo in "mainstream" children's literature, but which are, sadly, real components of children's lives.

The Demon Headmaster by Gillian Cross (1982) was published six years before the National Curriculum was instituted by the Education Reform Act 1988, which established curriculum content and the testing of pupil performance in a very structured manner. Some view this as a restrictive and overly-controlling educational system which limits the creativity and the freedom of both students and teachers. Cross's novel preempts this critical view and reflects the sense of disquiet prior to the National Curriculum being instituted. *The Demon Headmaster* shifts between realism and fantasy. The school setting is realistic; the Demon Headmaster is a creation of fantasy. The Headmaster is a megalomaniac who hypnotizes his pupils so that they achieve perfect test results. The children subvert his methods and win out for creativity and imagination. Cross's novel makes a humorous and powerful critical and political comment on contemporary education.

J. K. Rowling's *Harry Potter* books return to the boarding school as the dominant setting for the development of the characters and the adventures. Rowling combines realism and fantasy and the conventions of the school story, with the structure and mores of a "public" school (the pupils are selected by their being young wizards and witches). Here the Gothic and magic are interwoven in a series of books which depict a projected "English" cultural consciousness which leans upon the history of the school story and a projection of what "Englishness" is believed to "be" like. The readership is sympathetic towards the marginalized and downtrodden, yet heroic, Harry, who will finally win out because he is actually "all powerful." Harry is an archetypal "English" hero who echoes Tom Brown, Billy Casper, and Gillian Cross's intelligent, problem-solving young protagonists. Harry is shy, yet brave; downtrodden yet powerful; ethical, kind, vulnerable yet essentially strong and a wizard at what he does! Finally he can do "what he does" because the structuring format of the boarding-school story gives Rowling the devices and the narrative spatial opportunity.

Conventions in children's literature

From the above discussions it has become evident that children's literature is a diverse and complex field. In addition to the conventions and characteristics of genre and form which have a commonality with literature for adults, there are the parameters and constructs which are applicable to children's literature in its own right. Yet beyond children's literature primarily addressing the child reader and the constructs of the child and childhood, "absolute" conventions defy definition. Perry Nodelman has attempted to elicit such definitions for the field in *The Pleasures of Children's Literature* (1992) where he variously nominates characteristics and conventions. However, for each attempt at categorization one can cite texts which break those boundaries of expectation. Nonetheless, Nodelman's attempt provides invaluable points of reference which encourage interrogation, and help the academic to clarify their positioning towards and understanding of texts and the field. Selected examples from Nodelman's list demonstrate the complexity of the task.

Perry Nodelman states that children's literature is "simple but not necessarily simplistic"; "action-oriented rather than character-oriented." A host of texts ranging from the nineteenth-century to contemporary children's literature challenge that statement. Lewis Carroll's *Alice* texts and Charles Kingsley's *The Water Babies* (1863), for example, are multi-faceted and sophisticated works which challenge the reader with complex combinations of form and subject matter, where discussion of and challenges to subjectivity, social convention, religion, Darwinism, and the social and political matter of the period are integrated into texts for the child reader. Nina Bawden's *Carrie's War* (1973) is a sophisticated contemplation of the psychological effects on the child of the subject of war, evacuation, dislocation, love, and death. There is certainly action and adventure in these texts, but the pivotal concern is the construction of the child subject. The action and adventure are directed at the exploration and development of the child protagonist and thereby the reader.

Nodelman also nominates "presentation from the view of innocence" and the didactic nature of children's literature as defining characteristics of children's literature. These criteria are less open to challenge since the fact that books are written for children by adults means that the child reader is entering into the experience guided by the adult author, so they move from the view of "innocence to experience," and thus all texts for children are in some way didactic, to a greater or lesser extent. One could, however, conceivably make this argument for literature *per se*.

The criteria which stand out for me in Nodelman's list are "optimistic and with happy endings," with the emphasis being on "optimism." I believe that optimism and hope are key factors in writing for children, whether or no the actual ending is happy in itself. One certainly thinks of the sadness of the death of Charlotte in E. B. White's *Charlotte's Web* (White 1953) which is balanced by the solace and joy Wilbur takes in the next generation of spiders. A novel which stands out as an exception is Gudrun Pausewang's *The Last Children* (Pausewang 1988). This is a quasi post-holocaust world where the reader predicts that disease and destruction will finally overcome the remaining children. Pausewang's text points up the moral and emotional tenor of optimism which dominates writing for children, for if the upcoming generation loses hope, then all is lost.

Conclusion: children's literature as part of a cultural system

In conclusion, the study of children's literature is to examine, interrogate, and analyse this area of literature employing critical faculties as applied to adult literature, whilst also being aware that this is literature written *for* children, thereby taking into account Peter Hunt's call for a "childist" criticism.

It is a centrally important part of the endeavour to understand the cultural systems in which we do, and do not, and could possibly operate. Literature is essential to the well-developed and balanced human subject and to strive through the study of literature is to strive for understanding of the human subject. If we deny the study of children's literature as a serious academic subject, then we deny a fundamental part of such knowledge. As William Shakespeare succinctly observed, "What's past is prologue." All adult writers were children. They are writing from a past and projecting into the future, handing on their knowledge, experience, and vision. I have no doubt, nor do my colleagues in the field, that the academic study of children's literature has an important contribution to make well into our futures, and into shaping and helping to understand the possible development of the coming worlds.

Notes

1. See the National Curriculum Online at: http://www.curriculumonline.gov.uk. In a pressured professional life, the classroom teacher is, understandably, more likely to use that suggested list as "a canon." See also the associated approved National Curriculum site which provides materials and suggestions for teachers: www.teachit.co.uk/index.asp?t=m&m=2&a=1.
2. See *The Bookseller* (http://www.thebookseller.com) for annual publishing figures.
3. Even taking into account population differences, the proportion still emphasizes the paucity of translations into English.
4. P. W. Musgrave gives a clear and extensive discussion of the development of genres (Musgrave 1985).

Works cited

Armitt, Lucie. 1996. *Theorising the Fantastic, Interrogating Texts*. London: Arnold.

Auchmuty, Rosemary. 1992. *A World of Girls*. London: The Women's Press.

Avery, Gillian. 1994. *Behold the Child: American Children and Their Books 1621–1922*. London: Bodley Head.

Bawden, Nina. 1973. *Carrie's War*. London: Gollancz.

Blyton, Enid. 1953. *Five Go Down to the Sea*. London: Hodder Headline.

Butts, Dennis, ed. 1992. *Stories and Society*. Basingstoke: MacMillan—now Palgrave Macmillan.

Carroll, Lewis. 1865. *Alice in Wonderland*. London: Macmillan.

Crew, Hilary S. 2002. "Spinning New Tales from Traditional Texts: Donna Jo Napoli and the Rewriting of Fairy Tale." *Children's Literature in Education* 33.2:77–93.

Cross, Gillian. 1982. *The Demon Headmaster*. Oxford: Oxford University Press.

Cullinan, Bernice E. and Diane G. Person, eds. 2001. *The Continuum Encyclopedia of Children's Literature*. London: Continuum International Publishing Group—Academi.

Fine, Anne. 1997. *The Tulip Touch*. London: Puffin.

Frank, Anne. 1997. *The Diary of a Young Girl: Definitive Edition*. Translated by Susan Massotty. Edited by Miriam Pressler. Otto Frank Penguin Books.

Furst, Lilian R., ed. 1992. *Realism*. London: Longman.

Gardam, Jane. 1983. *The Pangs of Love*. London: Julia MacRae.

Goldthwaite, John. 1996. *The Natural History of Make-Believe: A Guide to the Principal Works of Britain, Europe, and America*. New York: Oxford University Press.

Grahame, Kenneth. 1908. *The Wind in the Willows*. London: Methuen.

Hines, Barry. 1969. *A Kestrel for a Knave*. Harmondsworth: Penguin.

Hughes, Thomas. 1857. *Tom Brown's Schooldays*. London: Macmillan.

———. 1989. *Tom Brown's Schooldays*. Edited by Andrew Sanders, *Oxford World Classics*. Oxford: Oxford University Press.

Hunt, Peter, ed. 1990. *Children's Literature: The Development of Criticism*. London: Routledge.

Hunt, Peter. 1991. *Criticism, Theory & Children's Literature*. Oxford: Basil Blackwell.
———, ed. 1992. *Literature for Children: Contemporary Criticism*. London: Routledge.
———. 1994. *An Introduction to Children's Literature*. Oxford: Oxford University Press.
———. 1995. "How Not to Read a Children's Book." *Children's Literature in Education* 26. 4:231–40.
———, ed. 1995. *Children's Literature: An Illustrated History*. Oxford: Oxford University Press.
———, ed. 1999. *Understanding Children's Literature: Key Essays from the International Companion Encyclopedia of Children's Literature*. London: Routledge.
———, ed. 2001. *Children's Literature: An Anthology 1801–1902*. Oxford: Blackwell.
———. 2001. *Children's Literature*. Blackwell Guides to Literature. Oxford: Blackwell.
Hunt, Peter, and Millicent Lenz. 2001. *Alternative Worlds in Fantasy Fiction*. Edited by Morag Styles, *Contemporary Classics of Children's Literature*. London: Continuum.
Hunt, Peter, and Sheila Ray, eds. 1996. *International Companion Encyclopedia of Children's Literature*. London: Routledge.
Jackson, Rosemary. 1988. *Fantasy: The Literature of Subversion*. London: Routledge.
Kelbie, Paul. 2003. " 'Parochial' Publishers Accused of Failing their Readers." *The Independent* (9 August).
Kingsley, Charles. 1863. *The Water-Babies*. London.
Kipling, R. 1899. *Stalky and Co*. London: Macmillan.
Kirk, Connie, ed. Forthcoming. *Encyclopedia of American Children's & Young Adult Literature*. 3 vols. Westport, CT: Greenwood Press.
Knoepflmacher, U. C., and Mitzi Myers. 1997. " 'Cross-Writing' and the Reconceptualisation of Children's Literature Studies." *Children's Literature Annual of the Modern Language Association Division and the Children's Literature Association* 25. Special Issue on Cross-writing Child and Adult.
Lange, Günter, ed. 2000. *Taschenbuch Der Kinder- Und Jugendliteratur [Handbook of Children's and Youth Literature]*. Baltmannsweiler: Schneider-Verlag Hohengehren.
Lawrence, Karen R., ed. 1992. *Decolonizing Tradition: New Views of Twentieth-Century "British" Literary Canons*. Illinois: University of Illinois Press.
Leavis, F. R. 1948. *The Great Tradition: George Eliot, Henry James, Joseph Conrad*. London: Chatto and Windus.
———.1969. *English Literature in Our Time & the University: The Clark Lectures 1967*. London: Chatto and Windus.
Lesnik-Oberstein, Karín. 1994. *Children's Literature: Criticism and the Fictional Child*. Oxford: Clarendon.
Lewis, C. S. 1950. *The Lion, the Witch and the Wardrobe*. London: Geoffrey Bles.
———. 1951. *Prince Caspian*. London: Geoffrey Bles.
———. 1952. *The Voyage of the "Dawn Treader"*. London: Geoffrey Bles.
———. 1953. *The Silver Chair*. London: Geoffrey Bles.
———. 1954. *The Horse and His Boy*. London: Geoffrey Bles.
———. 1956. *The Magician's Nephew*. London: Bodley Head.
———. 1956. *The Last Battle*. London: Bodley Head.
MacDonald, George. 1871. *At the Back of the North Wind*. London: Strachan & Co.
MacDonald, Ruth K. 1985. "Louisa May Alcott's *Little Women*: Who is Still Reading Miss Alcott and Why."13–20 in *Touchstones: Reflections on the Best in Children's Literature*. Vol. 1. Edited by Perry Nodelman. West Lafayette: Children's Literature Association.

Mangaro, Marc. 1992. *Myth, Rhetoric and the Voice of Authority: A Critique of Frazer, Eliot, Frye and Campbell.* London: Yale University Press.
Matthew, H. C. G. and Brian Harrison, eds. 2004. *Oxford Dictionary of National Biography.* Oxford: Oxford University Press.
Milne, A. A. 1926. *Winnie-the-Pooh.* London: Methuen.
Musgrave, P. W. 1985. *From Brown to Bunter: The Life and Death of the School Story.* London: Routledge and Kegan Paul.
Nesbit, E. 1906. *The Story of the Amulet.* London: T. Fisher Unwin.
Nikolajeva, Maria. 1988. *The Magic Code: The Use of Magical Patterns in Fantasy for Children.* Stockholm: Almqvist & Wiksell.
———. ed. 1995. *Aspects and Issues in the History of Children's Literature.* Vol. No. 60, *Contributions to the Study of World Literature.* Westport, CT: Greenwood Press.
———. 1996. *Children's Literature Comes of Age: Toward a New Aesthetic.* Garland Reference Library of the Humanities, v. 1816. Children's Literature and Culture, v. 1. New York: Garland.
———. 2000. *From Mythic to Linear: Time in Children's Literature.* Lanham MD: Scarecrow Press.
Nodelman, Perry, ed. 1985. *Touchstones: Reflections on the Best in Children's Literature.* Vol. 1. West Lafayette: Children's Literature Association ChLA Publishers.
———, ed. 1987. *Touchstones: Reflections on the Best in Children's Literature.* Vol. 2: Fairy Tales, Fables, Myths, Legends and Poetry. West Lafayette: ChLA Children's Literature Association.
———. 1988. *Words About Pictures: The Narrative Art of Children's Picture Books.* Athens: University of Georgia Press.
———. 1992. *The Pleasures of Children's Literature.* New York: Longman.
———. 2000. "Pleasure and Genre: Speculations on the Characteristics of Children's Fiction." *Children's Literature Annual of the Modern Language Association Division and the Children's Literature Assocation* 28:1–14.
O'Sullivan, Emer. 2005. *Comparative Children's Literature.* London: Routledge.
Pausacker, Jenny. 1981. "More Than Forty Years On: A Historical Study of the School Story." Ph.D. dissertation, Flinders.
Pausewang, Gudrun.1988. *The Last Children.* London: Julia MacRae.
Poultney, Clifford. 2003. *Muscular Christianity.* [cited November 2004]. Available from http://www.infed.org/christianeducation/muscular_christianity.htm.
Propp, V. 1969. *Morphology of the Folk Tale.* Austin: University of Texas Press.
Pullman, Philip. 1995. *Northern Lights.* Vol. 1, *His Dark Materials.* London: Scholastic Ltd.
———. 1997. *The Subtle Knife.* 3 vols. Vol. 2, *His Dark Materials.* London: Scholastic Press.
———. 2000. *The Amber Spyglass.* 3 vols. Vol. 3, *His Dark Materials.* London: David Fickling, Scholastic Ltd.
Quigley, Isabel. 1982. *The Heirs of Tom Brown.* London: Chatto & Windus.
Rosen, Michael, ed. 1991. *Culture Shock.* Harmondsworth: Penguin.
Rowling, J. K. 1997. *Harry Potter and the Philosopher's Stone.* London: Bloomsbury.
Sadler, Glenn Edward, ed. 1992. *Teaching Children's Literature: Issues, Pedagogy, Resources.* New York: Modern Language Association of America.
Sandis, Dominique. 2000. "A Review of the Portrayal of Greek Reality in English-Language Children's Books." In *Text, Culture and National Identity in Children's Literature,* edited by Jean Webb, 89–105. Helsinki: NORDINFO.

Scieszka, Jon. 1991. *The Frog Prince, Continued*. London: Viking.
Shavit, Zohar. 1986. *Poetics of Children's Literature*. Athens: University of Georgia Press.
Sherwood, Mrs. 1818. *History of the Fairchild Family*. 3 vols. Vol. 1. London: J. Hatchard.
Stevenson, Robert Louis. 1883. *Treasure Island*. London: Cassell.
Styles, Morag. 1998. *From the Garden to the Street: An Introduction to 300 Years of Poetry for Children*. London: Cassell.
Swindells, Robert. 1993. *Stone Cold*. London: Hamish Hamilton.
Townsend, John Rowe. 1965. *Written for Children: An Outline of English Children's Literature*. London: Garnet Miller.
———. 1987. *Written for Children: An Outline of English-language Children's Literature*. Third revised edition. Harmondsworth: Penguin.
Walton, Kendall L. 1990. *Mimesis as Make-Believe: On the Foundations of the Representational Arts*. Harvard: Harvard University Press.
Webb, Jean. 1993. "The Politics of Children's Literature." Paper presented at the Dreams and Dynamics, The International Association of School Librarianship Conference, Adelaide, South Australia.
Weinreich, Torben. 2000. *Children's Literature—Art or Pedagogy?* Translated by Don Bartlett. Frederiksberg: Roskilde University Press.
White, E. B. *Charlotte's Web*. Harmondsworth: Puffin Books, 1953.
Williams, Sandra. 1998. "An Investigation into Readings of Cultural Indicators Embedded in English Children's Literature Texts." Ph.D., University of Coventry.

Further reading

Hunt, Peter. *An Introduction to Children's Literature*. Oxford: Oxford University Press, 1994.
———. "How Not to Read a Children's Book." *Children's Literature in Education* 26.4:231–40, 1995.
———, ed. *Understanding Children's Literature: Key Essays from the International Companion Encyclopedia of Children's Literature*. London: Routledge, 1999.
Hunt, Peter, and Sheila Ray, eds. *International Companion Encyclopedia of Children's Literature*. London: Routledge, 1996.
Jackson, Rosemary. *Fantasy: The Literature of Subversion*. London: Routledge, 1988.
Nikolajeva, Maria. *Children's Literature Comes of Age: Toward a New Aesthetic*. Garland Reference Library of the Humanities, v. 1816. Children's Literature and Culture, v.1. New York: Garland, 1996.
Nodelman, Perry. *The Pleasures of Children's Literature*. New York: Longman, 1992.
O'Sullivan, Emer. *Comparative Children's Literature*. London: Routledge, 2005.
Shavit, Zohar. *Poetics of Children's Literature*. Athens: University of Georgia Press, 1986.
Styles, Morag. *From the Garden to the Street: An Introduction to 300 Years of Poetry for Children*. London: Cassell, 1998.
Weinreich, Torben. *Children's Literature—Art or Pedagogy?* Translated by Don Bartlett. Frederiksberg: Roskilde University Press, 2000.

4

Looking in the Mirror: Pedagogy, Theory, and Children's Literature

Roderick McGillis

The regular and fairly widespread teaching of children's literature in the university has a relatively short history, something in the order of thirty-five years. Even now, the teaching of children's literature is not securely placed in a specific academic unit; the subject finds location in English Departments, Faculties of Education, Schools of Librarianship, Foreign Language Departments, Departments of Sociology, and even in a Center for Children and Childhood Studies at Rutgers University, and similar centres at such institutions as the University of Reading and San Diego State University. The existence of Centres for the study of children, childhood, and children's literature indicates that although separate areas of research and pedagogy approach the literature from differing perspectives, and they have done so for a long time, they have not ignored each other; they have cross-fertilized the study of children's books. The study of children's books invites interdisciplinary activity. This should not surprise those of us trained as literary scholars because the study of literature came out of its closet thirty years ago when the New Criticism lost its place at the centre of interpretive activity in the Humanities. Of course, some things change slowly and the study of children's literature remained rooted in new critical reading until quite recently. The focus on plot, character, setting, and theme continues to surface in criticism of children's books. Like children's literature itself, the criticism of children's literature is stubbornly conservative. Because children, whatever they are, present a front line before the books we read and study, our concern is with the books' socializing effects on young readers, with ways to teach books to children, and with books as an impetus to reading. To be blunt, I argue that the study of children's literature desires to maintain the safety and security of social complicity and cohesiveness, but that we can get beyond this security.

In a recent book, Karín Lesnik-Oberstein asserts that critics and theorists of children's literature, up to the time of her book at least (Lesnik-Oberstein 2004), have been ultimately committed "to finding the right book for their child" (Lesnik-Oberstein 2004, 19). They have been unable to get beyond the socializing function of literature for the young, and unable to get beyond the notion that a "child" exists and needs stable and specific meaning in the books he reads. Instead, she asserts, we want a criticism that does not stabilize or put finality to meaning (Lesnik-Oberstein 2004, 20). My "want" here is not Lesnik-Oberstein's, for unlike her, I am in no doubt that all criticism, like all theory, is (whether it desires to be or not) temporary, contingent, and ongoing. "Desire" and "lack," constitute our wanting. We ought to know by now that that which we desire is always and ever that which we continue to lack. We may desire clarity and stability of meaning, but we will not be happy campers unless we accept this desire for what it is—ongoing, without end. Having said this, I do not consider that the observation that children's literature has and continues to have pedagogic implications contradicts the ongoing nature of criticism and theory. Teaching too does not end; it just takes many forms in its desire to find the elusive something that compensates for lack. We seek perfection in our performances, knowing full well that perfection must elude us.

What Zohar Shavit quite some time ago termed the literary polysystem of children's literature participates in the education of children; in other words, children's literature constitutes one of Althusser's Ideological State Apparatuses. But since children's literature is part of a polysystem, it offers some possibility of escape from one-dimensional conservatism. The State Apparatus is not singular: children receive education both inside the school system and outside the school system. The literary polysystem contains, as Shavit noted, both canonical and noncanonical books, but it also contains texts in a variety of media. Children "read" their culture through books and films and shop windows and magazines and video games. Culture and the market place are connected. Any of us involved with children's literature needs to be informed about cultural production for the young as it manifests itself in what I'll call the literate and secondarily literate array of textuality. And by "informed," I mean that we not only have to be familiar with this array of textuality (in films, video games, magazines, internet sites, and so on), but we also need to reflect on this textuality. In other words, we need to engage in theoretical thinking. We need theory. If I may be so bold, I would say that theory precisely allows us not to fret about "the choosing of good books for children" (Lesnik-Oberstein 2004, 4). The last thing I desire to do is convince others what books or any other form of textuality they should choose.

Theory, whatever this is, offers the only possibility of prying whatever children read or might read from its conservative and complicit position. One reason readers of children's books have been resistant to embracing theory is precisely theory's insistence upon a loss of innocence. Theory in its manifold positions (formalist, structuralist, psychoanalytical, feminist, Marxist, poststructuralist, and so on) may be conservative or radical, but theory as an activity of mind depends upon a loss of innocence. Theory demands that we step back from the innocent position of enthusiastic consumer; we must become that disappearing figure, the *flaneur* or *flaneuse*, he or she who wanders the streets and malls, the byways of cultural production, slowly taking in the secrets shared with those who take the time to notice things. As Keith Tester suggests, *flanerie* is "a nostalgia for a slower and more definite world" (Tester 1994, 15). Like *flanerie*, theory asks us to slow down and take in secrets. Its nostalgia is the productive nostalgia of leaning on and learning from the past. The *flaneur* and the theorist may be nostalgic, but their nostalgia in no way succumbs to the innocent view that the past is somehow better than the present, only that the past can inform the present.

Theory or theories

I'll return to innocence, but first I reflect on the teaching of theory. Should the teaching of children's literature necessarily involve the teaching of theory? Is there such a thing as a theory of children's literature? Or is theory something that exists independently of children's literature, like a flag or an ointment that we wave or apply when we begin to discuss children's books? Do we teach theory by itself and hope students then find it useful in their reading of books for the young? If we do this, then we will find ourselves teaching theories, not theory. When we introduce students to the main ideas associated with a range of theories, we take a taxonomical approach and line up various schools such as Marxism, psychoanalysis, feminism, New Historicism, postcolonialism, and such theories as queer theory and disability theory and so on. This is okay, but students might wonder what any of these high theories has to do with books for young and even younger readers. The study of theories can seem abstract. And so we might take a heuristic approach. Here we put theories into practice. We read *Where the Wild Things Are* from a psychoanalytic perspective or "His Dark Materials" from a feminist perspective and so on applying various theories to various books. This might provide the student with useful practice in using various theories, but such an approach begs the question as to why we might choose to use a specific approach to a particular text. Why read *Where the Wild Things Are* from a psychoanalytic perspective and not from a postcolonial perspective? Does a psychoanalytic approach nudge out a postcolonial approach? What is the best approach to use for any book or should we bring several approaches to each book? Can we approach any text from a theoretical standpoint that is pure? Such questions return us to the question of theory in and of itself. What good is a particular theoretical approach and why? If we do not return to the question of theory in all its abstract beckoning, then we are teaching readers how to read, and we are not teaching theory. I've been drawing on D. G. Myers in this paragraph, and I might as well turn directly to him for his conclusion regarding "both the taxonomical and heuristic approaches." He argues that both of these approaches "subtly encourage a pedagogical regime of authoritarianism" (Myers 1994, 2). Myers argues that to teach theory is to teach writers such as Derrida or Foucault or Butler or whomever as authorities with something correct in what they say, and to teach various ways of reading texts is to provide students with a sense of the proper way to read texts. "A pedagogy of authoritarianism comes into office when theory is studied and taught on the grounds of its being the dominant genre of knowledge at present" (Myers 1994, 2).

Myers wrote that last sentence in 1994. In 2004, we might breathe a sigh of relief. Now we have publications that announce the passing of high theory. Richard Rorty, in "Looking Back at 'Literary Theory,' " remarks that literary theory "has gradually become old hat" (Rorty 2004). Here is a sample of publications that inform us of theory's passing: *What's Left of Theory: New Work on the Politics of Literary Theory* (Butler, Guillory, Thomas 2000), *After Theory* (Eagleton 2003), *life.after.theory* (Payne and Schad 2003). Is there life after theory? Where do we go from here? Considering the state of children's literature as a newcomer in academic circles, do we continue to try to catch up or do we stretch and breath the new posttheory air? To breathe the posttheory air, we might hope, keeps us innocent; we can now just return to reading for the fun of it. Vain hope. So much depends upon how we define fun. The teaching of children's literature has always been more about values than aesthetics, although we have spoken of these values as if they were, perforce, themselves aesthetically pleasing to sugar the pill of instruction. In other words, children's literature people—whether these are what

Townsend long ago called "book people" or "child people" (Townsend 1980, 199)—talk much about maintaining the fun of reading while they insist on the usefulness of reading. And so we return again to the notion of pleasing instruction, and we ought to recognize just how this connection between pleasure and meaning demands reflection—theoretical reflection. How can pleasure be both "for itself" and "useful" socially? The question is theoretical (see Touponce 1995–96). If we think at all about books, about children's books, then we cannot avoid theory.

First a word about theory. Theory derives from the Greek *theoria*, which Raymond Williams defines as "contemplation, spectacle, mental conception (from *theoros*, Gk—spectator, rw *thea*, Gk—sight; cf. theatre)" (Williams 1976, 316). Williams goes on to consider the development of the meaning of theory and its relation to practice (often referred to as *praxis* these days because of this word's connection to a scheme or system of practice developed out of a theory). In short, theory exists in relation to practice; it does not exist as a separate activity related to mental activity, but unrelated to what we do in our material lives as human beings. To theorize is to contemplate the spectacle on the world's stage, and to do so in order to make us better players on that stage. All the world's a stage and even the players must watch the show now and then as they wait for their next cue. To put this simply, I draw on Terry Eagleton who reminds us that the rise of theory in the academy followed in the wake of the student revolts and political struggles of the late 1960s and early 1970s. These revolts and struggles changed the universities' and especially the Humanities Faculties' quiet assumptions concerning value and engagement; they also revealed the ways in which universities and humane studies were complicit with "military violence and industrial exploitation" (Eagleton 2003, 26). Eagleton goes on to say:

> The humanities had lost their innocence: they could no longer pretend to be untainted by power. If they wanted to stay in business, it was now vital that they paused to reflect on their own purposes and assumptions. It is this critical self-reflection which we know as theory. Theory of this kind comes about when we are forced into a new self-consciousness about what we are doing. (Eagleton 2003, 27)

Self-consciousness about what we are doing: this is theory. Sounds simple. But of course such self-consciousness is neither simple nor easy. The resistance to theory we sometimes meet in the classroom stems from an ingrained notion that literary activity ought to be natural, fun, and self-evident. We murder to dissect; we murder when we reflect too deeply. Or so the story goes. It seems that we are not to turn the gaze on ourselves because to do so will prove uncomfortable, like realizing we are showing signs of aging and turning from the mirror to look for the botox.

When we do look in the mirror, we see reflected back a figure who is both attractive and unattractive. Rather than ask the mirror for answers to our questions (who is the fairest of them all, for example), we would do better to think through the mirror. As Lacan has taught us, gazing into the mirror both allows for and suspends the gaze. We gaze at what we see, but we can also find ourselves gazed at by the figure in the mirror. We see our Imaginary and that Imaginary is both devoutly to be desired and intently to be feared. We see, in other words, mystery. That mystery is both an "other," a figure strangely attractive and eerily unsettling, and the mystery is ourselves, a figure familiar to each of us. The figure in the mirror is, you guessed it, uncanny in Freud's sense of both familiar and unfamiliar. Mystery is inescapable. This fact (shall I call it a fact?) should be both attractive and unsettling. Mystery pulls us forward, or it ought to pull us forward. If we take reading to be a reflective activity, a sort of looking in the mirror, then what the books we read reveal is both ourselves and the "other." In short, books are mysterious. So too is the activity of making sense of books. We read because we desire to understand what we read (at some level). What theory does for us is this: it reveals the mystery of textual interpretation, while at the same time it reflects interpretation's inevitable connections with desire. At one and the same time, theory is intellectual reflection and pursuit of desire. We attempt to think through problems, but we do so precisely because we desire answers to these problems. The catch is that no answers will ever close desire. I mean, the problems we seek to unproblematize are enduring problems; they will return and return again. If they did not return, then we would inhabit a world without mystery, surprise, or nuance; we would live life without repression. We would remain in infancy. The perennial nature of problems associated with questions of response to what we read (why do I like or dislike something? what does something mean? what does a reference suggest? why is my reaction different from my friend's reaction to a character or to a plot? etc.) is one reason why it is impossible to teach theory; we can only practise theory. We can only reflect.

An end to innocence

Why theory ends our innocence is because it asks us to consider what we do and why we do it. What does reading signify as a cultural practice?

What do interpretive activities imply about our preconceptions? Why do we read? Why do we have literature in the first place? What is literature? Theory generates questions and more questions. And our search for answers leads us into the mysteries of self-understanding. Theory precedes what we do and why we do it, every time. We cannot engage in thinking about the things we read or see or even fashion without having first, at some level, engaged in theoretical thinking. Once we choose to read for ourselves, we do so for a reason, and it is the reason that theory asks us to reflect on. Once we do this consciously and with some rigour in thinking, we can never return to a state of innocent choosing. We will now know why we choose what we choose. Or at least, we will now be part way to knowing why we choose what we choose. And children as well as adults can be self-reflexive. The usual argument I hear from students who resist theory is that innocence is bliss. Why destroy the bliss of a child's innocence by requiring or asking her or him to self-reflect? Why not allow children to be children? Why not indulge the glory and the dream? Well, the answer is simple. There is no glory and our life is no dream, although it may yet become one. Not to destroy the bliss of innocence, not to destroy the dream, is to leave children vulnerable to control, manipulation, coercion, and even exploitation. The innocent reader is the untheoretical reader; the innocent reader is the unreflective reader. And we might remember the kind of characters in fiction that do not reflect. The innocent are the ones sacrificed.

The twin designation "Children" and "Childhood" might well suggest, as Karen Coats argues, an awareness of both the materiality of our subject and its theoretical existence. Children are beautifully multifarious, and childhood is something we can only theorize about until we drag it into material conditions, at which point we are no longer speaking of childhood, but rather speaking about children living their lives in all its visceral intensity and difference. When we turn our attention to children's literature, we turn from lived lives to imagined lives. In literature, children and the child are local constructs and only distantly related to actual children whose lives are inflected with sorrow, joy, anxiety, downright fear, and material conditions of a variety of kinds. The children we encounter in the literature we read are simulacra, perhaps not the same order of simulacra as those we meet in news stories and magazines such as *Kids Wear*, but simulacra nevertheless. If I alter my language slightly, I designate these children as examples of the writers' (and I include the illustrators', the photographers' and film makers') and our Imaginary. We cannot hope to understand children's literature if we ignore the constructedness of the textual universe. And when we take note of literature's, of the text's, constructedness, we might make the short move to an acknowledgement that constructedness is just about all we have. Human life consists of stories and stories are constructions. Thomas King puts it this way: "The truth about stories is that that's all we are" (King 1992, 153). We have no existence outside of story—either adult or child.

Children, as Jacqueline Rose has argued, are constructed from adult desire; they do not exist as knowable entities in any unmediated way. Our sense of what constitutes childhood or "the child" at any given moment of history is contingent, dependent upon historical context. What we have are the signifiers "children," "the child," and "childhood," and these may signify any number of things, as long as that number is large. Just as we have for so long enforced a normalcy in the depiction of our Imaginary, we enforce a normalcy in the literature we think our children ought to read. We expect our literature for children to offer them something to sing about and something to socialize them. Children's literature has a pedagogic role to perform, and this performance is supposed to be fun. Education is fun. The children who are the audience for children's books and who do not exist as anything other than our Imaginary, pose a problem. On the one hand, these nonexistent children are the audience for the books we designate "children's books," and on the other, these books we designate "children's books" set out to create, that is to construct, the audience that will read them. In other words, children's literature is problematic in many ways, as others have noted. About the only way we can begin to understand children's literature is to theorize it. The catch is that theorizing children's literature will not get us any closer to understanding what children's literature is in any absolute sense. It will, however, get us closer to the literature we read than we would be were we not to theorize it. We can only come close to an "other" by reflecting on it. Innocence is unreflective.

Bricolage/pluralism

Children's literature criticism is *sui generis* a discipline that requires and rests on theory, and theory is just thinking with the information we have at hand to think with. The study of literature, arguably, cannot exist without theory. However, the study of mainstream literature can take place and has taken place without the foregrounding of theory. I think of the New Critical activity that largely held sway for most of the twentieth century in the academic study of literature. Close reading concentrated on aspects of form without necessarily leading to a thinking about form that we might identify as theoretical. Catherine Belsey's *Critical Practice* (Belsey 1980) identifies a kind of reading based on common sense, a reading that approaches literature "not as a self-conscious and deliberate practice, but as the 'obvious' mode of reading, the 'natural' way of approaching literary works" (Belsey 1980, 2). Early work on children's literature attempted to mimic the "obvious" mode of reading by concentrating on plot, character, setting, and theme. Representative of such mimicry is Rebecca J. Lukens's *Critical Handbook of Children's Literature* (Lukens 2002). But by the early 1980s, writing on children's books began to take notice of theory, at first trying to configure children's books to various familiar theoretical paradigms (Marxist, feminist, structuralist, etc.), and then noticing the special features of this literature, especially as these pertain to audience. One result of this turn to audience was Peter Hunt's call for a "childist" criticism. Ultimately, those who wrote about children's literature saw the need to think through this literature—i.e. to theorize it.

Theory is, to some extent, an act of *bricolage*. We might say that children's literature was one of the first academic disciplines to be interdisciplinary, and it was inevitable that such an interdisciplinary area of research should lead to amalgamation into Studies of Children and Childhood. What Studies of Children and Childhood offer the study of children's literature is an acute awareness of the historical development of our discipline with its emphasis on the connection between the literature young people read and the lives young people are expected to live and the ways adults conceive of children as either similar human beings or a race apart. Children's literature has evolved to such an extent that it is now impossible to neglect the reader herself. The reader children's literature "targets" (the implications of this word are sinister) is young, impressionable, curious, resistant, compliant, male, female, white, brown, black, other, experimental, not-so-young, buoyant, depressive, excitable, blue, green, reflective, and of course desiring. Sounds familiar? This reader occupies a great range of differences, of shifting and forming identities. I'm tempted to say that we have here a queer readership, but I know how volatile this descriptor is. In any case, children's literature situates itself between readers and the institutions those readers belong to: family, school, church. Reading does not take place in some isolated utopian space where innocence can rest unalloyed. Children's books are on the front lines, as lists of censored and embattled books indicate. I won't attempt a comprehensive list here, but familiar titles challenged by censors include Sendak's *In the Night Kitchen* (1970), Blume's *Are You There God, It's Me Margaret* (1970), Briggs's *Father Christmas* (1973),

Taylor's *Roll of Thunder, Hear My Cry* (1976), and Rowling's *Harry Potter and the Philosopher's Stone* (1997). To talk about children's books necessitates talking about issues, including censorship. And to talk about issues seriously, we need to reflect. And as I said at the outset, to reflect is to theorize.

Karen Coats has argued for a theoretical pluralism in the study of children's literature. She points out that:

> The questions undertaken by scholars of Children's Studies are necessarily philosophical, theoretical, and pragmatic, often at one and the same time. And their answers are always provisional and experimental, hinging on an ethical and methodological pluralism that must be maintained if we are to intervene effectively in the lives of children. (Coats 2001,140)

I'm not sure that provisional and experimental answers to difficult questions necessarily hinge on pluralism, but they do hinge on two necessary aspects of theory: 1) its inherently provisional character, and 2) its oppositional questioning. Pluralism has its attractions because it appears on the surface a sort of democratic surveying of the range of alternatives in approaching literature. And it is true that a knowledge of the range of alternatives is useful, even necessary. The problem surfaces when a pluralistic approach fails to negotiate the political implications behind the various approaches. Does this mean that we must select a particular critical and theoretical approach as the standard by which to judge all others? Must Marxism always trump psychoanalysis or feminism or formalism or whatever? Or must formalism always trump other approaches? Are we caught between either a single approach which assumes the authoritarian stance or a plural approach that fails to reveal the inequalities of power?

Myers offers a possible solution to this dilemma when he asserts that the "radical alternative to pluralism in the teaching of literary theory is a monistic one" (Myers 1994, 3). What Myers means by "monistic" is a genuinely exploratory and oppositional thinking. Such thinking is akin to the kind of critical examination of culture called for by critical pedagogues. As Myers points out, the "radical approach draws its inspiration from Paulo Freire's *Pedagogy of the Oppressed* (1994)" (Myers 1994, 3). The focus of a critical pedagogy is on the agendas that lurk between the lines of any text. So, for example, a book as innocent and attractive as Margaret Wise Brown's *The Runaway Bunny* (1942) ostensibly comforts the child by insisting on the inevitability of a mother's love, while it also calls for acceptance of this love and all its repressive satisfactions. The child reader is interpellated into the comforts of home and the status quo.

Two problems arise at this point. One is only a problem if we curry favour with notions of aesthetic value. How does a radical approach account for matters of form? The second problem is how do we teach a radical approach? The first problem strikes me as easily solved. In order to arrive at an understanding of any text's agenda, we need to be able to see *how* it communicates this agenda and to see the *how* of textuality is to give attention to matters of form in order to reach matters of content. In other words, a radical approach does not rule out the kind of reading taught by formalist and new critical pedagogies. The problem of how to teach a radical approach is also easily resolved, or at least as easily resolved as any question of how to teach anything is resolved. Obviously, teaching is itself a vexed topic, but the teaching of a radical approach to textuality calls for a genuine belief in the open-endedness of critical thinking. No conclusions will ever be final. Critical pedagogy rests on the assumption that thinking is an ongoing activity, and it is ongoing precisely because it can never rest in its testing of previous conclusions. Opposition is true friendship, and theory is friendly. It demands risk from everyone involved, but it does so with a smile. The instructor who is theoretically engaged will not rest easy with received opinion or yellowing lecture notes.

A case study: theory and critical practice

So let's take a risk. How might we approach a picture book such as *What's The Most Beautiful Thing You Know About Horses?* (1998), story by Richard Van Camp and pictures by George Littlechild? This is an innocent enough picture book published by Children's Book Press in San Francisco. Its premise is simple: "on January's coldest day of the year," in Fort Smith, Northwest Territories, Canada, the unnamed narrator decides to ask everyone he talks to on this day what is the most beautiful thing he or she knows about horses. He asks his dad and his mom, his brothers Jamie and Johnny, his buddy Mike, his friends Heather and George, and, before he goes for his nap, he asks his reader. That's it. To accompany this series of questions and answers, George Littlechild supplies simple drawings reminiscent of children's colourful work with gouache. Obviously, the book works in a way not dissimilar to the way a book such as Chris Van Allsburg's *The Mysteries of Harris Burdick* (1984) works. In Van Allsburg's book, the reader is drawn to speculate on the stories each picture might generate. In other words, *The Mysteries of Harris Burdick* seeks to activate the reader's imagination, to create an interactive reading experience. This interactive aspect of books for the young is not unusual, and we can find examples of it going back at least two centuries. In *What's the Most Beautiful Thing You Know About Horses?*, the narrator's address to the reader at the end makes it clear that this book wants the reader engaged in imaginative activity. And the innocent view of childhood has, since at least the end of the eighteenth century, placed great value on the word "imagination." Books for the young should appeal to the child's imagination. Children are imaginative creatures; adults are rational creatures. Childhood is a time of wonder, a precious moment in our lives when things are fresh, and all things bright and beautiful surround us. Children are precious creatures precisely because they are imaginative. This is the depiction of childhood Jacqueline Rose speaks about when she investigates the depth of adult investment in children and childhood. Children do not exist except as categories of the adult Imaginary. They are what we want them to be.

Mention of Jacqueline Rose should raise an eyebrow here. Perhaps we should reflect a moment on the nonexistent child in this book. The child-narrator in *What's the Most Beautiful Thing You Know About Horses?* does not exist, not in any material sense. We might wish to give this narrator a name, and the text encourages us to do so because one of the narrator's friends in the text is George Littlefield, a Cree. The book cover tells us the pictures in the book are by George Littlefield and the author's and illustrator's brief biographies at the end of the book tell us that the artist George Littlefield is "from the Plains Cree nation." The narrator is from the Dogrib nation, and Richard Van Camp's bio at the end informs us that he is from the Dogrib nation. Why would we not, then, assume that the narrator is Richard Van Camp? The thing is, the situation in the book suggests a narrator who is still a child. Kept, or at least staying, indoors on a bitterly cold day, this speaker speculates about horses by asking various people in his family and in his circle of friends what they think is most beautiful about horses. Then as the book comes to a close, the speaker mentions taking a nap. We also have photographs of the various people the speaker asks his question of, and these photographs deliver people of undetermined ages, but certainly not children. In other words, the characters remain elusive, old and young at the same time. Not only are their ages undetermined, but their racial and ethnic origins are not always clear. We know the narrator's mother is Dogrib and George is Cree, but what about Heather and Mike and the narrator's father? Their racial and ethnic origins are about as definite as the reader's. In other words again, the characters in this book pretend to have existence in the world the reader inhabits, but really they exist only as constructs within the diegetic portion of the book, and we might also say something similar about the reader implied by the narrator's address. These characters exist and they do not exist. These are hybrid characters in the sense that they inhabit a zone between fiction and reality. Well, so what?

Let's remember that the book publisher is Children's Book Press, a self-described "nonprofit publisher of multicultural literature for children" (Van Camp 1998, Half title page). And we might also remember that George Littlefield is Cree and Richard Van Camp is "a member of the Dogrib nation from the Northwest Territories of Canada" (Van Camp 1998, Half title page). The narrator of this book is also a member of the Dogrib nation; he informs us that his "Mom is a Dogrib Indian" (Van Camp 1998, n.p.). He does not tell us his father's ethnic background, but he does say that he (the narrator) is "half Indian" and "half white" (Van Camp 1998, n.p.). He is neither and both native and white; he is hybrid. He says the "good news about all this is I could be the cowboy *or* the Indian when we used to play Guns." The "bad news" is that his family "never had any horses to ride up here" (Van Camp 1998, n.p.). Good news and bad news: the good news is that this book delivers a comfortable multiculturalism, maintaining the innocence that we are all pretty much alike, and this "we are all" is unthreatening to any one group of people. The narrator reassuringly says that his "granny" taught him "that handshakes are hugs for strangers," and that if he could he would "shake hooves with all the horse tribes" (Van Camp 1998, n.p.). Unlike, say, Thomas King's *Coyote Columbus Story* (1992), a picture book that is openly critical of white colonization of Native North Americans, *What's The Most Beautiful Thing You Know About Horses?* appears uncritically to embrace everyone. It seems to maintain the innocent vision of imaginative childhood. The bad news is that this book insists on difference. Some people are dog people and some are horse people. Climate and geography are responsible for such a difference. We might find similarity in that the word for horse in Dogrib is tlicho (tlee-cho) "which means 'big dog'," and the word for horse in Cree is mista'tim (mis-ta-im) which means "big dog." The narrator thinks it is "neat how both languages call horses 'big dogs' " (Van Camp 1998, n.p.). Maybe the bad news is good news; difference disguises similarity.

But the English word "horse" has the same etymology as Latin *currere*, "to run." As far as I can find, "horse" in English has no connection with "dog." We know the Greek word *hippos* means "horse," but not dog. It is not much of a stretch to see that the Cree and Dogrib words for horse share a meaning that connects to dogs, but the same connection does not appear in the English word. If we reflect on this, we might trot back to the narrator's good news that he could be either the cowboy or the Indian. If this is good news, then it is so only because the narrator has a choice. The question is—which does he choose to be? Does he choose to be a "big dog" person or a "runner"? This question really leaves him little choice; historically, the Native people were forced to be runners, and half-Native people had the decision as to their race decided for them. Littlechild's picture of the half cowboy/half Indian picks up the familiar binary of white man and native. Each half of the person is distinguished by the stereotypical look of film figures. The Indian half has long black hair and wears a feathered headband. His cheek appears to be painted. He wears a buckskin shirt with fringe and on his foot he wears a moccasin. In his raised hand is a bow, and above the bow we see an arrow. On the left, behind the central figure, we see a teepee. Now for the cowboy half. He wears a Stetson under which we see his blond hair. His shirt has a designed pocket and cuffs. He wears tailored jeans and a big pointed-toe, high-heeled cowboy boot. In his hand he appears to carry an object that is most likely a piece of wood serving as the child's pistol. To his right and behind we see a rudimentary building, perhaps a barn. The two halves of the figure are connected by the neck scarf, and the reinforced inner thighs of the trousers. If anything connects the two halves of this figure, it is testosterone. The association of the cowboy half with the words "stick' em up," the association of the cowboy half with store-bought clothes and wooden buildings, and the narrator's comment that they used to play "guns" might just remind us of the unequal nature of the two halves. One half always seems to win, at least this has most often been the case in the stories of cowboys and Indians children have grown up with. One half has the gun, the other has the bow and arrow.

I've moved some way from the word "horses." My point is the emphasis the narrator places on the fact that "We are not horse people" (Van Camp 1998, n.p.). It may be that the Dogrib language has something in common with the Cree language, but Dogrib and Cree people are definitely not the same when it comes to knowing horses, and we can extrapolate and say that Dogrib, Cree, and white people are definitely not the same when it comes to the history of justice and equality. When it comes to playing guns, inequality has been the order of the times. I think the assertion of difference also appears in the various answers the narrator receives to his question concerning the beauty of horses. I won't rehearse all the answers, but generally we have answers that refer to horses having secrets and beautiful eyes, having a homing instinct, having beautiful hair, having the ability to run sideways, and having breath that communicates their soul. One person, buddy Mike, states that he does not like horses because after riding them all day "you feel bowlegged" (Van Camp 1998, n.p.). Littlefield's picture of a bow-legged Mike shows a blond cowboy astride an irritated-looking horse, and below this we see the horse smiling in the background while a bowlegged set of legs occupies the foreground. Another respondent, friend Heather, does not answer the question. Instead, she says that her "favorite horse is the Appaloosa because an Appaloosa is a horse with freckles" (Van Camp 1998, n.p.). And so tucked away inside the various answers are indications of the characters who provide the answers, and each is different. I think the point is underlined when the narrator sums up his questioning. He says that we could go on to "find out about all the animals of the earth if we called everybody in the whole world." Then he offers three secrets he learned the last time it was cold: "an eagle has three shadows," "frogs are the keepers of rain," and "there's an animal on this earth who knows your secret name" (Van Camp 1998, n.p.). Mention of "your secret name" could refer to the new name "which no man knoweth saving he that receiveth it" (Rev. 2:17), but I'm quite sure that it does not. It refers, I suspect, to Native beliefs. And here we come to the nub of things. This book may be for everyone, but it contains a sensibility and grounding in beliefs that are not fully open to me. I read this book as an outsider.

The book's cover makes it clear that this book is about love, the love of horses, the love of family and friends, the love of tolerance and difference, and the love of nature and the larger context of nature. By the larger context of nature, I refer to the many pictures that offer stylized representations of the galaxy. But the repeated mention of secrets should remind us that ultimately this book is about unknowing. Some things will remain secrets: the differences between people or between animals remain. And perhaps the most pronounced difference apparent in this book is its narrative. Unlike most narratives offered to children, this one is unformed by plot. The story has the rudiments of plot, but no conventional plotting. Instead, the book is a series of answers to the question posed by the book's title. The narrator makes no attempt to close the answers; in fact, the book ends with a question: "And what's the most beautiful thing you know about you?" (Van Camp 1998, n.p.). Only one person can answer this question and the answer will be unique to that one person. To put this in theoretical terms, the question addresses a "you" who is unknown, implied, existent, nonexistent, known. The question addresses a reader who is both singular and plural;

the "you" is both singular and plural. "You" is never just singular and never just plural; it is one and both. This "you" should teach us that no child exists, only children, and that children differ from one you to another you. Near the close of the narrative, the narrator says: "Well, partners, puppies need lots of sleep and so do I. But before I go for my nap, let me ask you: 'What's the most beautiful thing *you* know about horses?' " (Van Camp 1998, n.p.). These words address a community of partners; they connect human and animal; and they seek activity of response. These words are truly dialogic.

On the book's final page, the half-title, Richard Van Camp writes a note in which he remembers when his publisher, Harriet Rohmer, asked him to write a book about horses. Being a stranger to horses, Van Camp promised himself "to ride my first horse before this book came out" (Van Camp 1998, n.p.). And he did. This note allows Van Camp to extol the trust between horse and rider, and to compare this to the trust he shared with his illustrator, George Littlefield. Once again, we have the deep connection between animal and human that informs the book. But we also have explicit evidence of the connection between writing and acting. Writing has its effect in the material world. We might speculate that had Van Camp not written this book, he might not have ridden a horse, or at the very least, the writing of the book prompted the act of riding a horse. We might also speculate and say had not Van Camp written this book, then I might not have tried to work my way to an understanding of how the innocence of multiculturalism (its assumption of what Louise Saldanha terms "white innocence" (Saldanha 2004, 26–62); we are all the same under our skins) comes under interrogation in Van Camp's book. And to locate an interrogation of multiculturalism is to keep awareness of difference active in material reality. We move from book to context. We move from nonexistent characters to a sense of their relationship to "real" children. I must place the word "real" here in quotation marks because of its temporal and local significance. In other words, we shift from strictly theoretical concerns to what Karen Coats calls "the material effects of historical and ideological change" (Coats 2001, 140).

Theory before and theory after

And so my reading of *What's the Most Beautiful Thing You Know About Horses?* takes form in a theoretical context. In a *Horn Book* article not long ago, Cathryn Mercier earnestly points out that her "conscious application of theory to reading assists [her] in crafting the best possible understanding of a book's ambitions and achievements," and she goes on to say that "the more I understand the book, the better able I am to bring that book to a child" (Mercier 2002, 1). The application of theory does not have to be consciously the application of one "ism" or another to that which we read. My reading of the picture book will show signs of Marxism, postcolonialism, formalism, deconstruction, and even psychoanalysis to the reader who looks closely at it. You may even be able to find a trace of gender studies slyly hiding in an aside. Other aspects of my reading involve, implicitly, the notion of a canon. Why do I choose this book to examine in this essay? I could have chosen any number of books. First, I choose a picture book because I want to acknowledge that any reading of what we term children's literature necessitates an understanding of visual representation as well as verbal representation. I also want to acknowledge that the reading of visual images is a necessary skill beyond the book. Children, and all of us, live in a deeply visual environment and we need to know how to read visual signals just as much, maybe even more, than we need to read verbal signals. My students too often assume that a picture is transparent, whereas words are or can be tricky. They need to learn visual codes just as much as they need to learn verbal ones. For example, the two horses on the cover of the picture book are male and female, but we know this only from one conventional detail.

Second, I choose this book because I want to indicate that any canon we might acknowledge in the field of children's literature needs always to expand and change. To put what I wish to say another way, any choice that shatters a sense of a strict canon is a good choice as far as I am concerned. We need to embrace books by minority peoples just as we need to embrace books that challenge what Ghassan Hage calls the " 'White Nation' Fantasy" (Hage 2000, 78–104). Theory allows us to take whatever is at hand, like considered and considering *bricoleurs*, and make something happen. As it happens, *What's the Most Beautiful Thing You Know About Horses?* was given to me just about three weeks before my writing of this essay began. In other words, my decision to incorporate this book into this essay has an aspect of serendipity to it.

Third, I choose this book because I do not fully understand it. Mind you, I don't think I understand any book fully. None of us fully understands what we read; theory serves to remind us of this. In the case of *What's the Most Beautiful Thing You Know About Horses?*, I know that much of the book eludes me because I am an outsider to Dogrib and Cree cultures. What's more, something I do know about also eludes me here. I refer to intertextuality. I have no doubt that many of Littlechild's pictures in this book are intertextual references to Van Camp's novel, *The Lesser Blessed* (1996). The cover picture is an example, but so too is the picture of Littlechild as a horse just three pages from the end. The relevant passage in *The Lesser Blessed* concerns "the Horse's Head Nebula" (Van Camp 1996, 90), and the main character's desire to be an astronomer. I am confident that Littlechild serves us an intertextual reference in his illustrations, but his reference also serves to remind me that I don't fully grasp what he is driving at, and that I can be certain other intertextual references escape me. My failure to understand this book's intertextuality does not mean that I fail to understand the book at some level, but it does mean that I am reflecting and that reflection takes me to a place where innocence cannot survive. *The Lesser Blessed* is a novel that chronicles dysfunction in families; it is about scarring and desire and failure and hope. My reading of the novel infects my reading of the picture book. Why does the narrator name his mother's ethnic background but not his Dad's? Why does the narrator note that his brother Jamie has allowed the fire to go out? Can we find clues to life's difficulties as opposed to the cosy vision of imaginative sharing in *What's the Most Beautiful Thing You Know About Horses?*

And so my conclusion appears to be twofold: 1) we need theory in order to think self-consciously about the things we encounter, including literature, and 2) we need to teach theory in order to end the innocence of reading for fun. This is, I think, what my conclusion appears to be. However, appearances are notoriously deceiving. In the first place, I am arguing here for a separation between theoretical discourse and theoretical activity. Theoretical discourse, as Althusser, points out, is necessarily difficult because it takes common words and gives them uncommon or complex meanings (Althusser 1990, 45). This is why we need to have the taxonomy of theories that often takes place in theory classrooms. It is useful for us to know the general vocabulary of critical theory for the advanced level of conversation that takes place in university classrooms. But theory as an activity of mind does not require a full knowledge of theoretical discourse; it requires only self-consciousness. It requires a willingness to reflect, to look at what we are doing and think about it. If we do this, then we will gradually grow comfortable with theoretical discourse. And as we are growing comfortable with theoretical discourse, we are learning that theory is a form of play, a play with ideas, dare I say it, a freeplay. Bingo, we can have fun with theory. "Fun" is not necessarily a synonym for "unthinking." Reflection need not be a chore. If I may borrow again from those I love, theory is an indication that the faculties have been roused to act, and such activity can lead to an organized innocence. Theory is not some removed and distant abstraction; it is rather just another tune in the singing game. And remember: we sing to celebrate this thing called life.

Acknowledgement

My thanks to June Scudeler for the gift of *What's The Most Beautiful Thing You Know About Horses?*, and for the gift of friendship.

Works cited

Althusser, Louis. 1971. "Ideology and Ideological State Apparatuses (Notes Towards an Investigation)." 127–86 in *Lenin and Philosophy and Other Essays*. Translated by Ben Brewster. New York: Monthly Review Press.

———. 1990. "On Theoretical Work: Difficulties and Resources." (1967) 45–67 in *Philosophy and the Spontaneous Philosophy of the Scientists and Other Essays*. Translated by Ben Brewster et al. London/New York: Verso.

Belsey, Catherine. 1980. *Critical Practice*. London & New York: Routledge.

Blume, Judy. 1970. *Are You There God? It's Me, Margaret*. New York: Dell Yearling.

Briggs, Raymond. 1973. *Father Christmas*. London: Hamish Hamilton.

Brown, Margaret Wise. 1972. *The Runaway Bunny*. (1942) Pictures by Clement Hurd. New York: Harper Trophy.

Butler, Judith, John Guillory, and Kendall Thomas, eds. 2000. *What's Left of Theory: New Work on the Politics of Literary Theory*. New York: Routledge.

Coats, Karen S. 2001. "Keepin' It Plural: Children's Studies in the Academy." *Children's Literature Association Quarterly* 26 (Fall):140–50.

Eagleton, Terry. 2003. *After Theory*. London: Allen Lane (Penguin).

Freire, Paulo. 1994. *Pedagogy of the Oppressed*. (1970.) Translated by Myra Bergman Ramos. New York: Continuum.

Freud, Sigmund. "The 'Uncanny.' " (1919.) 336–76 in *Art and Literature*. The Pelican Freud 14. Translated by James Strachey. Harmondsworth: Penguin.

Hage, Ghassan. 2000. *White Nation: Fantasies of White Supremacy in a Multicultural Society*. New York: Routledge.

Hunt, Peter. 1984. "Childist Criticism: The Subculture of the Child, the Book and the Critic." *Signal* 43 (January):42–59.

Kid's Wear: The Junior Style Magazine. 2002. No. 14 (Spring/Summer).

King, Thomas. 1992. *Coyote Columbus Story*. Pictures by William Kent Monkman. Toronto/Vancouver: Groundwood.

———. 2003. *The Truth About Stories: A Native Narrative*. Toronto: Anansi.

Lacan, Jacques. 1977. "The Mirror Stage as Formative of the Function of the I as Revealed in Psychoanalytic Experience." (1949). 1–7 in *Ecrits: A Selection*. Translated by Alan Sheridan. New York and London: W. W. Norton.

Lesnik-Oberstein, Karín, ed. 2004. *Children's Literature: New Approaches*. London & New York: Palgrave—now Palgrave Macmillan.

Lukens, Rebecca J. 2002. *Critical Handbook of Children's Literature*. (1972). Seventh edition. New York: Allyn & Bacon.

Mercier, Cathryn M. 2002. "Critical Connections: Professional Reading From 2001." *Horn Book Magazine* 78 (May/June):301. Accessed online 17 June 2004 http://80-web25.epnet.com.ezproxy.lib.ucalgary.ca:2048/DeliveryPrintSave.asp?tb=1&_ug=sid+9BCB25C8-8652-45CF-908C-8477C8C07FC2@session.

Myers, D. G. 1994. "On the Teaching of Literary Theory." *Philosophy and Literature* 18 (October):326–36. Accessed online 17 June 2004 http://www.-english.tamu,edu/pers/fac/myers/teaching_theory.html.

Payne, Michael and John Schad, eds. 2003. *life. after. theory*. London & New York: Continuum.

Rorty, Richard. 2004. "Looking Back at 'Literary Theory.' " Response to the American Comparative Literature Association 2004 State of the Discipline Report (a work in progress, last updated 14 April 2004). Accessed online 17 June 2004 http://www.stanford.edu/~saussy/acla/.

Rose, Jacqueline. 1984. *The Case of Peter Pan or the Impossibility of Children's Fiction*. London: Macmillan—now palgrave Macmillan.

Rowling, J. K. 1997. *Harry Potter and the Philosopher's Stone*. London: Bloomsbury.

Saldanha, Louise. 2004. "Colouring Outside the Lines: Children's Literature Written by Women of Colour in Canada." Ph.D. thesis, University of Calgary.

Sendak, Maurice. 1963. *Where the Wild Things Are*. New York: Harper and Row.

———. 1970. *In the Night Kitchen*. New York: Harper and Row.

Shavit, Zohar. 1986. *Poetics of Children's Literature*. Athens & London: University of Georgia Press.

Tester, Keith. 1994. "Introduction," 1–21 in *The Flaneur*, ed. by Keith Tester. London and New York: Routledge.

Touponce, William F. 1995–96. "Children's Literature and the Pleasures of the Text." *Children's Literature Association Quarterly* 20 (Winter):175–82.

Townsend, John Rowe. 1980. "Standards of Criticism for Children's Literature," 193–207 in *The Signal Approach to Children's Books*, ed. Nancy Chambers. London: Kestrel Books.

Van Allsburg, Chris. 1984. *The Mysteries of Harris Burdick*. Boston: Houghton Mifflin.

Van Camp, Richard. 1996. *The Lesser Blessed*. Vancouver/Toronto: Douglas & McIntyre.

———. 1998. *What's The Most Beautiful Thing You Know About Horses?* San Francisco: Children's Book Press.

Williams, Raymond. 1976. *Keywords: A Vocabulary of Culture and Society*. London: Fontana Press.

Further reading

Althusser, Louis. *Philosophy and the Spontaneous Philosophy of the Scientists and other Essays*. Translated by Ben Brewster et al. London: Verso, 1990.

Bakhtin, Mikhail. *The Dialogic Imagination*. Translated by Caryl Emerson and Michael Holquist. Austin: University of Texas Press, 1981.

Davis, Lennard J. *Enforcing Normalcy: Disability, Deafness and the Body*. London and New York: Verso, 1995.

Eagleton, Terry. *Literary Theory: An Introduction*. Oxford: Basil Blackwell, 1983.

Fiedler, Leslie A. (1960.) *Love and Death in the American Novel*. New York: Stein and Day, 1966.

Frye, Northrop. *The Secular Scripture*. Cambridge, MA: Harvard University Press, 1976.

Genette, Gerard. *Narrative Discourse: An Essay in Method*. Translated by Jane E. Lewin. Ithaca, NY: Cornell University Press, 1980.
Jameson, Fredric. *The Political Unconscious: Narrative as a Socially Symbolic Act*. Ithaca, NY: Cornell University Press, 1981.
Said, Edward. *Culture and Imperialism*. New York: Alfred Knopf, 1993.
Williams, Raymond. *Keywords: A Vocabulary of Culture and Society*. London: Fontana Press, 1976.
Wimsatt, W. K. (1954.) *The Verbal Icon: Studies in the Meaning of Poetry*. London: Methuen, 1970.
Zizek, Slavoj. *Looking Awry. An Introduction to Jacques Lacan*. Cambridge, MA: MIT, 1991.

5
Word and Picture

Maria Nikolajeva

This chapter will discuss the various approaches to picturebooks, and the many existing tools for analysing these, mainly focusing on the text/image interaction. Picturebooks are an extremely gratifying subject to teach, since students often come to this module with preconceived opinions about picturebooks being simple and geared toward very small children, and they are surprised at the variety and complexity of picturebooks they meet in class. Further, because of their volume, the instructor can deal with a larger number of texts as compared to novels, which allows a deeper and more comprehensive discussion of the various kinds of texts. In my experience, students point out in their evaluations that the picturebook module or session was the most exciting part of the course. Furthermore, many insights gained during the study of picturebooks can be transposed onto other text types.

In the context of children's literature, picturebooks are a special kind of book in which the meaning is created through the interaction of verbal and visual media. In many reference sources, picturebooks are treated as identical with books for small children, who cannot yet read themselves. While many picturebooks do indeed address the youngest readers in their themes and issues, picturebooks should not be defined through their implied readership, but rather through their aesthetic characteristics. Until recently, the studies of picturebooks have been strictly divided into two separate categories: carried out by art historians and by children's literature experts. While the first group paid attention to aspects such as line, colour, light and dark, shape, and space, ignoring not only the textual component, but frequently also the sequential nature of the picturebook narrative,[1] the second group treated picturebooks as any other children's books, applying either literary or educational approaches without taking into consideration the importance of text/image interaction.[2] A number of influential recent studies of picturebooks demonstrate that picturebooks cannot be satisfactorily analysed with tools either from art history or literary criticism, but need a theory and a scholarly metalanguage of their own.[3]

Most researchers distinguish between picturebooks and illustrated books. In the former, a preexisting text has been supplied with illustrations, and pictures are subordinated to words. The same story, for instance a fairy tale, can be illustrated by different artists, and although these may impart different interpretations to the text, the pictures have primarily a decorative function; the story can still be understood without pictures. It is a good idea to let the students explore this by browsing through several illustrated versions of the same story. In a picturebook proper, words and images constitute an indivisible whole, and the overall impact of the work is achieved by the interaction of the two expressive means. This process and the result of the interaction have been described in terms such as iconotext, imagetext, composite text, synergy, polysystemy, counterpoint, contradiction, and congruence, which all emphasize that the true meaning of a picturebook is created only by the joint efforts of the verbal and visual communication. The variety in the terminology reveals clear difficulties: while "iconotext" or "composite text" refer to the static unity of text and pictures, "counterpoint" or "synergy" emphasize the complex dynamics of interaction in the process of meaning-making. The recently established solid spelling "picturebook" captures its terminological usage, as distinguished from picture books, or books with pictures.

I usually demonstrate the interdependence of word and image in a genuine picturebook by reading aloud to the students the text of Pat Hutchins's *Rosie's Walk* (1968), containing one single sentence: "Rosie the hen went for a walk across the yard, around the pond, over the haystack, past the mill, through the fence, under the beehives, and got back in time for dinner." As anticipated, the students do not find the text particularly funny. I then show the pictures and let them discover how the images tell a completely different story and how the humorous effect is created by the incongruence between what the words and the images convey.

It is, however, essential to emphasize that in terms of the relationship between words and images, picturebooks present a wide continuum, from wordless picturebooks, in which the title offers the only verbal guidance to the interpretation (for instance, Mitsumasa Anno's *Journey*, 1978; Jan Ormerod's *Sunshine*, 1981, and *Moonlight*, 1982), or from nonsequential, nonnarrative picture dictionaries and concept books

(Helen Oxenbury's *I See*, 2000, *I Hear*, 2000, *Touch*, 1985), in which words and images repeat and support each other, to picture storybooks, in which the narrative is carried collaboratively by words and pictures. Yet the quantitative and qualitative ratio of text and images may vary substantially. Words and pictures may convey more or less the same information and thus be symmetrical and even mutually redundant. Conversely, words and images may be complementary, filling each other's gaps and compensating for each other's inadequacies. Images are far superior to words when it comes to descriptions of characters and settings, while words are superior in conveying relationships and emotions, as well as direct speech. Images are unsurpassed in conveying space, while words are indispensable for temporal aspects. A clever picturebook makes use of the best of both means. In other cases, pictures may substantially add to the story conveyed by words, expanding and enhancing it, or occasionally, words can expand the meaning of images. If words and images tell two different stories, besides *Rosie's Walk*, for instance, in John Burningham's *Come Away from the Water, Shirley* (1977), or David McKee's *I Hate My Teddy Bear* (1982), the tension creates an ironic counterpoint, which can occasionally go so far as to become contradictory and even confusing, as in McKee's *Not Now, Bernard* (1980).[4] While different scholars suggest a variety of typologies concerning the balance between text and image, all the approaches clearly demonstrate that the corpus of picturebooks is far from homogeneous.

In this chapter, I have chosen to provide as complete an analysis as possible of one single book, Anthony Browne's *The Tunnel* (1989).[5] I have chosen the book for its complexity on many levels, which allows a discussion of various aspects and dimensions.[6] I have also successfully taught it in a variety of courses, from general overview courses of children's and juvenile literature to specifically focused courses on picturebooks. The students' responses to the book have provided many valuable thoughts; it is seldom that this book leaves them indifferent. I usually start the discussion of picturebooks by asking the students to submit a free response: simply say whatever they can say about the assigned books. The initial reaction to *The Tunnel* mostly concerns the plot and theme; frequently, the students interrogate gender stereotyping. It is only after my prompts and perhaps some discussions around other books that the students discover the complicated interaction of word and image that not only support and enhance the plot, but create additional facets and layers of meaning.

Normally, a somewhat comprehensive analysis of a picturebook would most probably not separate the discussion into the aspects I have singled out, but this distinction serves a pedagogical purpose, showing, among other things, how the interaction of word and image works differently within one and the same book when we speak about composition, setting, characterization, or point of view. During an actual classroom discussion, I would show and consider a great number of other picturebooks, illustrating the same elements of the narrative as in *The Tunnel*. The assessment of this module would be an individual or group investigation of all the relevant aspects of one specific picturebook from a selection provided (this to ensure that the chosen book includes complexity similar to that of *The Tunnel*).

The picturebook as an object

I always start the exploration with the picturebooks as an object, an artefact. The students are rarely aware of the fact that not only the pictures accompanying the words, but the cover, the back cover, the title page, and the endpapers may contain significant information, as can the size and format of the book, page layout, and other purely formal qualities.

Picturebooks come in many sizes and formats. There are two radically different ideas about what is suitable to children: one view says "small books for small hands" resulting in the typical Beatrix Potter format; while the other attitude is that large books are easier for children to handle, which gives us the oversized Babar books. Whatever the argument, the choice of format is by no means accidental: are Beatrix Potter's elegant watercolours conceivable if blown up to a Babar size? Or can the richness of detail in *The Tunnel* be appreciated if resized to the format of Peter Rabbit? *The Tunnel* is "normal-sized," yet there is a reason to consider the issue of format. There are several format possibilities for picturebooks, which are seldom applied in novel publishing. The most common are landscape (horizontal) format and portrait (vertical) format; other formats also occur, such as square. Some picturebook artists have a preference for just one format, while Anthony Browne varies according to the nature of the book. In the *Willy* books, which focus on single episodes, he uses vertical format. The horizontal format is better suited for narratives involving movement, like *The Tunnel*, where the artist also utilizes the whole doublespread to create a sense of a wide space.

The cover of a novel is normally merely decorative. The cover of a picturebook is a highly significant part of it. A picturebook cover is the door into the narrative, and it can occasionally carry information essential for understanding the story. In *The Tunnel*, the cover illustration repeats one of the most dramatic episodes inside the book, the girl entering the tunnel. The reader sees her disappearing into the darkness; the picture creates suspense and invites the reader to follow. The title traces the curved line of the tunnel vault (in some paperback editions, this important detail is ruined: Figure 5.1). The title does not reveal the particulars of the plot, but focuses on the central object of the story and its foremost symbol.

Normally the students quite reasonably assume that the narrative begins on the first page. Picturebooks, however, may make use of endpapers to create an establishing scene or even start the plot. Before we get to the first words of the narrative, we are given a glimpse of the main conflict depicted symbolically by visual means. The facing pages of the front endpaper depict two backgrounds revealing contrasting styles, the first a flowery pattern, the second brick (Figures 5.2 left and 5.2 right). As we will soon learn, the first background is wallpaper, symbolizing the indoor space where the girl prefers to be, while the brick wall is outdoors where her brother plays. (Incidentally, the brick wall is Browne's trademark, appearing in different contexts in almost every picturebook of his, as I show to the students.) At the front endpaper, we also see a book in front of the flowery wallpaper. The book, as we will discover from the story, is the girl's attribute. The back endpaper is seemingly the same, with the wallpaper on the left and brick on the right (Figures 5.3 left and 5.3 right). However, the book has moved from the left to the right and has been joined by the ball, the boy's attribute. Just as the visual story preceded the verbal one on the front endpaper, the back endpaper presents a somewhat didactic conclusion without the use of words. This is a very clever way of confirming the resolution of the plot by visual means. The discussions of the endpapers makes the students aware of the importance of visual details in picturebooks, and they also realize that pictures can and must be "read," that is, decoded, just like words.

The page layout can be significant, and a variation of layout may serve a number of purposes. In early picturebooks, text and pictures were normally separated (mostly for technical reasons, to facilitate printing); pictures were placed on the recto (right-hand page) and text on the verso (left-hand page). Beatrix Potter chose to create a special rhythm by alternating text and picture pages between recto and verso. In most contemporary books, the variety of page layout contributes to the dynamism of the story. *The Tunnel* contains twelve openings, or doublespreads. The first is used to introduce the two characters in contrast to each other, and the most logical layout here is two small contrasting panels on each page. The second spread continues the introduction and amplifies the

Figure 5.1 The cover of the paperback edition corrupts the balance between the image and the title layout

conflict depicting the boy scaring his sister at night. The smaller panel on the verso shows the boy peacefully asleep in his bed, while the larger picture on the opposite page presents a full description of the girl's room. The girl is through this layout introduced more substantially than the boy, which is likely to make the reader perceive her as the main character.

On the third spread, the artist has chosen an interesting mirror layout with the boy's hand pointing to the left, back into the safety of home (suggesting that the sister's place is at home), while the mother's hand on the recto points further into the book, toward the unknown and the dangerous (Figures 5.4 left and 5.4 right). The pictures are equal in size, so the balance between home and away is so far undisturbed.

The fourth and fifth spreads are conventional, with the picture on the recto and text on the verso, but on the sixth, the girl's upset face on the verso is framed into a black vaulted panel, echoing the vault of the

Figure 5.2 left Front endpaper

Figure 5.2 right Front endpaper

Figure 5.3 left Back endpaper

Figure 5.3 right Back endpaper

Whenever they were together they fought and argued noisily. All the time.

Figure 5.4 left The secure home . . .

One morning their mother grew impatient with them. "Out you go together," she said, "and try to be nice to each other just for once. And be back in time for lunch." But the boy didn't want his little sister with him.

Figure 5.4 right . . . and the dangerous away

tunnel on the recto. The four small panels on the seventh spread are used to convey the girl's movement through the tunnel: they depict four consecutive moments. The next two spreads are also extremely dynamic as they open the narrative space from the small picture on the verso through the full-page picture on the recto into the wordless and frameless spread of the girl running through the frightening forest (Figures 5.5(a) left, 5.5(a) right, 5.5(b) left, 5.5(b) right). The black background around the small picture of the petrified boy emphasizes the stasis of the next spread. The penultimate spread is again formed as a sequence of four pictures, and the very last one is traditional with text on the verso and picture on the recto. Thus the artist makes great efforts in using page layout to convey the narrative space and the changes in setting and mood, the open and closed spaces, and the contrast between movement and stasis. By no means all picturebook makers employ such variation of layout, and even in Browne's oeuvre, *The Tunnel* is unique in this respect. Yet it is important to point out for the students that the layout decisions are not accidental, but contribute to the overall impact of the story. Once the students are aware of this, they start noticing the variety of layout patterns in other picturebooks and the effect these produce. A good parallel is the expansion of the panels in the beginning of Maurice Sendak's *Where the Wild Things Are* (1963).

None of the pictures in the book "bleed," that is, expand beyond the panel area, which otherwise has become a common device in picture books. Moreover, all illustrations except two are clearly framed, some of them even double-framed. Frames create a sense of detachment, as if the artist did not want us to come too close to the narrative. However, there is no frame on the wordless doublespread: in this case, the absence of a frame literally draws us into the picture (here again a parallel to Sendak's book can be made). Another frameless illustration is the last one, portraying the characters reconciled, and, presumably, we have now got to know them so well that no frames are required.

After this discussion of the formal elements of the book, the students are prepared to plunge into the story as such. They have now also acquired some basic terminology to discuss images, such as doublespread, verso and recto, frame, and so on.

The plot

Even though some types of picturebooks can be nonnarrative, such as picture dictionaries and ABC books, the majority have a plot, however minimal. The scope of a picturebook does not normally allow for a complicated plot, which is perhaps why picturebooks are often considered "simple." In *The Tunnel*, the plot is indeed uncomplicated and easily recognizable from fairy tales: a brother and a sister are forced to leave home and face the dangerous world; the brother is enchanted, and the sister saves him. The verbal opening of the story immediately leads the reader's mind toward a fairy tale: "Once upon a time there lived a sister and brother . . ." Indeed the Hansel and Gretel motif will be reinforced throughout the story,[7] not only in the girl's sacrificial rescue of her brother, but more significantly in the imagery. It is clearly anticipated by the gingerbread house in the girl's bedroom. In my courses, I deal with picturebooks after fairy tales, so I expect the students to recognize the fairy-tale elements in *The Tunnel*, and in most cases they do.

The plot presents the most common pattern in all children's books: home (safe, but boring)—away (exciting, but dangerous)—home again.[8] In *The Tunnel* the initial setting is ordinary, which is conveyed by images only (the text does not specify that the characters live in contemporary urban surroundings), while the "away" world is magic and weird. Unlike the fairy tale (for instance, *Hansel and Gretel*), the evil force that has enchanted the brother is never described, neither in words, nor in pictures. In fact, we do not know what happened to the brother, which only adds to the subtle mystery of the narrative.

In carrying the plot, words and pictures can duplicate each other, support or even contradict each other. In *The Tunnel*, words and images would seem relatively symmetrical on the plot level, yet a close reading reveals how skilfully Browne chooses between the two expressive means to develop the narrative. The plot as such, after the exposition in which the characters are presented, starts with the complication as the mother sends the children out. The pictures support the conflict between brother and sister, showing their postures and, on the next spread, the sister with her back turned to the brother, while the text conveys a conversation between them. In the picture, the girl is engrossed in her book. Thus the words and the picture are slightly asynchronic, the picture lagging behind the words. Some actions are only related by words: "He went off to explore" and, on the next page: "She walked over to him." On the other hand, the words do not say that the boy goes into the tunnel, they only convey his direct speech: "Come on, let's see what's at the other end." As pictures cannot convey direct speech (at least not directly), the verbal dialogue is used to carry the bits of the plot impossible to convey visually. Since pictures are better suited to show actions and events, the artist naturally uses the best medium to express these. Similarly, on the next spread, the text merely says, in free indirect

At the other end she found herself in a quiet wood. There was no sign of her brother. But the wood soon turned into a dark forest. She thought about wolves and giants and witches, and wanted to turn back, but she could not – for what would become of her brother if she did? By now she was very frightened and she began to run, faster and faster . . .

Figure 5.5(a) left The change in panel size . . .

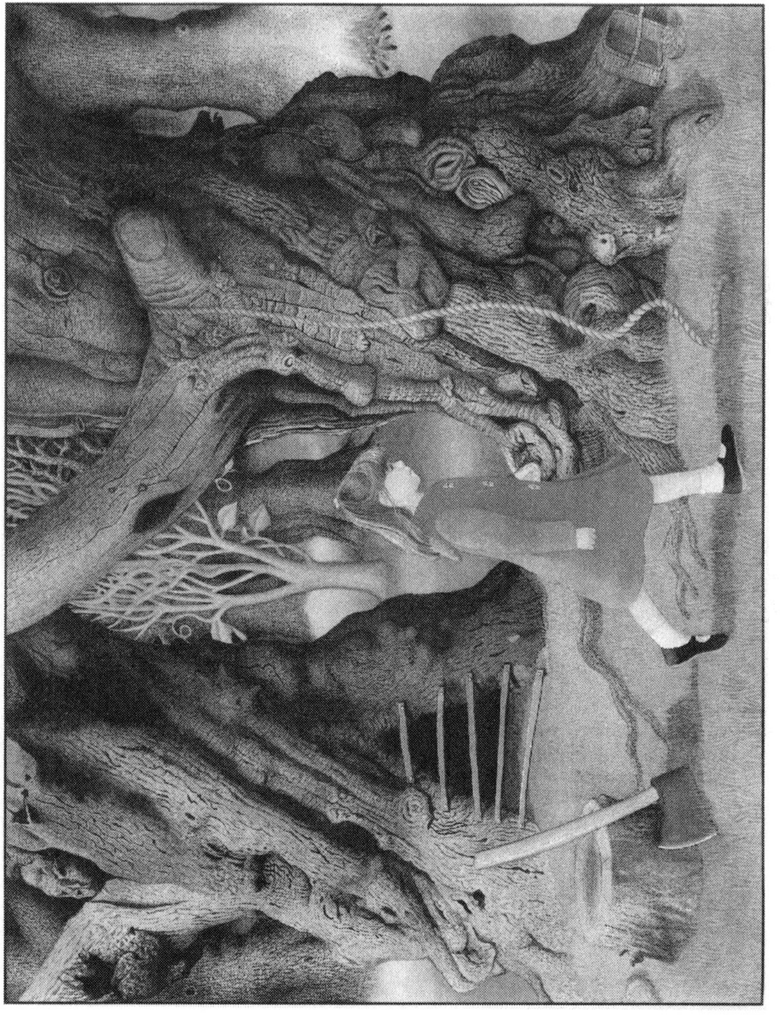

Figure 5.5(a) right

Figure 5.5(b) left

Figure 5.5(b) right . . . opens the narrative space

discourse: "What could she do? She *had* to follow him into the tunnel" (Browne's emphasis). The picture shows her doing so; it also shows that she has left her book behind, her most important attribute, which obviously has a deep symbolic significance. As she crawls through the tunnel, the text states: "The tunnel was dark, and damp, and slimy, and scary." The four adjectives match the four pictures, and in the last picture, we only see the girl's feet, while she is already out of the tunnel and in the next spread, where the "scary" things await her. The plot then takes the girl through the horrible forest, where the wordless spread is perhaps the most eloquent expression of the text's simple statement "she was very frightened," while the two consecutive pictures duplicate the words "she began to run, faster and faster . . ."

An episode where the pictures show a significant happening not expressed by words is the brother's transformation, where the last panel in the sequence of four shows him turned around to face his sister and with his arms around her. The body language in this image substantially enhances the brother's direct speech: "I knew you'd come." The part of the plot showing the characters' return home is only rendered by words: "They ran back, through the forest, through the wood, into the tunnel, and out again." Apparently, the narrative would not gain anything by showing the homecoming in pictures, since it would not add anything to the conflict. Finally, the token of home security is expressed verbally as: "When they reached home, their mother was setting the table." The significance of food in children's literature has been pointed out repeatedly.[9] In *The Tunnel*, the lunch, promised in the beginning, is never denied, but seriously jeopardized if the children were stuck forever in the weird world behind the tunnel. The food thus becomes, as often in children's books, the superficial reward for good behaviour. However, neither the set table nor the mother is depicted visually. Instead, the picture amplifies—literally, by using a close-up—the moral reward the children are given, their finding each other's affection: "Rose smiled at her brother. And Jack smiled back." As already mentioned, the back endpaper, showing the book and the ball together, is part of the plot, corresponding to the fairy-tale coda "lived happily ever after."

Setting

In a picturebook, setting can be conveyed by words, by pictures, or both. The visual text of a picturebook is naturally well suited to the description of spatial dimensions, the mutual spatial relations of figures and objects, their relative size, position, and so on. Setting demonstrates very well the difference between communication by diegesis (telling) and communication by mimesis (showing). While words can only *describe* space, pictures can actually *show* it, doing so more effectively and often more efficiently. In narrative theory, a description is one of the signs of the narrator's presence in the text. The verbal narrator forces the reader to "see" certain details of the setting, while ignoring others. Visual representation of setting is "nonnarrated," and therefore nonmanipulative, allowing a considerable freedom of interpretation from the reader.

As should be clear from the analysis of the plot, a good picturebook chooses cleverly between the two media to express whichever either can do best. It is obvious that pictures are far superior to words in presenting settings, and indeed a detailed verbal setting description in a picturebook would be completely redundant. The visual description has on the contrary unlimited possibilities. However, even in the visual setting we can observe a wide spectrum of pictorial solutions ranging from no setting at all, either verbal or visual (in books where only the characters and occasional objects necessary for the plot development are present) to a fully depicted setting which may be predominantly visual, predominantly verbal, or use a variety of combinations and permutations. *The Tunnel* is one of those books where visual setting is essential and significant on many levels.

The setting of a picturebook establishes the situation and the nature of the world in which the events of the story take place. At the simplest level it communicates a sense of time and place, through a more or less detailed description of exterior or interior scenes. As in a novel, picture book settings can be integral or used as a backdrop. In *The Tunnel*, the setting is of the backdrop kind: we do not know—and it is not important—exactly where and when the action takes place. We assume it to be an indeterminable present, judging from the characters' clothes, the scarce interiors and the urban exteriors, not least the dump, which is both a criticism of modern civilization, and symbolizes the conflict between the characters. The function of the setting as support for characterization begins on the first spread, as the characters are introduced within their specific settings: the girl against the flowery wallpaper, the boy against the brick wall; the girl indoors, the boy outdoors. The interior of the girl's room tells us about her interests, or maybe the interests her parents encourage: the classic illustration from "Little Red Riding Hood" and a nightshade in the form of a gingerbread house. The pattern on the wooden wardrobe anticipates the distorted tree stems beyond the tunnel. The two upside-down shoes look as if someone is crawling under the bed, just as the girl will eventually crawl into the tunnel. They may also remind one of the witch crushed under Dorothy's house in *The Wizard of Oz*. There is a rope—obviously an object out of place in a child's room—that will reappear in the magical wood. Thus the setting of the second spread, domestic as it is, prepares the reader for something other than a tame sibling drama. The contrast between the domestic and the alien, beyond-the-tunnel world is the main function of the setting in this book. In discussing this and subsequent spreads, it is important to let the students study them closely and at length, discovering every detail that may prove significant. It is remarkable how many details escape one's attention at first reading.

The pictures may expand on what the text describes, but they may go far beyond this, so that the entire setting is conveyed visually rather than verbally. Picturebooks can make use of a variety of pictorial solutions in the depiction of setting, for instance panoramic views (especially on the so-called establishing pages), long shots, middle-distance shots, close-ups or multiple scenes (that is, two or more different settings on the same spread or page). Picturebooks can even have contrasting settings on verso and recto. Many of these devices are used in *The Tunnel*. Mostly, words and pictures cooperate. As the girl emerges on the other side of the tunnel, she finds herself "in a quiet wood. There was no sign of her brother." The picture enhances the words by the sunlit grass and tree stems and the light sky between the trees. The picture is peaceful and in no way threatening, except that we perhaps share the girl's anxiety as we do not see her brother either. The words immediately turn our attention to the full-page recto picture: "But the woods soon turned into a dark forest." The picture expands the words, showing the details of the "dark forest" that would certainly take too many words to describe. The visual setting is perceived immediately and as a whole.

Time and movement

Picturebooks present a unique challenge and opportunity in their treatment of temporality. This area is also an excellent illustration of word and image filling each other's gaps, or, of even greater significance, compensating for each other's insufficiencies.

I start the discussion by asking the students whether one single picture can convey movement and the flow of time; a variety of images from picturebooks can be shown here. We soon arrive at the conclusion that there are two essential aspects of narrativity impossible to express definitively by visual signs alone: causality and temporality, for the visual sign system can indicate time only by implication. The flow of time can be expressed visually through pictures of clocks or calendars, of sunrise and sunset, or of seasonal changes, that is, through a *sequence* of pictures. However, in most cases, the verbal text serves to extend meaning and reveal time's progress by creating a definitive temporal connection between pictures.

Unlike film, the picturebook is discontinuous, and there is no direct way to depict movement. However, unlike decorative art, the picture book is narrative and sequential, and intends to convey a sense of movement and of duration. There are a number of techniques used in pictures alone, as well as a variety of options employed in the interaction of words and pictures, to imply movement and changes that take place over time. Different graphic codes, many borrowed from comics and photography, have been adopted by picturebook authors: blurs, motion lines, and the distortion of perspective, as clearly seen in the wordless doublespread in *The Tunnel*. Otherwise, the most frequent device to express movement within a single picture is *simultaneous succession*, a sequence of images depicting moments disjunctive in time, but perceived as belonging together, in an unequivocal order. The changes occurring in each subsequent image are supposed to indicate the flow of time between it and the preceding one. Browne does not use this device in *The Tunnel* (but does in some other books, such as *Changes*). Instead, he employs a sequence, for instance the girl crawling through the tunnel—(Figures 5.6 left and 5.6 right). Several pictures on the same doublespread encourage us to perceive a temporal—and often causal—relationship between them, even when the accompanying words have no clear temporal indications. It is "natural" to read the sequence left to right, as we read text. The temporal relationship is especially tangible in the sequence where the stone figure is turning back into the boy: his static, awkward pose with a wide-open mouth and face distorted by horror is changing into a "softer and warmer" figure, as the verbal text suggests (Figures 5.7 left and 5.7 right). The words claim that the transformation happens "very slowly," "little by little," and the sequence of four pictures with very little movement conveys this slow and painful process.

Unless the doublespread in a picturebook is one single panel, the creator may use the tension between verso and recto to imply movement as well as temporal and causal relations. In *The Tunnel*, we see the girl facing us on the recto, holding the book tight to her; on the opposite page she is disappearing into the tunnel. The words support our understanding that the event on the recto takes place after the event on the verso, but even without words the order would be obvious. Similarly, the

The tunnel was dark,

Figure 5.6 left   A sequence of pictures conveys movement . . .

and damp, and slimy, and scary.

Figure 5.6 right . . . and the flow of time

She threw her arms around the cold hard form, and wept. Very slowly, the figure began to change colour, becoming softer and warmer.

Figure 5.7 left A sequence with small changes . . .

Then, little by little, it began to move. Her brother was there. "Rose! I knew you'd come," he said. They ran back, through the forest, through the wood, into the tunnel, and out again.

Together.

Figure 5.7 right . . . conveys a slow and painful process

juxtaposition of images with "a quiet wood" and "a dark forest" clearly convey a temporal order (Figures 5.8 left and 5.8 right). Some scholars have suggested the notions of "home page" (or secure page) for verso and "away page," or "adventure page" for recto. This is not an absolute rule, but quite often the verso establishes a situation, while the recto disrupts it; the verso creates a sense of security, while the recto brings danger and excitement. In *The Tunnel*, we see it clearly in the spread with the breakfast scene (home, secure) on the verso and the children sent away on the recto; or once again, the contrast between "a quiet wood" and "a dark forest."

As noted above, the conventional way to decode movement is left to right, the way we read words (at least in our Western culture). Many picturebook authors seem to have accepted this convention when they arrange the book in a single movement from left to right. *The Tunnel* is tangibly based on the left-to-right movement, not only in the sequences of panels on some spreads, but also in the position of the characters, turned to the right and moving toward the right edge of the page. It may prove illuminating to reverse some of the images and let the students discover how the movement becomes distorted. The only significant deviation from the left-to-right movement is presented in the two pictures in which first the boy and then the girl crawl into the tunnel: away from the reader, into the unknown and dangerous, leaving their ball and book behind, that is leaving behind their identities in order to go through a rite of passage. Otherwise, the journey goes consistently from left to right, and the narrative tempo created by this composition is disturbing, which conveys the psychological charge of the book. However, the homecoming (logically right to left) is only depicted by words. It can be compared to the away and back home movement depicted visually in *Where the Wild Things Are*.

However, the spatio-temporal relationship in words and pictures is more complicated than this conventional solution. While the verbal text, even though it may contain temporal ellipses, is largely continuous and linear, pictures are always discontinuous. From the visual text alone there is no way to judge how much time has passed between two pictures. For instance, do the two events on the first spread, "The sister stayed inside" and "The brother played outside" take place simultaneously? And how much time has passed between the breakfast scene and the "one morning" when the mother loses her patience and sends the children out? Further, the duration of a verbal text is relatively determinable. Determining the duration and speed of a visual text presents considerable difficulty: how long a time does the action in a picture last?

It is equally hard to assess the discourse time: how long a does it take to narrate a picture? Since a picture is static we might suggest that its story time is zero, while its discourse time is indefinitely long. That is, in narratological terminology, the duration pattern of a picture is a pause.

Dealing with a sequence of pictures, either on the same spread or different spreads, we encounter various forms of ellipses. Verbal ellipses can be either definite (when it is specified that two hours, five days, or ten years have passed) or indefinite, in *The Tunnel*, for instance, "Just when she could run no further." Without devices such as the image of a clock, visual ellipses can only be indefinite and implicit. Depending on layout and other conventional devices, readers fill the ellipses between individual pictures, sometimes deciding that the ellipsis is very short, perhaps just a few seconds, or indeterminably long, up to several months. The wordless spread in *The Tunnel* is supposed to create a sense of a long duration before the girl comes to a clearing and sees her brother turned into a statue.

We may further decide that the pictures express the iterative, that is, something happening repeatedly, which is apparently the case with: "The sister stayed inside" and "The brother played outside," where the iterative marker "always" is implicit. The iterative is expressed verbally in sentences such as: ". . . she *would* lie awake," "*Sometimes* he crept . . ." and "*Whenever* they were together . . ." (emphasis added). Pictures cannot express iterative actions, but from the interaction of words and images we understand that the pictures show repeated events. Verbal statements compensate for the insufficiency of the visual signs and enhance our interpretation by specifying that the events take place "One morning . . ." (a singular event, unlike the earlier iterative ones). However, it is exactly the indeterminacy and ambiguity of visual temporality that makes picturebooks exciting and complex. While the words encourage the reader to go on (". . . she began to run, faster and faster . . ."), the images demand that we stop and devote a considerable time to reading the picture.

Whether an individual picture is static or conveys motion, the more details there are in a picture, the longer its discourse time. The common prejudice is that children do not like descriptions, preferring action scenes and dialogue. This must be an acquired preference, imposed on children by adults, since all empirical research shows that children (as well as adults) appreciate picturebook pauses and eagerly return to them. Many contemporary picturebook creators deliberately overload their pictures with details to make readers contemplate them at length. This is what Browne does in the wordless spread. We have previously

At the other end she found herself in a quiet wood. There was no sign of her brother. But the wood soon turned into a dark forest. She thought about wolves and giants and witches, and wanted to turn back, but she could not – for what would become of her brother if she did? By now she was very frightened and she began to run, faster and faster . . .

Figure 5.8 left Tension between verso and recto . . .

Figure 5.8 right . . . enhanced by words

agreed that that we normally read pictures left to right, as we read words. At this point, it seems necessary to problematize the whole issue of decoding pictures by presenting a counterargument, which also emphasizes the fact that all statements made earlier about how we perceive images are arbitrary. If a picture is totally symmetrical with the words, that is, functions as mere decoration and does not contribute any new information, we may indeed read it left to right and quite quickly. In pictures without a persuasive linear pattern and with many details, as the wordless spread in *The Tunnel*, our reading is arbitrary. The artist may deliberately or unconsciously place a detail in the picture that will attract our attention and compel us to start reading the picture from this point. The bright red colour of the girl's coat in the bottom right corner immediately catches the viewer's eye and makes us "run" through the spread following the figure. However, the abundance of details forces us to backtrack, pause, and browse over the spread at some length. The obvious speed of the running girl, conveyed graphically by a blur, and the inflicted pause of the viewer's eye are in conflict.

Characterization

The students are assumed to be familiar with the principal characterization devices in literature; if not, it can merely be noted that characterization can be external and internal, the former including description, narrator's comments, actions, and speech, while the latter employs different modes of mental representation. Characterization devices acquire a specific dimension in picturebooks.[10] For instance, external description can be both verbal and visual, each confirming or contradicting the other. Most often, verbal external description is omitted in picturebooks, and visual description only is used, being more efficient. Duplicating the description in words creates redundancy and diminishes the impact of characterization. In *The Tunnel*, the brother and sister are not described verbally, and it is only from the pictures that we know that they are human. It may seem natural to assume that they are human; however, picturebooks often feature anthropomorphic animals, occasionally without mentioning it in words. It is never mentioned in Browne's *Willy* books that Willy is a monkey. Without illustrations, and with the previous knowledge of the *Willy* books, we could just as well assume that the brother and sister in *The Tunnel* are animals. There is nothing in the plot that would preclude it.

Whatever the reason, the characters in *The Tunnel* are human children, and their appearance, including their clothes, emphasizes gender: soft pastels for the girl, bright sporty colours for the boy. The boy has short hair, the girl long. As earlier observed, they are also introduced against contrasting backgrounds symbolizing their inner qualities, as well as, once again, gender stereotypes: soft flowers versus hard brick. The visual description is quite sufficient, and the didactic verbal duplication of it feels rather unnecessary: "not at all like. In every way they were different." The juxtaposition continues on the facing page, both in pictures and in words: "stayed inside"—"played outside," "on her own"—"with his friends," "reading and dreaming"—"laughing and shouting, throwing and kicking, roughing and tumbling." Not only is the sister presented as passive and static, matching the female stereotype, the boy is described with three times as many action verbs. The two friends are the only figures, besides the main characters, portrayed in the book. They have a backdrop function, but they support the characterization of the boy as socially well-adapted, and in the picture, he is presented as the leader. The girl is apparently a loner.

Pictures have no denominative function, that is, they cannot tell us the characters' names. Neither can they express concrete facts about characters, such as age, or family relations. Browne makes excellent use of this in the book. He tells us that the characters are siblings, and he depicts the boy taller so that we can infer that he is older than his sister. We are not given their names, and throughout the story they are referred to by the generic "sister" and "brother," and on just one occasion "boy." In my classroom discussions, if the students refer to the characters as "Rose" and "Jack," I point out that the names only appear in the very end, and make the students contemplate the reasons and consequences. Apparently, this device amplifies the fairy-tale atmosphere of the story, but in the first place allows the overwhelming psychological transformation in the end, when the rescued brother addresses his sister by name: "Rose!" At this point he is still nameless himself, but he has acknowledged his sister as an individual rather than the neutral "sister." On the next page, the boy receives a name too, as Rose smiles at him: "And Jack smiled back."

A unique feature of picturebook communication is that pictures can show characters not mentioned by words, which may contrast with the protagonist, amplify our understanding of their relationships, or merely provide a credible background. There are no such characters in *The Tunnel*, mainly because the plot is totally focused on the siblings; but examples from many other picturebooks can be shown here. On the other hand, I point out that a character can be mentioned by words, but not portrayed in the pictures, a very efficient narratological device, which may be called visual paralipsis (omission). The mother in *The Tunnel* is only present in her direct speech, in the narrator's comment "grew impatient" and in the final action of setting the table. The most we see of her is her hand. It is interesting to ask ourselves why Browne chose not to portray the mother. Presumably, he did not want to give the mother a concrete shape, leaving this to the reader's imagination. Yet another comparison with *Where the Wild Things Are* is appropriate.

I also make the students think whether pictures can convey a state of mind. The logical answer is no: psychological description works best by words. Certain permanent human qualities (brave, clever, innocent) are difficult to communicate visually; however, the characters' poses, gestures, and facial expression can disclose emotions and attitudes, such as happiness, fear, and anger, as seen clearly in *The Tunnel*. Most often the narrative needs the subtleties of words to capture complex emotion and motivation. External and internal speech as a means of characterization is by definition verbal, although some interesting visual devices can be used to convey speech. Yet visual images can sometimes be more efficient in conveying the characters' inner life, especially vague, unuttered wishes, fears, daydreams, and other complex psychological states.[11] Pictures can make use of universal and unique symbols, of colours, shapes, and visual associations that would otherwise demand many pages of words. Such a picture communicates with the viewer immediately, which cannot be achieved through a verbal narration. The wordless spread of *The Tunnel* is an excellent example of this device.

Finally, pictures have the unique possibility to elaborate with close-ups, so that we literally can come closer to characters and almost feel as if we were talking to them. Very few picturebooks actually use this device, but Anthony Browne really exploits them, and in *The Tunnel*, the significant final image is a close-up (Figure 5.9).

We can generally say that picturebooks allow little room for thorough characterization in the conventional sense. Picturebooks tend to be plot-oriented rather than character-oriented. Further, the plot itself is often too limited to allow much development, which means that most characters are static rather than dynamic, and flat rather than round. Yet we see that *The Tunnel* successfully employs complex characterization through the interaction of word and image.

Perspective

It would by now be evident that in the discussion of *The Tunnel* we are moving from the less complex aspects of the word/image narrative, such

Figure 5.9 Close-up as characterization device

as plot and setting, toward the more complex and ambivalent. The consideration of the depiction of inner life brings us to the question of narrative perspective. Perspective, comprised of the narrative voice and the point of view, presents an extremely interesting dilemma in picturebooks, which once again has to do with the difference between visual and verbal communication, between showing and telling. In narratology, the term *point of view* is used in a more or less metaphorical sense, to denote the assumed positions of the narrator, the character, and the implied reader. With pictures, we can speak of perspective in a literal sense: as readers/viewers, we behold the picture from a certain fixed vantage point, imposed on us by the artist. Even though we can by eye movement "read" the picture left to right or right to left or in a circular pattern, the basic point of view is unchanged. It can, however, change within a sequence of pictures, both in direction and in distance ("zoom").

Presumably, the students are already familiar with the basic concepts and terms of narrative analysis. If not, it might be pointed out for them that narratology makes an essential distinction between point of view ("who sees") and narrative voice ("who speaks"). While this distinction is somewhat metaphysical in a novel, in a picturebook we should probably treat the words as *primarily* conveying the narrative voice, and pictures as *primarily* conveying the point of view. Pictures for obvious reasons lack the possibility of internal focalization, at least in a direct sense—the characters' feelings may, as mentioned earlier, be conveyed by facial expression, position in the page, tone, colour, and other graphic means. While the introspective narrator has, together with the first-person narrator, become one of the most common narrator types in contemporary psychological children's novel, the picturebook is essentially restricted in its use of introspection. It does, however, have its specific ways of conveying a subjective point of view.

On the other hand, pictures have unlimited possibilities of conveying literally an omnipresent perspective by giving a panoramic view of the setting, depicting several parallel events or several characters at different places, etc., that is, expressing something that the verbal text only can express indirectly. The iterative episodes in *The Tunnel*, "The sister stayed inside . . ." and "The brother played outside . . ." are a good example.

Most picturebooks would be normally classified as having an omniscient, omnipresent visual perspective. However, even in the seemingly simple cases, we often notice that the verbal and the visual perspective are not in accord with each other. Sometimes, while the words pretend to convey the point of view of the child (or the anthropomorphic animal representing the child), the visual point of view seems to be that of a condescending adult, or the other way round. Analysing narrative perspective in *The Tunnel*, we immediately notice that the words and pictures are not in consonance. The narration blends the narrator's relatively calm and matter-of-fact tone in the words with the characters' emotionally charged perception, conveyed by pictures. The verbal text is seemingly written from an omniscient perspective, with a didactic narrative voice explaining, as already noted, things that we easily can see from the pictures, for instance, that the brother and sister "were different," which seems to exclude the interpretation of these pictures as a depiction of a subjective view. However, both pictures are framed and clearly detached from each other. It is not at all impossible that the characters are in fact presented through each other's eyes. This provocative statement on my part usually causes a strong reaction from the students, as they are reluctant to ascribe the story still further complexity. I always emphasize that this is just one of many possible interpretations and is neither better nor more correct than any other; I simply take the opportunity to explore different options, even though they may feel a bit far-fetched.

Thus I go on to argue that the second pair of pictures, with the girl reading and the boy playing soccer, may have an omniscient perspective, but they can similarly reflect the way the characters see each other, literally and figuratively. We can thus read the verbal text as the characters' free indirect speech, transforming the first sentence: "The sister stayed inside on her own" into the somewhat irritated: "My sister always stays inside," and the second: "The brother played outside with his friends" into the envious and resigned: "My brother always plays outside." This reading, not at all self-evident, adds to the complexity of the story, creating an interplay of subjective narrative voices and perspectives (Bakhtinian heteroglossia[12] can be complemented by the neologism heteroscopia) rather than ascribing the narrative agency to a single objective narrator.

As the story progresses, the possible shifts in perspective become more intricate. The picture of the brother sleeping "soundly in his room" while his sister lies "awake, listening to the noises of the night" must be interpreted as having an omniscient perspective, as do the following spreads in which both appear together. However, in the picture where the brother crawls into the tunnel, the girl is watching him, with her back turned to the viewer—we share her literal point of view. One might assume that this picture now firmly establishes the girl's point of view; however, the next spread shows another frontal image of the frightened girl on the "secure" page and the rear view of her crawling into the tunnel on the "dangerous" page. The story seemingly describes external events, the changing of visual setting supporting the conflict and using the imagery of brick versus greenery to symbolize the characters' spatial spheres. Although this change in surroundings does reflect the characters' mood, for instance the dump referring to the broken relationship, it is not until the entrance to the tunnel that the words explicitly convey the sister's thoughts: "There might be witches . . . or goblins . . . or *anything* down there" (author's emphasis). The metamorphosis from the ordinary world to a surrealistic one begins in words with the sister's uttered fears, but is taken entirely into the visual realm as words fail. The words express the girl's state of mind as she prepares to look for her brother: "His sister was frightened of the tunnel and so she waited for him to come out again. She waited and waited, but he did not come. She was close to tears. What could she do? She *had* to follow him into the tunnel" (author's emphasis). But it is the setting itself, portrayed both in words and images, that reveals her sensations; her fear is communicated to the reader by the description of the tunnel: "dark, and damp, and slimy, and scary." This use of the surroundings to echo the emotion is reinforced by the reader's sharing of the experience pictorially, watching the sister literally disappear into the darkness as her feet catch the last of the light, and then her laborious progress through the tunnel which emphasizes the sense of claustrophobia. The four framed panels of the girl crawling through the tunnel are presented as if in cross-section—formally an omniscient, omnipresent perspective, but equally a subjective experience in correspondence with the words.

Yet another visual depiction of high emotion is of course the presentation of the forest. As the verbal text describes the girl's feelings, "she thought about wolves and giants and witches . . . By now she was very frightened and she began to run, faster and faster," the growing sense of fear is projected onto the metamorphosis of the trees. They change from an everyday appearance to gnarled, twisted, knotted trunks that take the shape of increasingly grotesque animals. Undifferentiated limbs, tails, and eyes seem to stretch out to grasp her as she passes or trip her as snaky roots, and the incipient transformation takes the shape of bears, wolves, boars, weasels, snakes, and gorillas emerging from the trees. The setting begins to take on allusive aspects: a fallen basket and a woodcutter's axe bring the girl's red-hooded coat into another fairy-tale dimension, anticipated by the Little Red Riding Hood painting in her bedroom. A barred hole in one tree, a rope hanging from another, and a fire burning feverishly near another (echoing Browne's version of *Hansel and Gretel*) provide hints of hidden life, while roots with tendrils spread out to trip and tangle. The wordless doublespread with a lone tombstone and the gingerbread house in the background completes the fearful transformation. The picture presents the girl's terror in a way that the simple statement "she was very frightened" cannot, and communicates the sense that it is the terrors in her mind, spawned of her imagination, that are of greatest significance here.

An excellent exercise at this point might be using the somewhat trite expression: "A picture says more then a thousand words," and asking the students to narrate the visual image: not to *describe* the picture, but attempt to convey by words the same emotions that the picture evokes in the viewer.

The last picture, reestablishing the realistic setting, is a close-up of the two characters, facing each other and, the text duplicating the picture, smiling at each other. In the picture, we share Jack's point of view, and this time there is no doubt about it: he is looking at Rose, seeing her, after the tunnel experience, with new eyes. Since this is the final picture of the book, its point of view compels us to consider still another possibility: have we witnessed Jack's imaginary story, following the horrors of his little sister through the enchanted woods and making him realize her vulnerability? Was the seemingly omniscient view of the surrealistic spreads indeed Jack's view, his inner vision, evoked by her words: "There might be witches . . . or goblins . . ."? Thus, the fluctuation in verbal as well as visual point of view in the story creates considerable ambiguity, while the uncertainty in the figural point of view provides additional complexity. Although, as we have discovered, on the levels of plot and characterization *The Tunnel* does not seem to contain any exciting clashes between words and images, and in some places even shows redundancy, in its totality the iconotext appears to use a high degree of counterpoint.

Fantasy and reality in picturebooks: modality

The question of narrative perspective leads us to the most complex, but also the most exciting, level of interpretation, that of the contradiction between the objective and subjective perception of the narrative, which both can be prompted by words or by pictures. Another way of addressing this question would be to speak about mimetic versus nonmimetic, or symbolic, representation, that is, statements which we interpret as a direct reflection or imitation ("mimesis") of reality as opposed to statements which we know we must interpret on different levels, for instance as symbols or metaphors.

The essence of this opposition can be conveyed by the concept of modality, a linguistic notion covering categories such as the possibility, impossibility, contingency, or necessity of a statement. Modality enables us to decide on the degree of truth in the communication we receive. Mimetic, or literal, interpretation means that we decode the received communication as true ("this has happened," indicative modality). Symbolic, transferred, nonmimetic interpretation encourages us to decode texts as expressing possibility ("it may have happened"), impossibility ("this cannot have happened"), desire ("I wish it happened"), necessity ("it should have happened"), subjective experience, or probability ("I believe that it has happened") and so on. As empirical research demonstrates, unsophisticated readers tend to interpret texts mimetically, identifying with protagonists and sharing their subjective perception. For instance, the girl's experience beyond the tunnel will be perceived as actually having occurred rather than taking place in her imagination. Many students are resistant to nonmimetic reading of novels as well as picturebooks, therefore I find it gratifying to take up the issue in *The Tunnel*.

I choose to speak about modality rather than genre, since picture books, more than any other kinds of children's fiction, effectively blur the common distinction between genres, doing so by verbal as well as by visual means. I find that the concept of modality enables us to examine the intricate way picturebooks convey subjective perception of reality, external or internal, without resorting to the artificial and obsolete division of narratives into fantasy and realism.[13] Most students find the concept of modality difficult at first, but as they grasp the implications, they quickly master this analytical tool and find it helpful in applying to other complex picturebooks.

As always, the dual narrative of picturebooks presents us with an additional problem. Since modality is a purely linguistic category, a visual image in itself cannot convey modality. That is, beholding a single picture not accompanied by words, we cannot as a rule decide whether what we see is real or unreal, a dream, a wish, a prescription, a permission, or a doubt. However, even in isolated pictures artists have means, based on conventions, to manipulate the viewers to interpret the image in a certain way, for instance as a fantasy. Pictures of mythical creatures, or unfamiliar or distorted objects, are automatically perceived as unreal, while photographic and other true-to-life images are perceived as real. Unnatural colours, for instance red sky and blue grass, will also prompt us to interpret the picture as imaginary. Pictures of familiar scenes which we can relate to will be interpreted as real. A sequence of visual images immediately creates a potential for modality. By adding verbal statements, the author can further force the viewer to adopt a particular interpretation. For instance, a landscape painting entitled "A Dream" will most probably be interpreted as imaginary, even through the picture itself may be true-to-life.

In picturebooks we cannot decide from the pictures alone whether the narrative is objective or not, that is, whether we should apply mimetic or symbolic interpretation. However, complex modality can be achieved through the interaction of words and images. While the verbal story is often told from a child's point of view presenting the events as true, the details in pictures may suggest that the story only takes place in the child's imagination. The pictures thus subvert the verbal narrative as an objective story, as already shown with the details in the girl's room anticipating her beyond-the-tunnel experience.

In analysing picturebooks, three modalities are of special interest: indicative (expressing objective truth), optative (expressing desire) and dubitative (expressing doubt). In *The Tunnel*, nothing in the first seven spreads suggests that the story is anything but real. Recognizable details of interior and exterior settings, the human shape of the characters, and the everyday events establish the indicative mode.

The words do not directly suggest that the transformed setting is the product of the girl's imagination; however the successive change prompts the reader to apply a different modality in interpretation. A mimetic reading would suggest that the girl indeed finds herself in another world where her brother has been enchanted and turned into stone. Yet the obvious connection of the imagery of the surrealistic pictures to the images appearing earlier in the realistic setting implies that we are dealing with the girl's projected horrors. The pictures elicit a sense of hesitation in the reader—the modality of the narrative is the dubitative, evoking doubt. The pictures subvert the verbal narrative's intended objectivity. The temporal indeterminacy created by the wordless double-spread adds to the ambiguity. When I get to this point, I try not to come with my own statements but let the students draw the conclusion themselves, which always proves more or less a revelation and can cause heated debates.

Intertextuality and metafiction

Some of the foremost characteristics of contemporary picturebooks reflect their connection with postmodern thought.[14] Already the spatio-temporal indeterminacy of *The Tunnel* is a typically postmodern trait, as is the suggested intersubjectivity of the two characters. Intertextuality—or intervisuality, a more appropriate term in connection with pictures—is another trademark of postmodern picturebooks, with references to other works of children's literature as well as famous works of art.[15] The visual connection to fairy tales in the girl's bedroom has already been discussed; as has her red hooded coat. In the picture of the "quiet wood" we see some birds on the ground, pecking at small white pebbles. An informed reader will recognize the allusion to *Hansel and Gretel*: the pebbles that Hansel drops and that will lead the children back home. A reader familiar with Browne's books will also recognize the pebbles from his illustrations to *Hansel and Gretel*. In *The Tunnel*, the pebbles lead the girl to her brother and reappear as a magical circle around him as he is petrified. It is hard to say exactly what the circle signifies, but the self-allusion is obvious. Moreover, it is not the only visual allusion to Browne's *Hansel and Gretel*, as the distorted trees appear already there, and the little picture of the fire in the "dark forest" panel is a direct visual self-quotation.

The students generally agree that the intervisuality is deliberate. The question remains as to its purpose. Superficially, the sister saves her brother just as Gretel saves Hansel. But from whom? There is no witch in *The Tunnel*. In Browne's *Hansel and Gretel*, the pictures suggest that the evil stepmother and the witch are the same person. The mother in *The Tunnel* is only depicted as a pointed hand, so she may just as well be the invisible evil force behind the enchantment. However, this is perhaps going too far in speculation.

Finally, if I feel that the students are receptive enough, I might attempt a rather far-fetched metafictional interpretation. Metafiction is a postmodern feature that implies a deliberate subversion of fictionality and the text's self-consciousness about being an artistic construction. In contemporary picturebooks, metafiction has become a prominent trait,[16] often taking the form of frame-breaking and blurring the boundaries between the various levels of the narrative, including breakthrough into the reader's space. Often it also means the character's consciousness about being part of a fictive narrative. *The Tunnel* is, unlike many other books by Browne, not overtly metafictional, yet with the whole oeuvre as a background, as within the context of postmodern Western picture books, we can try to apply the concept of metafiction to this book. In the picture of the dump, the sister is reading a book. It is a fairy-tale book that we have already observed on the endpaper, in the establishing picture of the sister "staying inside, reading," open on the bed as she is trying to sleep, and carried under her arm as she is forced to go out and play with her brother. A purely metafictional interpretation, not directly suggested by either words or pictures, is that the adventure behind the tunnel is not merely prompted by her reading, but is in fact the story she is reading. When she suggests that there "might be witches . . . or goblins" beyond the tunnel, she is also aware of the genre in which she participates. Browne does not, however, go so far as make his heroine read *The Tunnel*, which would have been an overt metafictional device.

The dual audience

The questions that inevitably appear in the discussion of *The Tunnel* is for whom this complex book is written, whether children understand the various levels of it, or whether they get scared of the imagery. Teaching picturebooks as literature, I normally do not dwell on the pragmatic aspects, such as how to use this book in school, for what age group it is suitable, or whether it is suitable at all. Instead, I suggest considering in what way this book addresses its primary and secondary audiences, that is, children and adults.

Picturebooks are more likely than books for older readers to be shared by children and adults, as the latter read the books to children who cannot as yet read for themselves. It is perhaps one of the strongest assumptions that picturebooks equal books for the youngest. As is hopefully clear from the analysis of *The Tunnel*, picturebooks can be extremely complex, and they can also be read and enjoyed on different levels. However, instead of questioning their suitability for the young audience, I would argue that picturebooks, more than any other form of children's literature, demonstrate its most prominent inherent feature, dual address.[17] Since picturebooks are assumed to be read by an adult to a child, textual and visual gaps in picturebooks are deliberately left to be filled differently by child and adult, in the process described by scholars as crosswriting. Contemporary picturebook creators seem to be very much aware of this reading situation, addressing the adult co-reader parallel to the child, for instance, through specific intertextual and intervisual references. It has become common for picturebook makers to include extensive and ironic visual allusions to famous art objects as well as aspects of popular culture, as for instance in Browne's *Gorilla* (1983) and *Piggybook* (1986), which most likely are not immediately perceived by young readers. There are few visual (or verbal for that matter) elements in *The Tunnel* that deliberately address adults only. Yet the book obviously addresses the various reader categories on different levels. Where a young—or unsophisticated—reader will only see an exciting and slightly scary adventure and perhaps also perceive the simple moral evolving from the trivial story of sibling rivalry, a reader better trained in visual literacy will discover the psychological depth that we normally do not associate with books for the youngest children.

Does this make this picturebook "unsuitable" for young children? Here the dual nature of the picturebook narrative emerges as superior in some respects. A novel is dependent on the complexity of the language to be understood and interpreted; a reader who does not master this complexity will not be able to decode the text. Images affect our senses in a more immediate way and are not dependent on language to be understood. The fact that young readers cannot articulate their understanding of a picturebook narrative does not imply that they lack understanding or empathy. This is presumably the premise from which picturebook authors such as Anthony Browne create their work.

As I mentioned at the beginning, students frequently judge the picturebook section of the course as the most stimulating and even overwhelming. Most often, their previous experience of picturebooks is limited to simple, mass-market-type products that provide no challenge and hardly show any literary qualities. When exposed to complex, psychologically-charged picturebooks, such as Browne's *The Tunnel,* and *Gorilla,* or *Outside Over There* (1981) by Maurice Sendak, or *Granpa* (1984) and *Aldo* (1991) by John Burningham, or *Looking for Atlantis* (1993) by Colin Thompson, they realize that not only "a picture says more than a thousand words," but, more important, "there is more to the picture than meets the eye." The common response after discussing picturebooks that I get from students is: "I will never again view children's literature as simple."

Notes

1. See for example Klemin 1966; Cianciolo 1970; Alderson 1973; Feaver 1977; Lacy 1986; Cianciolo 1990.
2. For example Spitz 1999.
3. See Schwarcz 1982; Roxburgh 1983; Moebius 1986; Nodelman 1988; Doonan 1993; Sipe 1998; Kümmerling-Meibauer 1999.
4. For a more detailed discussion of the word/picture interaction see Nikolajeva and Scott 2001b and 2000; and Nikolajeva 2002.
5. For an overview of Anthony Browne's picturebook production see Doonan 1986 and 1998; Perrot 2000. For Browne's self-reflections see Browne 1994.
6. Some of the observations in this chapter have been earlier made in my copublications with Carole Scott.
7. It is interesting to know that Browne illustrated *Hansel and Gretel* in 1981. See Doonan 1983.
8. See Nodelman and Reimer 2003, 201.
9. See, for example, Nikolajeva 2000, 11–16.
10. For a more detailed discussion see Nikolajeva 2003.
11. See Nikolajeva and Scott 2001a.
12. See Bakhtin 1981.
13. I should make it clear at this point that my use of the term "modality" differs radically from the one proposed by Gunther Kress and Theo van Leeuwen in *Reading Images. The Grammar of Visual Design* (1996) and adopted in picturebook analysis, for instance, by John Stephens and Jane Doonan. Kress and van Leeuwen discuss the way images convey the sense of reality, ascribing photography a higher degree of modality ("closer to truth") and abstract or surrealist art a lower degree ("far away from truth"). While this use of the term is certainly acceptable and perhaps fruitful for reading visual images, I find it less applicable to word/image interaction.
14. See Bradford 1993; Lewis 2001.
15. See Beckett 2001.
16. See Lewis 1990; Mackey 1990.
17. See Scott 1999.

Works cited

Alderson, Brian. 1973. *Looking at Picture Books*. London: National Book League.

Anno, Mitsumasa. 1978. *Anno's Journey*. London: Bodley Head.

Bakhtin, Mikhail. 1981. *The Dialogic Imagination*. Austin: University of Texas Press.

Beckett, Sandra. 2001. "Parodic Play with Painting in Picture Books." *Children's Literature* 29:175–95.

Bradford, Clare. 1993. "The Picture Book: Some Postmodern Tensions." *Papers: Explorations in Children's Literature* 4.3:10–14.

Browne, Anthony. 1981. *Hansel and Gretel*. London: MacRae.

———. 1983. *Gorilla*. London: Julia MacRae.

———. 1986. *Piggybook*. London: Julia MacRae.

———. 1989. *The Tunnel*. London: Julia MacRae.

———. 1994. "Making Picture Books." 176–98 in *The Prose and the Passion*. Edited by Morag Styles, Eve Bearne and Victor Watson. London: Cassell.

Burningham, John. 1977. *Come Away from the Water, Shirley*. London: Jonathan Cape.

———. 1984. *Granpa*. London: Jonathan Cape.

———. 1991. *Aldo*. London: Jonathan Cape.

Cianciolo, Patricia. 1970. *Illustrations in Children's Books*. Dubuque, Iowa: Wm. C. Browne.

———. 1990. *Picture Books for Children*. Third edition. Chicago: American Library Association.

Doonan, Jane. 1983. "Talking Pictures: A New Look at Hansel and Gretel." *Signal* 42:123–31.

———. 1986. "The Object Lesson: Picture Books of Anthony Browne." *Word and Image* 2:159–72.

———. 1993. *Looking at Pictures in Picture Books*. Stroud: Thimble Press.

———. 1998. "Drawing Out Ideas: A Second Decade of the Work of Anthony Browne," *The Lion and the Unicorn* 23.1:30–56.

Feaver, William. 1977. *When We Were Young. Two Centuries of Children's Book Illustrations*. London: Thames and Hudson.

Hutchins, Pat. 1968. *Rosie's Walk*. London: Bodley Head.

Klemin, Diana. 1966. *The Art of Art for Children's Books*. New York: Clarkson N. Potter.

Kress, Gunther, and Theo van Leeuwen. 1996. *Reading Images. The Grammar of Visual Design*. London: Routledge.

Kümmerling-Meibauer, Bettina. 1999. "Metalinguistic Awareness and the Child's Developing Concept of Irony: The Relationship Between Pictures and Texts in Ironic Picture Books." *The Lion and the Unicorn*, 23.2:157–83.

Lacy, Lyn Ellen. 1986. *Art and Design in Children's Picture Books. An Analysis of Caldecott Award-Winning Illustrations*. Chicago: American Library Association.

Lewis, David. 1990. "The Constructedness of Texts: Picture Books and the Metafictive." *Signal* 62:131–46.

———. 2001. *Reading Contemporary Picturebooks. Picturing Text*. London: Routledge.

Mackey, Margaret. 1990. "Metafiction for Beginners. Allan Ahlberg's Ten in a Bed." *Children's Literature in Education* 21.3:179–87.

McKee, David. 1980. *Not Now, Bernard*. London: Arrow.
———. 1982. *I Hate My Teddy Bear*. London: Andersen.
Moebius, William. 1986. "Introduction to Picturebook Codes." *Word and Image* 2.2:141–58.
Nikolajeva, Maria. 2000. *From Mythic to Linear: Time in Children's Literature*. Lanham, MD: Scarecrow.
———. 2002. "The Verbal and the Visual. The Picturebook as a Medium." 85–108 in *Children's Literature as Communication*. Edited by Roger Sell. Amsterdam: John Benjamin.
———. 2003. "Picturebook Characterization: Text/Image Interaction." 37–49 in *Art, Narrative and Childhood*. Edited by Morag Styles. London: Trentham.
Nikolajeva, Maria and Carole Scott. 2000. "Dynamics of Picturebook Communication." *Children's Literature in Education* 31.4:225–39.
———. 2001a. "Images of the Mind: The Depiction of Consciousness in Picturebooks." *CREArTA* 2.1:12–36.
———. 2001b. *How Picturebooks Work*. New York: Garland.
Nodelman, Perry. 1988. *Words About Pictures. The Narrative Art of Children's Picture Books*. Athens, GA: University of Georgia Press.
Nodelman, Perry, and Reimer, Mavis. 2003. *The Pleasures of Children's Literature*. Third edition. Boston: Allyn & Bacon.
Ormerod, Jan. 1981. *Sunshine*. Harmondsworth: Kestrel.
———. 1982. *Moonlight*. Harmondsworth: Kestrel.
Oxenbury, Helen. 1985. *I Touch*. London: Walker Books.
———. 2000. *I Hear*. London: Walker Books.
———. 2000. *I See*. London: Walker Books.
Perrot, Jean. 2000. "An English Promenade." *Bookbird* 38.3:11–16.
Roxburgh, Stephen. 1983. "A Picture Equals How many Words? Narrative Theory and Picture Books for Children." *The Lion and the Unicorn* 7-8:20–33.
Schwarcz, Joseph H. 1982. *Ways of the Illustrator: Visual Communication in Children's Literature*. Chicago: American Library Association.
Scott, Carole. 1999. "Dual Audience in Picture Books." 99–110 in *Transcending Boundaries: Writing for the Dual Audience of Adults and Children*. Edited by Sandra Beckett. New York: Garland.
Sendak, Maurice. 1963. *Where the Wild Things Are*. New York: Harper & Row.
———. 1981. *Outside Over There*. London: Bodley Head.
Sipe, Lawrence R. 1998. "How Picture Books Work: A Semiotically Framed Theory of Text–Picture Relationships." *Children's Literature in Education* 29.2:97–108.
Spitz, Ellen Handler. 1999. *Inside Picture Books*. New Haven: Yale University Press.
Thompson, Colin. 1993. *Looking for Atlantis*. London: MacRae.

Further reading

Bader, Barbara. *American Picturebooks: From Noah's Ark to the Beast Within*. New York: Macmillan, 1976.
Bang, Molly. *Picture This: How Pictures Work*. New York: SeaStar Books, 2000.
Bennett, Jill. *Learning to Read with Picture Books*. Stroud: Thimble Press, 1982.
Cotton, Penni, ed. *Picture Books Sans Frontièrs*. London: Trentham, 2000.

Hearn, Michael, Trinkett Clark, and H. Nicholas B. Clark. *Myth, Magic, and Mystery. One Hundred Years of American Children's Book Illustration*. Boulder, CO: Roberts Rinehart, 1996.

Hürlimann, Bettina. *Picture-Book World*. Translated and edited by Brian W. Alderson. London: Oxford University Press, 1968.

Kiefer, Barbara. *The Potential of Picturebooks: From Visual Literacy to Aesthetic Understanding*. Englewood Cliffs, NJ: Prentice Hall, 1995.

Marantz, Sylvia and Kenneth Marantz. *The Art of Children's Picture Books: A Selective Reference Guide*, 2nd edn. New York: Garland, 1995.

McCann, Donnarae and Olga Richard. *The Child's First Books: A Critical Study of Pictures and Texts*. New York: Wilson, 1973.

Nikolajeva, Maria. "The Verbal and the Visual Literacy: The Role of Picturebooks in the Reading Experience of Young Children." 235–48 in *A Handbok of Research in Early Childhood Literacy*. Edited by Jackie Marsh et al., London: Sage, 2003.

Schwarcz, Joseph H. and Chava Schwarcz. *The Picture Book Comes of Age*. Chicago: American Library Association, 1991.

Stewig, John Warren. *Looking at Picture Books*. Fort Atkinson, WI: Highsmith Press, 1995.

Styles, Morag, ed. *Art, Narrative and Childhood*. London: Trentham, 2002.

Whalley, Joyce Irene and Tessa Rose Chester. *A History of Children's Book Illustration*. London: John Murray, 1988.

6
Children as Readers

Judith Elkin

Introduction

This chapter focuses on the individual child reader, and the role of children's literature in the child's educational, social, and cultural development. It looks at why children need to read in the twenty-first century; a century which will be increasingly dominated by technology. The values of wide, diverse reading in the educational, emotional, and social development of the child and the joys and pleasures of reading are explored. It also considers how children's literature can transform the life of the individual child, as well as being a source of both learning and pleasure. The author deliberately explores individual reader responses to the values of reading as a child, making extensive use of quotations from individuals for whom reading was, and remains, a significant influence. This draws heavily on research conducted for *Reading and Reader Development: the Pleasure of Reading* (Elkin, Train, and Denham 2003) which looks at the theory of reading in the context of current reading initiatives and reader development practice.

This author, recently returned from a holiday in Umbria, was reminded of the pleasure of reading. She devoured books. Focused reading of novels, autobiographies, travel guides, phrase books, and dictionaries all contributed to a better understanding of Italy, whilst being enormous sources of relaxation and pleasure in a context of gorgeous self-indulgence! It is that intimacy of wide, diverse reading which all children should have the opportunity to indulge in. It is also part of the author's fundamental philosophy for teaching children's literature: a belief that the adult student has to experience a personal love of reading children's literature to enable them to pass that passion on to children, whether as a teacher, librarian, social worker, carer, parent, or grandparent.

This philosophy underpins this chapter and is explored as a model in the final section, on teaching children's literature.

Why do people read?

A number of eloquent writers have considered why reading is important to them. Gold describes the benefits of reading:

> Reading is not necessary to our survival, if by survival we mean eating and staying warm. It is necessary to our larger survival, however, to an enriched, aware life in which we exercise some measure of control over our well-being, our creativity and our connection to everything around us. (Gold 1990, 100)

Manguel concurs: "We read to understand, or to begin to understand . . . Reading, almost as much as breathing, is our essential function" (Manguel 1969, 7). So does the novelist, P. D. James, when she states: "To enjoy reading, to love books, is to have a source of joy, satisfaction and pleasure throughout the whole of life from childhood to old age, and a sure shield against its inevitable disappointments and griefs" (cited Van Riel 1992, 1–2).

These are strong assertions, but allow us to begin to assess the value of reading on children's well being in particular. Spufford, in his inspirational *The Child that Books Built* (Spufford 2002) is passionate about his reading as a child:

> The dominant sensation of reading was excited delight . . . They freed us from the limitations of having just one limited life with one point of view; they let us see beyond the horizon of our own circumstances . . . The books you read as a child brought you sights you hadn't seen for yourself, scents you hadn't smelled, sounds you hadn't heard. They introduced you to people you hadn't met, and helped you to sample ways of being that would never have occurred to you . . . And the result was . . . somebody who was enriched by the knowledge that their own particular life only occupied one little space in a much bigger world of possibilities. (Spufford 2002, 10)

He describes his mother's reaction to his reading as a child:

> 'I can always tell when you're reading somewhere in the house. There's a special silence, a *reading* silence.' I never heard it, this extra

> depth of hush that somehow travelled through walls and ceilings to announce that my seven-year-old self had become as absent as a present person can be. The silence went both ways. As my concentration on the story in my hands took hold, all sounds faded away . . . The silence that fell on the noises of people and traffic and dogs allowed an inner door to open to the book's data, its script of sound. (Spufford 2002, 1)

Readers often talk about being "lost in a book," a feeling of being so engrossed in an activity that nothing else matters. Manguel recognizes this state as being: "buried in books, isolated from the world of facts and flesh, feeling superior to those unfamiliar with the words preserved between dusty covers." (Manguel 1996, 296) Novelist Anita Desai, who as a child in India was known in her family as a Lese Ratte or "reading rat," a bookworm, remembers her own world receding, when she discovered *Wuthering Heights* at the age of nine:

> an old Delhi bungalow, its verandas and plastered walls and ceiling fans, its garden of papaya and guava trees full of shrieking parakeets, the gritty dust that settled on the pages of a book before one could turn them, all receded. What became real, dazzlingly real, through the power and magic of Emily Brontë's pen, were the Yorkshire moors, the storm-driven heath, the torments of its anguished inhabitants, who roamed therein in rain and sleet, crying out from the depths of their broken hearts and hearing only ghosts reply. (Cited Manguel 1996, 208)

This magic is beautifully described through Bastiona Nalthazar Bux's passion for books in Michael Ende's *The Neverending Story*:

> If you have never spent whole afternoons with burning ears and rumpled hair, forgetting the world around you over a book, forgetting cold and hunger—if you have never read secretly under the bedclothes with a flashlight, because your father or mother or some other well-meaning person has switched off the lamp on the plausible ground that it was time to sleep because you had to get up so early. If you have never wept bitter tears because a wonderful story has come to an end and you must take your leave of the characters with whom you have shared so many adventures, whom you have loved and admired, for whom you have hoped and feared, and without whose company life seems empty and meaningless—If such things

> have not been part of your experience, you probably won't understand what Bastian did next . . . Staring at the title of the book, he turned hot and cold, cold and hot. Here was just what he had dreamed of, what he had longed for ever since the passion for books had taken hold of him. A story that never ended! The book of books!! (Ende 1984, 10)

Literacy in the technological age

For avid readers, adults and children, the above quotations will send a tingle of recognition down the spine. But what about the noncommitted reader, particularly the child in the twenty-first century? Do books and reading any longer have the transformational power outlined above? Has the digital world finally sounded the death knell of reading apart from the purely functional reading, albeit now complex, required to survive in today's world?

Bettina Hurlimann writing in the 1960s, is much quoted for her view that:

> in this restless age of technology, when the emphasis is always on records of attainment and productivity, there is some danger of forgetting that a child does not require too much in the way of books . . . What he does need are the right books at the right time so that he may find in literature a true point of balance in an often disordered world. It is for us as parents or teachers, librarians or publishers, to recognize this need and to know how best, how most imaginatively, to fulfil it. (Hurlimann 1967, xviii)

Prophetic in the late 1960s, does this still hold good today, when technology has advanced beyond recognition and dominates our lives? Anstey claims:

> The changes in work, public and private lives indicate that during our working lives we will be required to change tasks, 'multiskill' or change occupations, and each of these changes will require us to acquire new literacy skills and interact in different ways. Furthermore, the changing technologies of our work, public and private lives mean the acquisition of literacies associated with these new technologies . . . Multiliteracies focus on the many modes of representation and forms of text that have been made available through multimedia and technological change. Therefore, being multiliterate requires not only the

> mastery of communication, but an ability to critically analyse, deconstruct, and reconstruct a range of texts and other representational forms. It also requires the ability to engage in the social responsibilities and interactions associated with these texts. (Anstey 2002, 446)

Arts Council England (ACE) endorses the role of reading in the twenty-first century, whilst acknowledging the changing context. Its recent review of children's literature, *From Looking Glass to Spyglass* (Arts Council England 2003) recognized the "transforming power of arts in relation to children and young people and the role the arts can play in developing confident, creative and articulate individuals" (Arts Council England 2003, 3). In particular:

> We see children's literature as the touchstone for a healthy and sustainable literary culture . . . It affords the means by which children can dialogue with their futures, not only through the printed word, but also through children's literature's intimate connections with the visual arts and design, film and television, theatre and new technologies. Its value is private and public, cultural and artistic, and also social and economic. (Arts Council England 2003, 3)

The review was widely welcomed as timely and positive, acknowledging the need to adopt a more modern and generous definition of children's literature, to accommodate new media, a mix of art-forms, mediated participation, and multiple audiences. The ensuing Strategy for Children's Literature (Arts Council England 2004) developed in the context of ACE's corporate priorities and will feed into their cross-sectoral youth strategy. Advocacy, access and diversity, professional development, networking, and sharing information and support for the individual artists are the key planks of the strategy.

The OECD (Organization for Economic Cooperation and Development) report, *Reading for Change* (OECD 2002) acknowledges the importance of literacy in a global context. "Reading literacy is a dynamic rather than a static concept that needs to parallel changes in society and culture. The reading literacy needed for individual growth, economic participation and citizenship 20 years ago were different from what is expected today" (OECD 2002, 16). The OECD use the following helpful definition:

> Literacy is no longer considered an ability only acquired in childhood during the early years of schooling. Instead, it is viewed as an expanding

> set of knowledge, skills and strategies which individuals build on throughout life in various situations and through interaction with their peers and with the larger communities in which they participate. (OECD 2002, 24)

Fasick echoes this:

> The modern world demands a literate workforce to perform the tasks necessary for modern industry. Literacy, therefore, is generally viewed as of great economic value both to nations and to individuals. [citing Frederico Mayor, Director-General of UNESCO speaking on International Literacy Day in 1996] Those societies that, over the past decades, have invested most heavily in the education of their citizens have been the ones that have advanced most rapidly and where the conditions of life have been fundamentally transformed. A literate world is not only one where people can read and write, it is a world in which the human potential has been liberated and placed in the service of progress. (Fasick 2000, 38)

UNESCO recognizes literacy as a fundamental human right. The UNESCO definition of literacy reflects a commonly held view that literacy should be synonymous with control. As Jackson puts it:

> Fully literate children have the potential to control themselves and their environment through access to information, ideas, opinions: such is the power of literacy that teaching it could be defined as 'empowerment.' (Jackson 1993, 4)

Alongside more conventional books, electronic books clearly have a role in literacy development. It is somewhat disappointing, therefore, to find De Jong and Bus's 2003 study of the value of electronic books for supporting literacy being highly critical of the current lack of choice. De Jong and Bus call for research to stimulate the development of high-quality electronic books:

> with many weak, ineffective examples, characterized by the low quality of their multimedia additions and with few possibilities for interaction with facets of the story . . . Multimedia options open an interactive vista that can support children's literacy development in a digital world and provide them with access to stories that may be beyond their reading level. (De Jong and Bus 2003, 147–64)

The value of reading

Assuming that the twenty-first century requires individuals to be highly literate to survive in a knowledge society, it is appropriate to assume that reading proficiency must begin in childhood, and at as early an age as possible. Let's turn back to the value of reading in developing literate individuals.

As both an adult and children's librarian in the 1960s and 1970s and as an academic from the mid-1980s onwards, this author worked with many groups of librarians, teachers, parents, children, and students, of Education, English, and Librarianship, in the United Kingdom and abroad. She taxed groups at numerous workshops and seminars to reflect on the value and meaning of reading to themselves as individuals and for children. By amalgamating their ideas we can provide a useful, internationally-generated, composite of the values of reading, both in general terms and for children in particular. In general terms, these include its capacity to stimulate the imagination and help develop a critical and thinking mind; to foster independence; and to aid emotional development. Reading offers an escape from the world, but it also helps us place ourselves in relationship with the world, giving a better understanding of human nature and insight into life; enabling the reader to appreciate other people's problems; and helping the reader to shape, store, and reflect on the past and the future. It offers an understanding of the complexities of relationships between individuals and cultures, and of different moral codes and values.

For children, whose imagination and understanding of things around them is changing at such a rate, reading fulfils many important functions.

A language and audio stimulus. Learning to read depends to a large extent on the child's experience of language. Storytelling and reading aid the child by expanding vocabulary; and by providing new sentence patterns, improving spelling, grammar, and writing skills; by creating an opportunity to learn to listen as distinct from merely hearing.

A visual stimulus. Picture books provide a valuable aid to encourage perception and discrimination. The activity of concentrating and looking at pictures aids the child in coming to terms with the text (apart from the purely aesthetic experience) and the structure of the book.

An enrichment to the imagination. Good stories can enrich the imagination, develop compassion, humour, and understanding; arouse curiosity and the ability to question. Books can foster racial and cultural understanding and offer positive role models.

A way of widening horizons. Children's limited experiences widen as they are presented with new experiences and answers to problems and fears. Stories evoke response, recognition, identification, stimulation; they educate the emotions (fear, greed, love, good, and evil are the basic ingredients of stories); they educate the imagination by stretching it to other dimensions.

Provision of information. Reading introduces wider knowledge, offering children the opportunity to think, to reflect, to ask questions, and to develop comprehension, stimulating curiosity, liberating the imagination, aiding natural learning and the educational process.

Social development. Reading can create a social sense, involving the whole family in learning together and developing life-long reading habits. Sharing is the best incentive to learning to read and continuing to read; the joy of books shared with another person, whether parents, teachers, siblings, friends, or grandparents. Books can demonstrate the value of different cultures and show the similarities between children playing, learning, and growing up anywhere in the world.

Compensation for the difficulties of growing up. The story can have the psychological value of showing the child that someone else has been there before them; story heightens the reader's awareness, shaping the raw material of life and so organizing even that which is sad or painful into satisfying experience. Different groups of children may gain particular benefits from reading. Teenagers, for example, may find opportunities for: exploring identity; subversion; the chance to be part of the crowd; comfort; opportunity to be alone; intellectual credibility.

Sharing reading and telling stories

Reading is often a solitary occupation but sharing has inestimable value, too. For example, Butler, the doyen of using books with babies, firmly believes that:

> there is no parents' aid which can compare with the book in its capacity to establish and maintain a relationship with a child. Its effects extend far beyond the covers of the actual book, and invade every aspect of life. Parents and children who share books come to share the same frame of reference. Incidents in everyday life constantly remind one or the other—or both simultaneously—of a situation, a character, an action, from a jointly enjoyed book, with all the generation of warmth and well-being that is attendant upon such sharing. (Butler 1998, xii)

> giving parents the idea of 'the book as a tool' will do more for the dual purpose of establishing the parent–child relationship and ensuring the child's adequate language development, than any amount of advice on talking to children . . . Shades of meaning which may be quite unavailable to the child of limited language experience are startlingly present in the understanding—and increasingly the speech—of the 'well-read-to' toddler. (Butler 1998, 6)

Meek reminds us that story is fundamental to all societies and storytelling is part of our heritage:

> Storytelling is a universal habit, a part of our common humanity . . . all cultures have some form of narrative. Stories are part of our conversation, our recollections, our plans, our hopes, our fears. Young and old, we all tell stories as soon as we begin to explain or describe events and actions, feelings and motives. (Meek 1991, 103)
>
> . . . in human remembering the past stays alive, so story-telling not only supplies children with memories they cannot yet have, it also gives them "virtual" memory, the idea of remembering what they have heard others tell . . . Story-telling lies at the back of all literacy, powerful in its effect and distinguished by its cultural differences. (Meek 1991, 65)

In his seminal *The Uses of Enchantment* (1976)—a "significant statement on the life-enriching force of story in childhood" (Moss 1980, 74)—Bruno Bettelheim suggests of fairy tales that they:

> start where the child really is in his psychological and emotional being. They speak about his severe inner pressures in a way that the child unconsciously understands and—without belittling the most serious inner struggles which growing up entails—offer examples of both temporary and permanent solutions to pressing difficulties . . . The fairy tale . . . confronts the child squarely with the basic human predicaments. (Bettelheim 1976, 56)

This view is reinforced by storyteller Grace Hallworth:

> We cannot take steps in life or literature without narrating . . . we cannot stir without telling stories . . . of dreams, of love affairs, trials and tribulations of the wife, the husband, the child . . . science and technology uses the anecdotal method of storytelling. Sharing is

> central to strategies of encouraging international understanding and developing heightened sensitivities to other cultures, as well as our own culture . . . We need to build a bridge between the culture of literature and the culture of life. (Hallworth 1985)

Language and early literacy

Meek notes that one of the distinguishing features of habitual readers and writers is their curiosity about language (Meek 1991, 54). But all children do not come naturally to reading, for a variety of reasons, and may need help. Manguel cites James Hillman's belief that:

> those who have read stories or had stories read to them in childhood: 'are in better shape and have a better prognosis than those to whom story must be introduced . . . coming early with life it is already a perspective on life . . . these first readings become something lived in and lived through, a way in which the soul finds itself in life. (Manguel 1996, 11)

Butler is convinced that it is the early years which have the most influence on the child's and subsequently adult's reading:

> There is nothing magic about the way contact with books in early years produces early readers. One would surely expect it to. A baby is learning about the way language arises from the page each time her parent opens a book, from earliest days. She is linking the human voice to the print at a very early age. Given repeated opportunity, she notices how the adult attends to the black marks, how he can't go on reading if the page is turned too soon . . . Skills come apparently unbidden as the toddler advances into three- and four-year old independence. Print is friendly and familiar for this child. She is already unconsciously finding landmarks, noting regular features, predicting patterns . . . Unbidden? Not a bit of it! This child has had her reading skills handed to her on a golden platter. (Butler 1998, 8)

Butler's *Cushla and her Books* (Butler 1987) is an inspirational book about how books helped her multiply-handicapped granddaughter and her parents to cope with the stressful early years of her life. Born with a chromosome deficiency, asthma, and eczema, Cushla was a sickly baby, who fed and slept poorly. She had hearing, sight, and mobility problems and was constantly distressed; her early development and growth and prognosis were poor. *Cushla and her Books* documents the way that picture books, stories, and poetry were entrenched in Cushla's everyday life:

> How can one assess the contribution of her books to the quality of Cushla's life? It seems clear that access to such a wealth of words and pictures, in a setting of consistent love and support, has contributed enormously to her cognitive development in general and her language development in particular . . . But, perhaps, most of all, Cushla's books have surrounded her with friends; with people and warmth and colour during the days when her life was lived in almost constant pain and frustration. The adults who have loved her and have tried to represent the world to her when she could not do this for herself have played their parts. But perhaps it was the characters themselves who went with her into the dark and lonely places that only she knew . . . And perhaps they will always be with her; Peter Rabbit and Grandmother Lucy, Mr Gumpy and James, James, followed by a procession of cats and kings, tigers and bears, with Davy and Emma and Naughty Agapanthus bringing up the rear. If so, she will be well fortified. (Butler 1987, 102)

Reading in school

Chambers' views on the quality of a mediator in the process of acquiring literacy, whether teacher or librarian, were expressed emphatically over thirty years ago but still carry considerable weight:

> The effectiveness of any teacher in the encouragement of the reading habit varies in proportion to the teacher's depth of knowledge of children's books and literature generally . . . The teacher who reads avidly himself, the teacher who knows and reads children's books, invariably fosters a similar interest in a high percentage of his pupils . . . The teaching profession is a profession of reluctant readers. They are rarely seen to read a novel, purr over it with pleasure, dwell on it with interest, talk about it with enthusiasm or anger; worse, they are never even seen carrying one . . . They are heard hacking a set book to pieces. (Chambers 1969, 117)

Thirty years on, Meek, echoing this, is sceptical about current mechanistic methods of teaching reading in English schools, blaming the system rather than the teachers. Meek wants children's literature moved back to the centre of the curriculum:

> The main problem for teachers is that their best and most effective skills in teaching reading are constantly undervalued: observing, interacting, taking children's thinking further, making split-second decisions at significant points of learning and following these up with reflection shared in discussions. To learn to read better than ever before, as they surely must, children need space and time to think about what they are reading and also about reading itself . . . This is not a rejection of confirmed ways of teaching reading. My proposal is about texts, and the difference books make to children's views of the task of learning to read; a simple shift, to bring the writers and artists who care about readers into closer contact with those who have to engage with new texts . . . Those who emphasise the functional nature of literacy, who believe that there is a set of "basic" competences to be taught and learned according to a single pattern of instruction, will have difficulty with the underlying concept that literacy is too important to be taught or to serve as an instrumental commodity. I am persuaded that the best practice includes reading with children the texts that they are not yet experienced enough to read for themselves, and that the best evidence of reading progress comes from the observations of good teachers who take time to discuss reading with their pupils and who teach them to write. (Meek 1998, 123)

Whilst being rather more restrained in their comments, recent research commissioned by the Teacher Training Agency showed that the most effective literacy teachers were those who were more likely to "embed their teaching of reading into a wider context and to show how specific aspects of reading and writing contribute to communication" (Wray et al. 2002, 132). Such teachers contextualized what they taught and made language features meaningful, building on a sound basis of knowledge of children's books.

Teaching of reading in schools in England has been the focus of increasingly intense debate, with many children's writers entering the fray, as evidenced by the recent publication, *Meetings with the Minister* (Powling et al. 2003), in which five children's authors discuss their ideas about the National Literacy Strategy and its negative impact on children's reading with the Minister of State for Education, Charles Clarke. Their main complaint is that reading is becoming utilitarian:

> It is done to extract information, to find something out, to be tested. It is not undertaken for pleasure. What is odd about this is that

> almost any teacher you know understands that the child who reads for the sheer exhilaration of immersing themselves in a good story absorbs, almost by osmosis, the rhythms and cadences of language. It is far easier to teach a reader the principles of grammar. Finally, vocabulary widens immeasurably. A blessed spin-off, in other words, is that the reading child is a successful child. (Gibbons 2004, 4)

Arts Council England's Children's Literature Strategy (Arts Council England 2004) supports increasing access to children's literature during initial teacher training and the need for more creative reading and writing opportunities as part of teachers' continuing professional development, across the curriculum. There was concern about the dominance of an instrumental approach to children's literature in schools, with schools being concerned that time spent on reading and writing did not contribute to school objectives and achieving targets. Properly resourced and respected school libraries and school library services were seen as needing to be at the heart of any long-term cultural shift in the relationship between creativity and education.

The literature on literacy teaching is generally sparse in its coverage of the value of libraries and librarians in the promotion of reading and literacy. And yet libraries can be seen as the UK's most significant providers of the reading experience, with around 121 million books in the public library service and 430 million loans per annum including 107 million children's books (Library and Information Commission 1998). Research for *A Place for Children* (Elkin and Kinnell 2000) found that libraries contribute to the child's reading development in numerous ways. They offer a welcoming, safe, socially-inclusive place in which to read, and a neutral ground for those disaffected from school. As well as providing access to books and other facilities, they are active in promoting reader development, supporting family reading and literacy groups, giving advice to parents, helping with home-educated children, and encouraging love of books and reading. Library provision also complements the educational opportunities offered in schools (Elkin, Train, and Denham 2003, 24).

Teaching children's literature

Where does the teaching of children's literature fit into this complex world of reading literacy? Inevitably there are different approaches to the teaching of children's literature, depending partly, but not exclusively, on whether children's literature is seen as a study in its own right, usually as part of an English literature or cultural studies course, or as part of a professional course, particularly for teachers or librarians.

Hollindale helpfully addresses some of the pedagogical implications for university and college teachers of children's literature, especially those which concern the pastoral rather than the academic element of teaching, and the personal rather than the critical element of student learning, identifying the tensions for undergraduate students, hovering between maturity and adolescence:

> Because it involves revisiting known books and a past but still living self, the study of children's literature has no refuge in the treaty of agreed academic distance which forms the implicit basis for most tutorials and seminars in university English . . . At their best, undergraduate courses on children's literature become complex inquiries into the nature of reading, of a kind which cannot easily be replicated in the more established courses devoted to unfamiliar, "adult" and canonical texts. (Hollindale 1996, 62–63)
>
> It seems to me very important that the process of re-entering childhood reading should be one of integration with the adult critical self, which leads to continuities and connections being accepted and better understood . . . if the process of integration works, the student will have a hands-on direct experience of reader response theory and will understand that all readings of all works, including re-readings, are individual and unique. (Hollindale 1996, 65)
>
> We may not realize in adult life how influential the pre-critical experience of narrative can be. These early stories provide structures which we use to shape our lives, and among other things they partly govern our responses to later texts . . . When children's literature courses bring favourite childhood reading into the open play of critical discussion, they are dealing with far more important things than literary texts. (Hollindale 1996, 71)
>
> What children's literature courses can do is to reconnect not only childhood and adult life but the amateur and the professional reader, restoring the personal dimension to recently and rapidly acquired professional critical skills . . . perhaps we underestimate the problems and losses that we cause when we professionalize reading in the later years of school . . . We cannot understand ourselves as readers (or, perhaps, as people) if we date our understanding from the point where we become critically proficient. (Hollindale 1996, 73)

One of the most useful and practical books for teachers on teaching and exploring children's literature, is *Exploring Children's Literature* by

Gamble and Yates. It gives a very wide range of examples and exercises in using texts to develop an understanding of narrative, character, language, and genre. They focus on helping the teacher through an exploration and development of their own wide and diverse reading to help the child to interpret the text and make sense of what has been read. They start with a belief that:

> children's learning of language, reading and their writing, was greatly improved when they studied in detail the books they were reading as a class and as individuals . . . a deep knowledge of how literature works, of the language and literary theory is a necessary foundation for teaching and learning from literature . . . Many of those working with children have a love and breadth of knowledge of children's books. This is evidenced through visiting schools and libraries where the children buzz with excitement about books and engage readily in book talk; where the classroom and library book shelves are well stocked and reflect a wide range of texts including old favourites and recent arrivals . . . to work effectively with children to develop their knowledge and responses to literature, adults require sound knowledge of a range of literature and how it can be shared with children to inspire and challenge . . . It would not, for example, be acceptable for a teacher or student to claim "I don't do fractions" or "the Romans", or "forces". But it is possible to find teachers who are not at ease with choosing books and reading aloud to children, who do not have regular shared story times outside formal lessons, and do not feel comfortable in exploring books with children. (Gamble and Yates 2002, 1–2)

Sutcliffe, teaching initial teacher-training students, agrees that:

> no student should qualify without having taken a substantial course in children's books . . . teaching will depend on knowledge of the literature. The courses have been designed to enable students to know the books intimately by making time to think and talk and write about them. We believe that it is not possible, or desirable, to divorce reading and thinking about books from considering how they will be read by children and mediated by adults. (Sutcliffe 1995, 135)

The written work of Sutcliffe's students takes the form of a reading journal in which students record details of all the books they have read, and they are able to build on these journals throughout the four years of their course, as well as using them actively with children in the classroom. Sutcliffe uses examples from her own journal, and examples from the student's reading journals, to demonstrate how an intimate experience of reading children's books, in this reflective way, whilst sharing with fellow students, can give students enormous confidence in their own teaching of reading and formulating reading policies. Sutcliffe cites a particular student, handing in her reading journal kept over three years, "showing evidence of a most remarkable reading journey." "I think this is the most important thing of all—the literature *has* to be at the center of the children's learning" (Sutcliffe 1995, 150).

DeCandido analyses her experience of teaching children's literature online. The course was largely aimed at teachers and school librarians, attracted by an online course because of a range of domestic and logistical problems. Coming from a background where her preferred teaching style called for plenty of interaction with students, DeCandido found:

> The single hardest thing about teaching online was creating the entire course in my mind from beginning to end and then reproducing it, whole and entire, before classes even began, for the online environment . . . It's a struggle to find ways to describe . . . the particular intensity of an online literature course. It was as if we had our fingers on each other's pulses, all the time. I could log in to class at any hour of the day or night and find new comments, new questions, and different responses to what we were reading. I cherish that experience . . . A great gift of online teaching is the chance it gives to those of a more retiring nature to reflect on their answers and then post them . . . This absolute emphasis upon the Word—if you wanted to be heard, you had to write it down and send it forth for all to see—is what transmutes the virtual, paperless environment into one where books are the center. I was teaching about books: this was not a course in multimedia. What kept us focused in the disembodied cyberspace we inhabited was those books. We all read the same ones, we all faced the same questions, we all heard one another's answers. We read together and then we talked about it, applying our ideas to classroom situations, to library booktalks, to the work of our days. (DeCandido 2002, 297–98)

Brown writes about teaching children's literature on a final year undergraduate programme as an:

> extraordinarily stimulating and productive topic for comparative and interdisciplinary study . . . One aspect of teaching a course of this nature to undergraduates is different from teaching other literary topics. In discussing books written by adult writers for a specific young audience

> and often with a clearly implied child reader, many complex questions arise about authorial aim, narrative tone and reader response. The situation is further complicated because the texts are being (re)-read by a young adult audience most of whom have read some or all of these books in the not too distant past as children or adolescents. For students, the challenge lies in confronting, dissecting and assessing texts from a different perspective, which sometimes involves interpreting and perhaps overcoming childhood responses. (Brown 2002, 191)

Brown deliberately selects set texts for the course chosen for the scope they offer to explore both the social and literary context and narrative technique:

> Students are forewarned to consider the extent to which a text aimed at an essentially passive and impressionable readership can be seen as an instrument of social control and to interrogate assumptions and ideologies that are explicit (content) and implicit (narrative strategies and tone). (Brown 2002, 199)

The set texts chosen for comparative study are largely from the nineteenth and early twentieth centuries:

> For both teaching and research purposes, I have found that children's literature and the comparative approach, both of which present a challenge to conventional modes of interpretation, are an enticing and mutually enriching combination. (Brown 2002, 199)

Denham writes about teaching children's literature to students of librarianship and English. Denham's aim was to enable students to take a creative and critical approach to imaginative and pleasurable literature of all kinds for children of different ages and abilities. She is critical of courses, particularly those aimed at future teachers and librarians, which offer a "dispassionate approach to children's literature [which] frequently appears to neglect the perspective of the child" (Denham 1994, 90).

Denham encourages students to take a reflective and affective approach. The course was assessed through student-led seminars, each covering a different genre of children's books and by all students keeping an analytical reading diary and review of their learning experiences. Feedback from students was positive:

> The diary that we were asked to keep over this period . . . was an extremely valuable learning method. It complemented the process of

> discovery that was already taking place through the teaching and reading of books, by making me translate my learning into practice through having to critically judge the "quality" of children's books through the formulation of my own criteria. This task was . . . something that my [English] degree course had not equipped me for. (Denham 1994, 101)
>
> I have evolved from somebody who did not know very much about the extraordinary world of children's literature or recognize the treasure box that it is to someone who now has reconsidered and recognizes the importance of children's literature and just how important it is for a child's intellectual, social and emotional development, virtually from the day they were born. (Denham 1994, 102)

Concluding remarks

That final quote from an undergraduate student brings us full circle. This chapter has focused on the child reader and the individual pleasure and joy to be gained from reading. It has looked at the life-enhancing opportunities to be gained from reading and taken the stance that no child should miss out on such pleasures: children should be empowered to enjoy, to share and to expand their reading; prereaders should be caught during babyhood to ensure they become readers for life; children should be helped to understand that reading is a very personal experience and to be confident in their own interpretation of a text. Reading remains an important skill in the twenty-first century, as part of expanding literacies. The teaching of reading in schools needs attention to ensure it remains a focal point of the curriculum. The teaching of children's literature at universities and colleges similarly needs attention, to ensure that teachers and librarians are well prepared for the future reading generation.

Works cited

Anstey, Michele. 2002. "It's Not all Black and White: Postmodern Picture Books and New Literacies." *Journal of Adolescent and Adult Literacy* 45.6 (March):444–57.

Arts Council England. 2003. *From Looking Glass to Spyglass: A Consultation Paper on Children's Literature*. London: Arts Council England.

———. 2004. *A Strategy for Children's Literature*. London: Arts Council England.

Bettelheim, Bruno. 1976. *The Uses of Enchantment: The Meaning and Importance of Fairy Tales*. London: Thames and Hudson.

Brown, Penny. 2002. "Teaching Children's Literature as a Comparative Literary Subject in a British University." *Signal* 99 (September):189–99.

Butler, Dorothy. 1987. *Cushla and her Books*. London: Penguin Books.

———. 1998. *Babies need Books: Sharing the Joy of Books with Children from Birth to Six*, revised edition. London: Bodley Head.

Chambers, Aidan. 1969. *The Reluctant Reader*. Oxford: Pergamon.

DeCandido, Graceanne. 2002. "A Particular Intensity: Teaching Children's Literature Online." *Horn Book Magazine* 78.3 (May/June):293–8.

De Jong, Maria and Adriana Bus. 2003. "How Well Suited are Electronic Books to Supporting Literacy?" *Journal of Early Childhood Literacy* 3.2:147–64.

Denham, Debbie. 1994. "Children's Literature: A Reflective Approach to Learning." *The International Review of Children's Literature and Librarianship* 9.2:88–103.

Elkin, Judith and Margaret Kinnell. 2000. *A Place for Children: Public Libraries as a Major Force in Children's Reading*. British Library Research and Innovation Report 117. London: Library Association Publishing.

Elkin, Judith, Briony Train, and Debbie Denham. 2003. *Reading and Reader Development: The Pleasure of Reading*. London: Facet Publishing.

Ende, Michael. 1984. *The Neverending Story*. Translated by Ralph Manheim. London: Penguin Books.

Fasick, Adele. 2000. "Is Literacy For All an Achievable Goal?" *The New Review of Children's Literature and Librarianship* 6: 38.

Gamble, Nikki and Sally Yates. 2002. *Exploring Children's Literature: Teaching the Language and Reading of Fiction*. London: Paul Chapman Publishing.

Gibbons, Alan. 2004. "What's reading for anyway?" *Books For Keeps* 144 (January):4–5.

Gold, Joseph. 1990. *Read for your Life: Literature as a Life Support System*. Ontario: Fitzhenry & Whiteside.

Hallworth, Grace. 1985. Unpublished paper delivered at UNESCO/IFLA conference, *The Library, a Centre for Promoting International Understanding*. Salamanca, Spain (June).

Hollindale, Peter, with Rhianon Howells, and Jacqui Newby. 1996. "Re-reading the Self: Children's Books and Undergraduate Readers." *Signal* 79 (January): 62–74.

Hurlimann, Bettina. 1967. *Three Centuries of Children's Books in Europe*. Translated and edited by Brian Alderson. London: Oxford University Press.

Jackson, Margaret. 1993. *Literacy*. London: David Fulton.

Library and Information Commission. 1998. *Libraries: the Lifeforce for Learning*. London: Library and Information Commission.

Manguel, Alberto. 1996. *A History of Reading*. London: Viking.

Meek, Margaret. 1991. *On Being Literate*. London: Bodley Head.

———. 1998. "Important reading lessons" 116–24 in *Literacy is Not Enough: Essays on the Importance of Reading*. Edited by Brian Cox. Manchester: Manchester University Press.

Moss, Elaine. 1980. "Seventies in British Children's Books." 48–80 in *The Signal Approach to Children's Books: A Collection*. Edited by Nancy Chambers. London: Kestrel.

Organization for Economic Cooperation and Development. 2002. *Reading for Change: Performance and Engagement across Countries, Results from PISA 2000*. Paris: OECD.

Powling, Chris, Bernard Ashley, Philip Pullman, Anne Fine and Jamila Gavin. 2003. *Meetings with the Minister: Five children's Authors on the National Literacy Strategy*. Reading: The National Centre for Language and Literacy.

Spufford, Frances. 2002. *The Child that Books Built: a memoir of childhood and reading.* London: Faber.
Sutcliffe, Mary. 1995. "Children's Books in Teacher Education at Westminster College, Oxford." *Signal* 77 (May):134–50.
Van Riel, Rachel, ed. 1992. *Reading the Future: A Place for Literature in Public Libraries.* A report of a seminar, organized by the Arts Council of Great Britain in association with the Library Association and the Regional Arts Boards of England.
Wray, David, Jane Medwell and Louise Poulson. 2002. *Teaching Literacy Effectively in the Primary School.* London: Routledge Falmer.

Further reading

Elkin, Judith and Margaret Kinnell. *A Place for Children: Public Libraries as a Major Force in Children's Reading.* British Library Research and Innovation. Report 117. London: Library Association Publishing, 2000.
Elkin, Judith and Ray Lonsdale. *Focus on the Child: Libraries, Literacy and Learning.* London: Library Association Publishing, 1996.
Elkin, Judith, Briony Train, and Debbie Denham. *Reading and Reader Development: The Pleasure of Reading.* London: Facet Publishing, 2003.
Gold, Joseph. *Read for your Life: Literature as a Life Support System.* Ontario: Fitzhenry & Whiteside, 1990.
Manguel, Alberto. A *History of Reading.* London: Viking, 1996.
Meek, Margaret. *On Being Literate.* London: Bodley Head, 1991.
Spufford, Francis. *The Child that Books Built: A Memoir of Childhood and Reading.* London: Faber, 2002.
Trelease, Jim. *The Read Aloud Handbook.* London: Penguin, 1982.
Wray, David and Jane Medwell. *Teaching Literacy Effectively.* London: Teacher Training Agency, 2002.

7
Children's Literature at Postgraduate Level in the United Kingdom

Pat Pinsent and Kimberley Reynolds

Undergraduate courses in children's literature were offered, generally as parts of degrees in either English literature or education, fairly widely throughout Britain by the mid-1980s, and it is unsurprising that the graduates from such courses, together with other professionals in the area—teachers, librarians, writers, editors, and publishers—frequently expressed the desire to study the subject at a higher level. This demand coincided with an educational climate in which universities were encouraged to set up Masters level courses, and led to the inauguration of several programmes in which children's literature formed the whole or a significant part. In the United Kingdom, Reading University was the first to respond to this need, followed by a course (now no longer running) from the University of Warwick. The then Roehampton Institute (now Roehampton University) established a children's literature MA in the early 1990s, the first group of students beginning their studies in January 1993. Subsequently, as will be seen below, many other universities have followed suit.

Factors involved in the establishment of an MA in children's literature

Since key issues of syllabus and student uptake are likely to be common to most courses (though they will have been met by different responses), it is probably more useful to describe the development of a specific, internationally popular, course, the MA at Roehampton, than to attempt to collate details from too wide a range of institutions. At its inception, the kind of aspects which needed to be considered, either by the university administration or by the course team, or both, may be categorized under the following headings:

a) Devising a syllabus
b) Qualifications required from students
c) Teaching mode and staffing
d) Maintaining standards.

Devising a syllabus

From its inception, the MA in Children's Literature at Roehampton was seen as an award in Literature, rather than Education, and consequently the syllabus needed to incorporate all the critical theory, period, and genre knowledge that this emphasis implies. Although the students on the course, many of whom came from a background in teaching or librarianship, often intended to use their studies towards their professional advancement, it was always understood that pedagogical issues were only touched on incidentally. Since at that time there were few British precedents for a course at this level, a number of factors had to be taken into account:

1. The desire of many students to study contemporary children's literature had to be set against the desirability of giving them a background in the history of the genre.
2. Students whose main interest lay in the written text had to be reminded of the importance to children of visual elements and of the performance of children's stories in various other media.
3. Given the scathing attitude of many academics, even those in the area of English Literature, towards what they sometimes termed "kiddielit," it was particularly important to establish a culture in which assessed work would not be purely descriptive of the texts but would incorporate an element of analysis, provided either by the traditional approaches of literary criticism or by an encounter with more recent literary, linguistic, feminist, psychoanalytic, sociological, philosophical, or other theory.
4. Increasingly, within the academic culture of the late twentieth century, there was a need to familiarize students with research methods. This has become an indispensable element both for students to pursue their own research, and for them to interpret the research of others.
5. The danger of a syllabus becoming fossilized had to be faced.

In the devising of the Roehampton MA in children's literature, these factors were addressed in the following ways:

1. From the inception of the programme, the modules offered included several with an historical emphasis, notably one on the Origins and Development of Children's Literature. Although such modules were never compulsory, initially the number of choices offered was relatively small and the majority of students took at least one module with an historical emphasis. Some element of historical perspective is also inevitably present to contextualize the study of more recent periods.
2. In order to provide a good range of texts, students have had to choose at least one of the two modules related to visual texts—on the History of Book Illustration or on Contemporary Picture Books—or a module devoted to various forms of adaptation of children's literature for performance.
3. A major priority was the devising of a course on critical and theoretical perspectives, involving not only approaches prevalent in literature courses generally, but also including a substantial section devoted to the response of children to their reading. From the beginning, this module has also involved the application of these approaches to specific children's literature texts, notably fairy tales and animal stories. This module is normally the first taken by Masters students, partly because of the importance of these approaches to their reading of literature in general, but also on the principle that it involves abstract material which is often unfamiliar to them, so that it can act as a test of student commitment to the programme.
4. Our initial expectation was that through their coursework (particularly that related to the Critical and Theoretical Perspectives module) and the dissertation, students would learn in practice the Research methods they needed, though sessions were arranged in the library to help with Internet searches as well as library use. However it soon became apparent (and was made a requirement by the University authorities) that for the general acceptability of the course as a qualification for entering on study for a doctorate, or in relation to job applications, a more specific taught Research Methods element was required. Material had to be devised which was relevant both to those who planned in their dissertations to make use of textual criticism and to those who wanted to make practical investigations. An additional factor was that both categories of student need to be able to interpret published research with a full understanding of its

limitations. The challenge of ensuring that the Research Methods assignments should prepare the students for their own research seems to have been met. Students are asked to comment on a relevant piece of published research, to comment on resource provision at a research centre, and to produce a relevant annotated bibliography. There is also a study day including talks from professional researchers and from students who have successfully completed their dissertations.

5. New elements have continually been incorporated, notably in the areas of literature in translation and of postcolonialism. Because of the number of students on the course, these have not necessitated cutting out other existing elements, though module syllabuses have constantly been revised to allow for developments and recently published texts.

Qualifications required from students

Because not all universities teach children's literature at undergraduate level, it was impossible to demand specific knowledge as a prerequisite. We also wanted, without lowering the standards, to allow the admission of students who did not have a degree in a relevant subject such as literature or education, or indeed in some instances did not have a degree at all. In the case of teachers who had begun their careers before teaching became an all-graduate profession, the problem has been tackled by asking for a further certificate or diploma, but other students who lacked the appropriate qualifications are normally asked to begin by taking a module as an Associate student and, subject to satisfactory completion, then changing to either the MA programme or the Certificate or Diploma in Children's Literature, both of which involve modules from the Masters course.

A more difficult question is that of openness to students whose first language is not English, of whom there have been many, notably Japanese, Greek, Korean, French, German, and Spanish. Inevitably their language abilities vary considerably. There is no easy answer to this, as even those who on paper reach the required standard in examinations of linguistic proficiency may prove to have inadequate language skills to follow seminars or to produce essays displaying a command of English appropriate to the material they are discussing. Again, asking students to begin their course without registering for the full MA is sometimes a solution.

Teaching mode and staffing

The proportions of full and part-time students on course have been very variable. The first cohort of students was entirely part-time except for one student from South Africa who, despite having English as his third or fourth language, was our first graduate. Course conveners have had to bear in mind the differing needs of those whose programme has to include all its components in a single year and others who may spread their studies over as long as four years, or even have an officially recognized year of interruption within their study period. Despite occasional student fears of lack of equity in assessment demands, the balance generally seems to have been successful, with students from different backgrounds learning a good deal from each other. In particular, since many of the sessions include seminar presentations, students can gain a variety of perspectives on the literature concerned.

Six years after the programme started, a Distance Learning mode was inaugurated, embodying a selection of the most popular, or compulsory, modules taught on campus. The production of the material involved a good deal of labour, but it has been very positively received by students, most of whom would have been unable to study the subject otherwise. A combination of book-type resources and online communication has generally been found the most appropriate to the students' needs, while cooperation from the Learning Resources Centre has prevented distant students from being disadvantaged.

Tutorial contact, whether face-to-face, or by telephone and email, has always been an essential element of the course, for both students on campus and those more distant. The needs of students vary considerably here too, especially as far as the writing of their dissertations is concerned.

The contribution of colleagues outside the department has been essential from the beginning. Whether for a single session or for a whole module, the expertise of people from other departments, notably Education, Drama, and Art, as well as some from outside the university, has been stimulating to students on course. Additionally, the MA students have been particularly encouraged to attend conferences, notably that held annually in conjunction with the British Region of the International Board on Books for Young People (IBBY), at which prominent authors and critics have spoken. Another link is that with the Children's Literature International Summer School (CLISS), held biennally.

Maintaining standards

To a considerable extent, the normal university processes of validation by outside experts and provision of external examiners ensures parity with comparable courses in other institutions. Other factors which reinforce the conviction of excellence are students' success with subsequent publication of material from essays and dissertations, and the fact that many have gone on to read for Ph.D.s or to experience improved career prospects. The range of subjects researched for dissertations is quite impressive; original work has been done on areas as diverse as Greek, Irish, Australian, Xhosa, and Taiwanese children's fiction, virtual reality, graphic novels, the representation of music—as well as a vast range of known and unknown authors and illustrators, ancient and modern. In the first ten years of the programme's existence, the number of graduates has been about one hundred and fifty, and numbers of applicants for both the on-campus and the distance learning modes of the course remain buoyant.

Current state of provision in the UK: Masters level

The following universities offer comprehensive graduate programmes in Children's Literature. It is possible to take individual units of study in Children's Literature elsewhere, but the programmes listed below provide degrees wholly or largely in the area of Children's Literature Studies. Programmes may be offered by Cultural Studies, Education, Literature, and Sociology faculties, or as interdisciplinary programmes. As a result, prospective students need to read the information supplied by each programme carefully to ensure that it has the emphasis and professional recognition they require. The majority of courses expect students normally to have a good first degree (2.1 or above) or equivalent (including professional qualifications in some cases) in a relevant subject. Students for who are not first-language English speakers are required to prove an appropriate standard of proficiency to meet the demands of studying and writing at postgraduate level (details of these requirements can be found on each university's web site).

University of Central England: www.uce.ac.uk
A Children's Literature programme within the Masters Degree in Literary Studies in the Faculty of Computing, Information, and English was validated in 2003. Areas covered are fantasy; folk and fairy tales, and picture books. Mode: full-time and part-time.

University of Cambridge: www.homerton.ac.uk
An M.Ed. in Critical Approaches to Children's Literature was launched in 2003 as part of the Cambridge Education Faculty's Modular M.Ed. The first year of this two-year course is open to suitably qualified candidates in teaching, librarianship, postgraduates in English working at higher degree level and those already on the M.Ed. who choose to take it as

their second year module. The second year is only open to those who have already taken the first year. The course covers a wide range of children's literature and critical theory; emphases include journal writing and writing for children; visual texts; poetry; oral texts; media texts; children's responses to texts. Mode: part-time over two years.

De Montfort University: www.dmu.ac.uk
The MA in Constructions of Childhood, running since 2000, is offered at both the Bedford and Leicester campuses. It is an interdisciplinary programme (combining English, History, and Education) which includes a large children's literature component, some of it based on the Hockcliffe Collection of early children's literature. The programme consists of a compulsory Research Methods module, three taught modules (Representations of Gender in Children's Literature; Twentieth-Century Childhoods, and Comparison of Fin de Siècle and Millennial Narratives of Childhood), and a dissertation. Mode: part-time over two years.

University of Manchester: www.art.man.ac.uk/SML/contact.shtml
The UK's only MA in European Children's Literature is offered in the School of Modern Languages. Students take four core courses: Arts Faculty Research Training; Research Methods in Modern Languages and Cultures; Critical Theory I; Critical Theory II followed by two Children's Literature options: Illustration in nineteenth-century children's literature and Instruction and Amusement in Early European Children's Literature, and a 12–15,000-word dissertation. Mode: full-time and part-time.

University of Nottingham: www.nottingham.ac.uk/education/courses/lit.htm
An MA in Children's Literature is offered by the School of Education. Students take four core modules: Becoming a Reader; History and Ideology of Children's Literature; Genre Studies, and Writing By and For Children, followed by a dissertation of 12–15,000 words. Mode: part-time over 2–4 years.

University of Reading: www.reading.ac.uk/english/MAchildrenlitprospectus.htm
The longest-established MA in the field. Students take three core modules: one on Critical Theory, and one each on nineteenth- and twentieth-century children's literature. They then choose three of six optional units: North American Children's Literature; Commonwealth Children's Literature; Children's Radio, Film, and Television; Myth and Folktale in Children's Literature and Popular Forms of Children's Fiction, before

writing a 20,000-word dissertation. Mode: full-time and part-time over 1–2 years.

University of Roehampton: www.roehampton.ac.uk/artshum/english/progs/childlit_ma.ap
Running since 1993, this is a flexible MA and the only one in the UK to be offered by Distance Learning as well as on site. It is supported by regular conferences and a biennial international summer school. Students take three compulsory modules: Research Methods, Critical and Theoretical Perspectives, and at least one of the three modules concerned with visual elements of children's literature: Visual Texts; History of Children's Book Illustration, and Children's Literature in Performance. Three more modules are then chosen from an extensive menu consisting of Origins and Developments of Children's Literature; Children's Literature 1900–1960; Children's Literature 1960 to the Present Day; Poetry Written for Children; Research Enquiry (all available by Distance Learning); and Contemporary Children's Literature Written in English; Children's Literature in Translation; American Children's Literature to 1933; American Children's Literature 1933 to the Present Day; Verse and Voice; Time and History in Twentieth-Century Children's Literature; Alternative Narratives; Children's Literature of Migration; and Children as Readers. A 20,000 word dissertation is submitted to fulfil the requirements of the programme. Mode: full-time and part-time over 1–6 years; on site and by Distance Learning.

Sheffield Hallam University: www.shu.ac.uk/cultural/english/maenglish.html
As part of the MA English Studies students may specialize in Children's Literature after completing a mandatory Research Methods course, two optional units with Children's Literature content, and a dissertation in the area of Children's Literature.

University of Sunderland: www.sunderland.ac.uk
The MA Education, running since 2000, offers a specific route for students who wish to focus on children, child development, and the professional application of children's literature. Although offered as an Education degree, this specialism is not designed exclusively for teachers but aims to be of interest and use to all those who have a personal and/or professional interest in children and children's literature. Students taking this route take three dedicated modules: Journey Towards Modern Fantasy; Authors and Themes, and Issues and Analysis in Children's Literature, together with a Research Methods module, before

submitting a 20,000 word dissertation. Mode: part-time, normally over three years.

Research and scholarship

Despite the relatively short period since the establishment of higher degree courses in children's literature, a considerable number of scholars with research interests in the field have added to its development, and also to its interconnections with other disciplines, such as colonial and postcolonial studies and feminism. They have been able to take advantage of the increasing availability of resources, especially online, and of the opportunities for publication of both books and articles.

Every university that offers taught graduate courses in children's literature will also supervise research for M.Phil. and Ph.D. degrees in the area. Institutions with particular expertise, not all of which offer graduate courses, are: University of Bolton; DeMontfort University, Bedford; University of Birmingham; University of Durham; Homerton College, Cambridge; University of Newcastle; University of Reading; University of Roehampton; University of Warwick; University of the West of England, Bristol; University College Worcester.

8
Children's Literature at Postgraduate Level in the United States

Richard Flynn

Until recently, postgraduate study of children's literature in North American English departments has been relatively rare and somewhat haphazard. For many professors in my generation and the generation before us, studying, teaching, and writing about children's literature often began by lucky accident. As graduate students, few of us would have been permitted to specialize in children's literature, but few of us would have even thought to do so. The more fortunate among us may have had mentors sympathetic to the emerging field. (Judith Plotz, for instance, was my dissertation advisor.) But our formal study of children's literature was either spotty or nonexistent. Because we went to school when children's literature was still generally considered beneath criticism, most of us experience a shock of recognition when we read the opening sentence of Beverly Lyon Clark's book *Kiddie Lit: The Cultural Construction of Children's Literature in America* (2003): "When I was in graduate school in the 1970s, I wouldn't have been caught dead reading children's literature."

Here in the twenty-first century, there are a number of graduate programmes at the master's level where one may specialize in children's literature—at Eastern Michigan University, Hollins University, Simmons College, and San Diego State University, among others. There are even Ph.D. programmes, most prominently those at Illinois State University, the University of Florida, and the University of Pittsburgh. In addition, there is now a well-established infrastructure of established journals, organizations, listservs, and scholarship opportunities available to graduate students and junior scholars working in the field of English that makes the systematic study of children's literature possible and even attractive.

That said, there are a number of factors the prospective graduate student should consider regarding the advanced study of children's literature. Despite the increased respectability of the field—it is no longer possible to refer to it as "the great excluded" (the subtitle of the annual *Children's Literature* in its early years)—there are still ways in which children's literature remains marginalized in many English departments. Frequently, courses in children's literature, while offered by the English department, are designated service courses for Education majors, and a number of schools even go so far as to forbid English majors from taking them for credit in the major. Graduate students who anticipate careers in college and university teaching need to think realistically about the potential for scholarly growth and major programme and graduate teaching assignments over what is likely to be a career of thirty years or more. The best-known children's literature doctoral programmes provide breadth in their programmes and foster students with training in secondary literary fields, composition and rhetoric, or cultural studies. Nevertheless, graduate students need to be aware of the dangers of specializing too narrowly, as they will seldom be required to teach only children's literature if they are fortunate enough to find a tenure-track position.

That said, there are many practical advantages to getting a graduate degree that includes training in children's literature. Foremost among them is the opportunity to work with established scholars in the field, who serve as generous mentors to deserving students. Although the children's literature field as a subspecialty in English is relatively small, there are numerous opportunities for graduate students to present papers and to publish. (Doing both while one is still in graduate school is imperative for those who hope to teach at the university level.) The more one knows about particular faculty in the programmes one is interested in, the better. A good plan for the prospective student would be to spend time reading the major scholarly journals in the field, such as *The Children's Literature Association Quarterly*, the *Children's Literature* annual, *The Lion and the Unicorn*, and *Children's Literature in Education*. There one may become familiar with the work of potential faculty mentors, but, even more important, one may become familiar with critical conversations in the field and learn about the field's concerns, debates, and theories that one will be engaged in over the course of graduate study.

The list of resources that follows is by no means comprehensive, but it should give prospective students a good idea of what is available, and should serve as a starting point for planning a postbaccalaureate degree in children's literature. One final caveat: because there are still pockets of disrespect for children's literature in many English departments, faculty outside the field who are unfamiliar with its academic rigour may give bad advice. I know of one student in a general MA programme who was discouraged from writing a thesis on children's literature. His professors advised him that Ph.D. programmes would only take him seriously if he wrote on a "major" figure like Keats or Shakespeare. Fortunately, the student rejected this advice, wrote the thesis he wanted to write, went on to one of the Ph.D. children's literature programmes, and is now a successful tenure-track assistant professor specializing in children's literature, with many articles published and a book forthcoming. There are likely more unemployed or underemployed Keats and Shakespeare scholars than there are children's literature scholars. It is best for students to pursue the course of study that truly interests them and to take all advice with a grain of salt, including mine.

Selected MA programmes in children's literature

It might well be advisable for the new college graduate interested in children's literature to begin formal graduate study in one of the many excellent masters-level graduate programmes. Information on selected formal children's literature programmes is provided below. The student should be aware, however, that there are good children's literature faculty in traditional MA programmes that offer graduate courses and the opportunity to write theses in children's literature. Some of these programmes, such as Texas State University in San Marcos, offer concentrations or minors in children's literature. Some programmes don't appear to offer a formal concentration, but have several accomplished faculty members in the field, such as Kansas State University and Southwest Missouri State University. The following are selected formal MA programmes in children's literature, with a few brief comments:

Eastern Michigan University
Department of English Language and Literature
612 Pray-Harrold
Ypsilanti, MI 48197
Phone: (734) 487–4220
Fax: (734) 483–9744
http://www.emich.edu/public/english/childlit/

This programme is one of the oldest children's literature programmes housed in an English Department. Besides the MA, there is a minor concentration in children's literature at the undergraduate level as well as an interdisciplinary undergraduate major in Major in Children's Literature and Drama/Theatre for the Young. Faculty include Ian Wojcik-Andrews, Sheila Most, and Harry Eiss.

MA Requirements for a Concentration in Children's Literature: http://www.emich.edu/public/catalogs/current/acaf/colleges/coa/eng/grad/macl.html

Hollins University
Graduate Studies Office
Hollins University
Roanoke, VA 24020
(540) 362–6575

Programme director: Amanda Cockrell
Phone: (540) 362–6024
E-mail: acockrell@hollins.edu

Hollins, a women's university at the undergraduate level, offers coeducational master's programmes, including a highly-respected programme in children's literature. The programme is notable in that students take classes only in the summer, and there are always a number of distinguished visiting professors in residence as well. In conjunction with its highly respected creative writing programme, Hollins offers a MFA degree in writing for children in addition to its regular MA in Children's Literature. Hollins is also home to the annual journal *Children's Literature*, perhaps the most prestigious journal in the field.

Programme web site: http://www.hollins.edu/grad/childlit/

San Diego State University
Children's Literature programme
Department of English and Comparative Literature
5500 Campanile Drive
San Diego, CA 92182–8140

Director: Dr Jerry Griswold
E-mail: childlit@mail.sdsu.edu
Phone: (619) 594–5443
Fax: (619) 594–4998

The web site for the programme says that it is "the only children's literature programme at the MA level in the western United States."

The programme has recently established the National Center for the Study of Children's Literature. The faculty includes such recognized scholars such as Jerry Griswold, Allida Allison, and June Cummins, with several other faculty members in the department doing research and teaching in the field. They have an active student group that organizes programmes and festivals. The MA degree is new, but the department's commitment to children's literature is longstanding.

Web site: http://www-rohan.sdsu.edu/~childlit/

Simmons College
College of Arts and Sciences
Office of Graduate Studies Admission
300 The Fenway
Boston, Massachusetts 02115–5898
Phone: (617) 521–2915
E-mail: gsa@simmons.edu
Director: Susan P. Bloom
Associate Director: Cathryn Mercier

Simmons offers the MA in children's literature, the MFA in Writing for Children, a dual MA/MFA, and a dual MA/MAT degree for those who wish to become teachers. Every two years they hold a symposium, led by a well-known scholar, culminating in a weekend institute with well-known authors and discussion sessions. According to their web site, graduates "pursue careers as authors, editors, scholars, and critics, as well as librarians and teachers. Students also use their children's literature degree as a stepping stone to doctoral programs and entrepreneurial work in children's literature." The programme combines academic rigour with an emphasis on contemporary children's literature, as both Bloom and Mercier write regularly for *The Horn Book*.

Programme web site: http://www.simmons.edu/gradstudies/childrens_literature/

Ph.D. programmes

The University of Florida
Department of English
4008 Turlington Hall
P.O. Box 117310
Gainesville, Florida 32611–7310
Phone: (352) 392–6650
Fax: (352) 392–0860

Florida offers concentrations in Children's Literature at both the MA and Ph.D. levels. It is particularly well-suited for students with an interest in cultural studies and for students who might wish to work with the vast archive housed in the Baldwin Library of Historical Children's Literature (http://web.uflib.ufl.edu/spec/baldwin/baldwin.html). In addition to that major resource, Florida is also the home to the Center for Children's Literature and Culture (http://www.clas.ufl.edu/cclc/). At present the director of graduate studies is a well-known children's literature and culture scholar, Kenneth Kidd. Noted scholar John Cech directs the Center for Children's Literature and Culture.

General information about graduate study: http://www.english.ufl.edu/programmes/grad/

Specific requirements of the children's literature tracks: http://www.english.ufl.edu/programmes/grad/ma_phd_tracks/childrenslit.html

Illinois State University
Stevenson Hall Room 409
Campus Box 4240
Normal IL 61790–4240
Phone: (309) 438–3667
Fax: (309) 438–5414

According to their web site, the children's literature programme at Illinois State "has long embraced both literary and educational approaches to children's literature." Their doctorate in English Studies requires a pedagogical component and the study of required and cognate fields that make their graduates particularly attractive to employers. The children's literature faculty is excellent, including such well-known literary scholars as Roberta Trites, Jan Susina, and Karen Coats. It also claims to be the oldest and best-established English children's literature programme in the country. They have an excellent track record in placing graduates into jobs in the academy.

For more information visit: http://www.english.ilstu.edu/childrenslit/index.html

The University of Pittsburgh
526 Cathedral of Learning
4200 Fifth Avenue
Pittsburgh, PA 15260
Phone: (412) 624–6506
Fax: (412) 624–6639

The Ph.D. in cultural critical studies at Pittsburgh offers a concentration in children's literature with a childhood studies focus. The children's literature programme is directed by noted scholar Valerie Krips. Children's literature faculty includes Troy Boone and Marah Gubar. According to their web site, the programme encourages study beginning with the MA: "Students who continue to the PhD may write a dissertation on the subject of children's literature, and, we believe, will be better prepared to do so by the work undertaken in the MA." The page also cautions: "Although it will be possible to further specialized interest in children, childhood, and children's books within the framework of the MA, it cannot be guaranteed that graduate classes which deal directly with the subject of children's literature will be offered frequently." Nevertheless, the programme has an excellent reputation for producing some of the most sophisticated scholars in the field.

Home page for Ph.D. in Cultural Critical Studies: http://www.english.pitt.edu/graduate/phd.html

Graduate Research page for children's literature programme: http://www.pitt.edu/~childlit/clgradresearch.html

The University of Connecticut
Dept. of English, Box U-4025
215 Glenbrook Road
Storrs, CT 06269–4025
Phone: (860) 486–2141
Fax: (860) 486–1530

The Ph.D. programme at UConn (as it is nicknamed) also emphasizes Cultural and Critical Studies, and unlike the others listed here does not have a formal concentration in children's literature. However, for many years, because of the presence of the late Francelia Butler, who was a driving force behind the establishment of children's literature as a field in English (as opposed to education or library science) many of the top children's literature scholars were graduates of the programme. The presence on the faculty of such accomplished senior scholars as Margaret Higonnet and such accomplished junior scholars as Katharine Capshaw Smith makes this still quite attractive as an option for prospective students. Also attractive is the presence of the Northeast Children's Literature Collection housed in the Thomas J. Dodd Research Center.

Graduate programmes home page: http://english.uconn.edu/site_files/html/main.html

Essential resources for the prospective and current graduate student

There are two organizations to which every graduate student in children's literature should belong: The Children's Literature Association, and the Children's Literature Division of the Modern Language Association.

Membership of the Children's Literature Association includes subscriptions to *The Children's Literature Association Quarterly* and the annual *Children's Literature*, as well as reduced rates for the association's annual conference. There is a reduced membership fee for graduate students, and the association sponsors the Hannah Beiter Graduate Student Research Grants competition.

Association home page: http://ebbs.english.vt.edu/chla/.index.html

One joins the MLA Division on Children's Literature by joining the Modern Language Association and checking off the division membership. While one must attend the annual MLA conference to become deeply involved in the division, it is a very friendly organization and welcomes graduate students who wish to attend its meetings and to propose panels.

Web site: http://www.mla.org/

The MLA has recently made available on line a Guide to Doctoral programs in English and Other Modern Languages available at: http://www.mla.org/gdp_intro

The above constitutes a mere selection of the resources and programmes available. As with any graduate programme, prospective students are advised to do careful and extensive research to ensure a good fit and a fulfilling graduate experience. The study of English beyond the bachelor's degree requires substantial intellectual, emotional, and financial investments, as well as a commitment of several years, after which there are uncertain rewards. But as the foregoing descriptions indicate, there are a number of excellent programmes for those committed to the advanced study of children's literature.

Work cited

Clark, Beverly Lyon. 2003. *Kiddie Lit: The Cultural Construction of Children's Literature in America*. Baltimore & London: Johns Hopkins University Press.

Appendix 1
Sample Undergraduate Syllabi

Charles Butler

There is a growing range of undergraduate courses being taught in children's literature throughout the English-speaking world. Some are general introductions to the field, while others specialize by period, genre, or the age group of the readership (for example focusing on contemporary books, on fantasy, or on books for young children). Some encourage close reading and personal response, others are more theoretically or culturally orientated. Some are aimed at education students intending to become teachers, others at students taking a course in children's literature as part of a general English degree. In terms of assessment, their methods range from academic essays, to journals and reviews, to workshop presentations. The selection presented here is intended simply to suggest something of the variety of approaches currently being followed, and to stimulate ideas for possible future developments.

Kiddult Fiction (Rachel Falconer, University of Sheffield)
"This course analyses twentieth and twenty-first century 'kiddult fiction' or crossover child–adult fiction, with a particular emphasis on the genre of fantasy fiction. A sub-genre of children's literature, 'kiddult fiction' is uniquely positioned on the border between serious and popular literature as well as between child and adult readers, and includes books which are as often compulsively devoured, as read for pleasure and education." The course combines formal analysis with a consideration of such matters as marketing and reception history. It has been run in tandem with the Kiddult Fiction Project, which involves students running workshops with children.
Assessment: a) a 2,000-word essay; b) a group project involving *either* a research presentation to a large group *or* a workshop session with children.

Picture and Word (Alice Mills, University of Ballarat)
The course introduces the academic study of children's literature through a focus on picture books. As well as exposing students to the language and issues involved in children's literature in general, it teaches them to extend and refine their appreciation and analysis of the visual, encouraging both creative and critical thinking.
Assessment: a) to produce six pages of an original story-book, and analyse it in a 1,500-word essay (only the essay to be assessed); b) an analytical essay of

2,000 words on a picture story book published within the last five years; c) weekly journal tasks.

Children's Literature into Film (Martha Stoddard Holmes, California State San Marcos)
The course combines an introduction to the history and criticism of children's literature with elements of film analysis, considering books in relationship to film versions that have been made of them.
Assessment: a) in-class "quizzes" (partly designed to ensure seminar attendance); b) five short "response papers" *or* one longer one, addressing the relationship between a book and a film; c) a group presentation; d) a take-home essay paper.

Children's Literature (Sally Bentley, Bishop Grosseteste College)
A "overview" course in children's literature, including novels from a range of genres and periods (from *Alice's Adventures in Wonderland* to contemporary Young Adult novels such as *Dear Nobody*), and a range of picture books by authors such as Sendak, Burningham, and Browne.
Assessment: Seminar papers and a Timed Assignment.

Children's Literature: History and Criticism (Amelia Rutledge, George Mason University)
An "advanced course in the history and the criticism of children's literature," which combines analysis of classic texts with theoretical considerations of the nature of fantasy, mimesis, narrative, and the social construction of childhood.
Assessment: a) two short analytical papers, b) one longer paper; c) short exercises based on questions specific to that session's topic; d) a final examination.

A History of Children's Literature (Jacqui Reid-Walsh, Concordia University)
"This course is organized around two conceptual 'bookends,' the immensely popular books *Little Goody Two Shoes* (1765) attributed to Oliver Goldsmith or John Newbery and *Harry Potter and the Philosopher's Stone* (1997) by J. K. Rowling. These two books, some two hundred and thirty years apart, were and are publishing phenomena of their respective periods. Both deserve scrutiny for this link between children's literature and commercial publishing, but more importantly they can be seen as forms of 'miscellanies' containing many aspects of literature for children popular in their respective periods."
The course combines historical and genre approaches, using Nodelman and Reimer's *Pleasures of Children's Literature* as a background text in order to provide "a dimension of critical and theoretical investigation."
Assessment: Assessment is made on a variety of activities, including research papers, reviews, and interviews with young readers.

Children and Literature (Morag Styles et al., University of Cambridge)
This an optional course run by the Faculty of Education. The course includes lectures, seminars, and supervisions on a wide range of genres and topics within the field. The focus is on texts, authors, and young readers, set within a historical and cultural context. A feature of the course is the contribution made by invited speakers, who have (over the years) included David Almond, James Berry, Melvin Burgess, Anthony Browne, Kevin Crossley-Holland, Anne Fine, Janni Howker, Jan Mark, Jan Ormerod, Gareth Owen, Philip Pullman, Michael Rosen, Jill Paton Walsh, Philippa Pearce, Robert Swindells, and Robert Westall.

Assessment: a) a short dissertation; b) an examination covering set books, genre-based questions, and an unseen text.

Children's Literature (Jackie Stallcup, California State University, Northridge)
The course is concerned with "developing criteria and resources for selecting and critiquing children's texts, exploring methods for engaging children with literature, and developing an understanding of the socio-political implications and controversies embedded in texts written for (or adopted by) children." It includes sections on issues (ideology, the relationship of text to illustration, censorship) and genres (folklore, realism, fantasy (auto)biography and historical fiction).
Assessment: a) journal; b) term paper; c) mid-term class-based test; d) project; e) participation and quizzes.

Online syllabi for teaching children's literature

Many university and college teachers now make their syllabi, reading lists, and even lecture notes available online. Given that such information is continually changing it is not desirable to attempt a comprehensive listing here; however, the following sites are particularly useful in presenting a range of different course descriptions:

www.scils.rutgers.edu/~kvander/Syllabus/index.html: a collection of syllabi developed by Kay Vandergrift, covering a variety of topics within children's literature, and aimed in some cases particularly towards education students.

http://io.uwinnipeg.ca/~nodelman/resources/index.htm: part of Perry Nodelman's and Mavis Reimer's *Pleasures of Children's Literature* site, describing courses developed by the authors for use in conjunction with their book.

www.northern.edu/hastingw/kidlitpg.htm: a selection of Waller Hastings's current and former children's literature courses at Northern State University, going back to 1997.

http://lilt.ilstu.edu/kscoat2/: Karen Coats's courses in children's literature and related topics at Illinois State University.

Appendix 2
Resources

Kimberley Reynolds, Pat Pinsent, and Charles Butler

This book is not intended as a handbook to pure research in children's literature. Nevertheless, good access to sources of information, whether in the form of books and journals, internet sites, centres of expertise, or collections, is crucial to the successful preparation of teaching programmes. The last decade has seen a proliferation of such resources, and the purpose of this chapter is to list some of the most useful, as well as to provide a jumping-off point for further enquiry.

Anthologies and reference books

Carpenter, Humphrey and Mari Pritchard. *The Oxford Companion to Children's Literature.* Oxford and New York: Oxford University Press, 1984. Now dated but still a useful source of information about authors, illustrators, texts, characters, periodicals, and some general topics; particularly strong on historical material.

Cullinan, Bernice E., and Diane G. Person. *The Continuum Encyclopedia of Children's Literature.* New York and London: Continuum, 2001.

Cullinan, Bernice E., and Deb Wooten. *The Continuum Encyclopedia of Young Adult Literature.* New York and London: Continuum, 2005.

Hunt, Peter, ed. *Children's Literature: An Anthology 1801—1902.* Oxford: Blackwell, 2001. For those interested in the history and development of the subject, this anthology introduces nicely chosen extracts from often hard-to-locate but influential texts and authors.

Hunt, Peter, ed. *Children's Literature: An Illustrated History.* Oxford and New York: Oxford University Press, 1995. Accessible overviews by well-qualified contributors of the development of children's literature from 1700 to the late twentieth century, organized by period, place (primarily the UK and the USA), and genres.

Hunt, Peter, ed. *The International Companion Encyclopedia of Children's Literature.* London and New York: Routledge, 2004. A wide-ranging collection on key areas to children's literature scholars, from critical theory to essays on the state of children's literature in selected countries.

Mark, Jan, ed. *The Oxford Book of Children's Stories*. Oxford University Press, 1993.

Something about the Author. Detroit: Gale. Provides biographical and bibliographical information about authors of children's literature: a yearly publication.

Watson, Victor, ed. *The Cambridge Guide to Children's Books in English*. Cambridge: Cambridge University Press, 2001. Similar to the *Oxford Companion*, but more recent and more comprehensive. It includes considerably more information on North American and other English-language texts, authors, illustrators, and periodicals, and contains numerous essays on topics such as nudity in children's literature, information books, and detective fiction.

Zipes, Jack, Lissa Paul, Lynne Vallone, Gillian Avery and Peter Hunt, eds. *The Norton Anthology of Children's Literature: the Traditions in English*. New York: W. W. Norton, 2005. A wide-ranging anthology of English-language children's literature from 1659, including many full-length texts.

———. ed. *Encyclopedia of Children's Literature*. Oxford: Oxford University Press, 2006.

Journals

Journals are invaluable for teachers who wish to keep abreast of key issues, critical approaches and research developments, as well as being a way of encountering new writers, illustrators, and critics. The list of English-language journals below has a bias towards those journals with an academic focus, although there are numerous general and review publications that may also be of relevance to the teacher of children's literature.

The ALAN Review: Assembly on Literature for Adolescents: http://scholar.lib.vt.edu/ejournals/ALAN/
Editors: James Blasingame (James.Blasingame@asu.edu) and Lori A. Goodson (lagoodson@cox.net).

Bookbird (www.ibby.org)
Journal of IBBY: the International Board on Books for Young People.
Editors: Siobhán Parkinson (parkbenn@eircom.net) and Valerie Coghlan (vcoghlan@cice.ie).

Canadian Children's Literature (ccl@uwinnipeg.ca)
Department of English, University of Winnipeg, 515 Portage Avenue, Winnipeg MB R3L 1V9, Canada. Editor: Perry Nodelman.

Children's Literature (annual)
The Children's Literature Association Quarterly http://ebbs.english.vt.edu/chla/quarterly.html
Children's Literature Association, PO Box 138, Battle Creek, MI 49016, USA.

Children's Literature in Education, Kluwer Academic Publishers, Journals Dept., PO Box 322, 3300 AH Dordrecht, The Netherlands.
Editors: Margaret Mackey (United States & Canada), P.O. Box 45034, Lansdowne Postal Outlet, Edmondton, Alberta, T6H 5YI, Canada; Geoff Fox (UK and

elsewhere excluding North America), Aller Down Cottage, Coppice Lane, Sandford, Crediton, EX17 4EG, UK.

CREArTA: Journal of the Centre for Research and Education in the Arts, www.crea.uts.edu.au/ University of Technology Sydney. Editor: Dr Rosemary Ross Johnston, Director, Centre for Research and Education in the Arts.

Horn Book Magazine (www.hbook.com)
56 Roland St., Suite 200, Boston, MA 02129, USA.
Editor: Roger Sutton, magazine@hbook.com

Inis: the Children's Books Ireland Magazine www.childrensbooksireland.com
Children's Books Ireland, 17 Lower Camden Street, Dublin 2, Ireland.
Editors: Siobhán Parkinson (parkbenn@eircom.net) and Valerie Coghlan (vcoghlan@cice.ie).

The Journal of Children's Literature www.childrensliteratureassembly.org/journal3.htm
West Virginia University, Department of Educational Theory & Practice.
607-C Allen Hall, Box 6122, Morgantown, WV 26501–6122, USA. Editor: Elizabeth Poe.

The Journal of Children's Literature Studies www.piedpiperpublishing.com/childlitcontributors.htm
Pied Piper Publishing Ltd., 80 Birmingham Rd, Shenstone, Lichfield, Staffs, WS14 0JU, UK Editors: Debbie Mynott & Glen Mynott.

The Lion and the Unicorn www.press.jhu.edu/journals/
The Johns Hopkins University Press, P.O. Box 19966, Baltimore, MD 21211–0966, USA. Editors: George Bodmer (Indiana University—Northwest); Lissa Paul (University of New Brunswick); Jan Susina (Illinois State University).

The Looking Glass: an Online Children's Literature Journal
www.the-looking-glass.net Editor: Jane Goldstein (the scholarly section, "Alice's Academy," is edited by Elizabeth Pandolfo-Briggs).

Marvels and Tales: Journal of Fairy Tale Studies www.langlab.wayne.edu/MarvelsHome/Marvels_Tales.html
Wayne State University Press, Leonard N. Simons Building, 4809 Woodward Avenue, Detroit M1 48201–1309, USA.
Editor: Professor Donald Haase (d.haase@wayne.edu), 443 Manoogian Hall, Wayne State University, Detroit M1 48202.

New Review of Children's Literature and Librarianship www.tandf.co.uk
Taylor and Francis, 11 New Fetter Lane, London EC4P 4EE, UK.
Editor: Dr Sally Maynard (s.e.maynard@lboro.ac.uk).

Papers: Explorations into Children's Literature
School of Communication and Creative Arts, Deakin University, Burwood 3125
Editor: Prof. Clare Bradford (clarex@deakin.edu.au).

Sankofa: A Journal of African Children's and Young Adult Literature
202-E Holmes Hall, Morgan State University, 1700 E. Eold Spring Road,

Baltimore, MD 21251, USA.
Editor: Dr Meena Khorana (meenakh@aol.com).

English-language Internet discussion lists

There are two general lists for the academic discussion of children's literature:

children-literature-uk: run by Roehampton University's National Centre for Research in Children's Literature as a discussion forum about children's books, largely by those with an academic interest in the subject: www.jiscmail.ac.uk/lists/CHILDREN-LITERATURE-UK.html

Child_Lit: hosted by Michael Joseph of Rutgers University (USA) to discuss the theory and criticism of children's literature: www.rci.rutgers.edu/~mjoseph/childlit/about.html

There are also numerous listservs devoted to the discussion of particular genres or authors. For example, Girlsown (Girlsown@home.it.net.au) discusses schoolgirl stories and series such as those by E. M. Brent-Dyer, D. F. Bruce, E. J. Oxenham and Enid Blyton; while the Child Whispers Fanlisting (http://www.too-manic.net/enidblyton/) concentrates on Blyton's work specifically. Many discussions also take place on fora such as Live Journal communities and Yahoo Groups, some of which are considerably more "fannish" than academic in content.

Academic and specialist web sites

ABC-Lit: An Index to Children's Literature Scholarship: www.abc-lit.com

Carol Hurst's Children's Literature site: www.carolhurst.com/

CHILDE: Children's historical literature disseminated throughout Europe: www.bookchilde.org

Children's Literature: A guide to the criticism: www.unm.edu/~lhendr/

Children's Literature Association: http://wiz.cath.vt.edu/chla/

Children's Book Council (USA): www.cbcbooks.org

Children's Literature Web Guide: www.ucalgary.ca/~dkbrown

International Board on Books for Young People: www.ibby.org

International Research Society for Children's Literature (IRSCL): www.irscl.ac.uk

Kay Vandergrift's Special Interest Page: www.scils.rutgers.edu/~kvander/

National Centre for Research in Children's Literature (NCRCL): www.ncrcl.ac.uk

Newbery Classroom: http://www.rci.rutgers.edu/~mjoseph/newbery.html

Nineteenth-Century Girls' Series: http://readseries.com/index.html

Once Upon a Time: www.bsu.edu/classes/vancamp/ouat.html

Organizations and research centres within the United Kingdom

The UK boasts a wide variety of organizations dedicated to aspects of children's literature, from those concerned with individual authors to those whose remit is to promote children's literature in general. While many are not academic in the strict sense, their members are often extremely knowledgeable and helpful. They issue newsletters and publications, have information and access to collections, organize conferences and events, and generally work to develop knowledge and activity about specific areas of interest to children's literature scholars.

Booktrust (Children's section) www.booktrusted.com
45 East Hill, London SW18 2QZ
A charitable organization designed to bring young people and books together. Produces booklists and publications; maintains a short-term depository for contemporary children's books published in the UK and related reference material; maintains cuttings; administers prizes; supports teachers and other professionals in the field by providing information.

Children's Book Circle (CBC) c/o Puffin Books, 80 The Strand, London WC2R 0RL
A discussion forum for anyone involved with children's books; holds regular meetings addressed by invited speakers on topical issues relating to children's books; administers the Eleanor Farjeon Award and organizes the annual Patrick Hardy Lecture.

Children's Books History Society (CBHS) c/o Daniels, French Section, British Library, 96 Euston Road, London NW1 2DB
Promotes appreciation of children's books in their literary, historical, and bibliographical aspects and encourages distribution and exchange of information about children's literature. Holds regular meetings; organizes visits to collections; runs occasional conferences; publishes a substantial newsletter and annual Occasional Paper.

Centre for the Children's Book (CCB) www.centreforthechildrensbook.org.uk
18 Quay Level, St Peter's Marina, Newcastle-upon-Tyne NE6 1TZ
An organization designed to preserve the work and document the creative process of contemporary British children's writers and illustrators; to mount, tour, and provide outreach activities based on exhibitions; to run lectures, workshops, and other children's literature events; to provide an archive and library for children's literature researchers.

Centre for International Research in Childhood: Literature, Culture, Media (CIRCL) www.reading.ac.uk/circl
Aims to promote and coordinate international and interdisciplinary academic research in childhood, focusing on research in children and culture, children's literature, and children and the media; organizes lectures, seminars, and conferences.

Centre for the Study of Children, Youth, and Media http://www.ccsonline.org.uk/mediacentre/main.html
Institute of Education, University of London, 20 Bedford Way, London WC1H 0AL.

Federation of Children's Book Groups 2 Bridge Wood View, Horsforth, Leeds, West Yorkshire LS18 5PE, E-mail: info@fcbg.org.uk
A national voluntary organization that aims to promote enjoyment of and interest in children's books and reading; brings together parents, professionals, and official organizations; operates through a combination of local groups which organize events, exhibitions, and a newsletter, and a national group which organizes an annual conference; runs the annual Children's Book Award; promotes National Share-a-Story Month; publishes anthologies, book lists, and information leaflets; supports the (nonacademic) children's book magazine, *Carousel*.

National Centre for Research in Children's Literature (NCRCL), University of Roehampton, Roehampton Lane, London SW15 5PJ (www.ncrcl.ac.uk)
An academic research centre promoting excellence in research in and study of children's literature in all its aspects. Runs undergraduate, graduate and postgraduate programmes; with the British section of IBBY runs an annual conference; initiates research projects and collaborations; runs the Children's Literature International Summer School; undertakes consultancy and evaluations; administers the Marsh Award for Children's Literature in Translation, and produces publications, including research reports and conference proceedings.

Societies devoted to the work of children's authors

Hans Christian Andersen Center: University of Southern Denmark, Campusvej 55,5230 Odense M, Denmark: www.andersen.sdu.dk/index_e.html

BB Society (Denys Watkins-Pitchford): 8 Park Road, Solihull, West Midlands B91 3SU: www.welford.org/bb.htm

J. M. Barrie Society: www.jmbarrie.net/

International Wizard of Oz Club: L. Frank Baum, Department E, P.O. Box 26249, San Francisco, CA 94126–6249, USA: www.ozclub.org

Enid Blyton Society: www.enidblytonsociety.co.uk/

The New Chalet Club (Elinor Brent-Dyor): www.newchaletclub.co.uk/index.html

The Jennings Society (Anthony Buckeridge): The Jennings Society, Darrell Swift, 37 Tinshill Lane, Leeds LS16 6BU

Lewis Carroll Society: www.lewiscarrollsociety.org.uk

The Roald Dahl Museum and Story Centre: 81–83 High St, Great Missenden, Buckinghamshire, HP16 0AL: www.roalddahlmuseum.org/

From the Punchbowl (Monica Edwards): The Punchbowl, Hurstpierpoint College, Hassocks, Sussex, BN6 9JS: www.punchbowl.org.uk/Society.html

Kipling Society: 6 Clifton Road, London W9 1SS: www.kipling.org.uk

The New York C. S. Lewis Society: www.nycslsociety.com

The Betsy-Tacy Society (Maud Hart Lovelace): P.O. Box 94, Mankato MN 56002–0094, USA: www.betsy-tacysociety.org/

George MacDonald Society: www.macdonaldsociety.org

Walter de la Mare Society: c/o Flat 15, Trinity Court, Vicarage Road, Twickenham, Middlesex TW2 5TY: www.bluetree.co.uk/wdlmsociety

John Masefield Society: www.sas.ac.uk/ies/cmps/projects/masefield/society/jmsws.htm

Anne of Green Gables Society (L. M. Montgomery): Kindred Spirits Dept. W, Box 491, Avonlea, Prince Edward Island, Canada C0B 1M0: www.annesociety.org/secure/society/index.cfm

Violet Needham Society: 19 Ashburnham Place, London SE10 8TZ

Edith Nesbit Society: 21 Churchfields, West Malling, Kent, ME19 6RJ. (Tel: 0208–698–8907)

Elsie Oxenham Appreciation Society: www.bufobooks.demon.co.uk/abbeylnk.htm

Beatrix Potter Society: www.beatrixpottersociety.org.uk

Arthur Ransome Society: Abbot Hall, Kendal, Cumbria LA9 5AL, www.arthur-ransome.org/ar/tars.html

The Friars' Club ("Frank Richards"): www.friarsclub.net/

Malcolm Saville Society: The Malcolm Saville Society, 24 Larkswood Rise, St Albans AL4 9JU: www.witchend.com

Robert Louis Stevenson Club: 37 Lauder Road, Edinburgh EH9 1UE (Tel: 0131–667–6256)

Tolkien Society: www.tolkiensociety.org/

Charlotte M. Yonge Fellowship: c/o 8 Anchorage Terrace, Durham DH1 3DL: www.cmyf.org.uk

Children's book collections

Britain
A comprehensive list of British collections of children's literature can be found on the National Centre for Research in Children's Literature web site: www.ncrcl.ac.uk/clcoll.htm.

USA
American Antiquarian Society: www.americanantiquarian.org/children.htm

Baldwin Library of Historical Children's Literature at the University of Florida: http://web.uflib.ufl.edu/spec/baldwin/baldwin.html

Cotsen Children's Library Research Collection at Princeton University: http://ccl.princeton.edu/research/e2/index.html

de Grummond collection at the University of Southern Mississippi: www.lib. usm.edu/~degrum/

University of Minnesota: http://special.lib.umn.edu/clrc/

Northeast Children's Literature Collection at the University of Connecticut: http://www.lib.uconn.edu/online/research/speclib/ASC/children/index.html

University of Washington: www.lib.washington.edu/specialcoll/collections/childrens/

Other collections can be found listed at: www.lib.washington.edu/subject/Childrens/websites/further.html#special.

Canada
University of British Columbia: www.library.ubc.ca/spcoll/childlit.html

Toronto Public Library's Osborne Collection of Early Children's Books: http://collections.ic.gc.ca/osborne/index.html

Eileen Wallace Collection at the University of New Brunswick: www.lib.unb.ca/collections/clc/

Australia
Australian Children's Literature collection of the State Library of New South Wales: www.sl.nsw.gov.au/doclifensw/culture/childrenlit.cfm

Deakin University, including the Children's Literature Research Collection: www.deakin.edu.au/library/spc/spcchildlit.php

Online collections
Digital resources for primary materials include:

the CHILDE project: www.bookchilde.org/

the ECLIPSE project on Mother Goose: http://eclipse.rutgers.edu/

Project Gutenberg: www.promo.net/pg

the Hockcliffe Project: www.cta.dmu.ac.uk/projects/Hockliffe/

Appendix 3
Children's Literature Criticism: Key Texts

Charles Butler

Although there are many fine studies devoted to individual children's authors and texts, considerations of space mean that this brief list has been confined to critical texts with a more general scope, or those that have had an influence far beyond their immediate subject.

Bettelheim, Bruno. *The Uses of Enchantment: the meaning and importance of fairy tales*. London: Thames and Hudson, 1976.

Carpenter, Humphrey. *Secret Gardens: a study of the golden age of children's literature*. London: Unwin, 1985.

Chambers, Aidan. "The reader in the book." (1977.) 250–75 in *The Signal Approach to Children's Books*. Edited by Nancy Chambers. (1980.) Metuchen, NJ: Scarecrow Press, 1981.

Cook, Elizabeth. *The Ordinary and the Fabulous: an introduction to myths, legends and fairy tales for teachers and storytellers*. Cambridge: Cambridge University Press, 1969.

Coveney, Peter. *The Image of Childhood: the individual and society: a study of the theme in English literature* (Revised edition). Harmondsworth: Penguin, 1967.

Darton, F. J. Harvey. *Children's Books in England*. Third edition, revised by Brian Alderson, Cambridge: Cambridge University Press, 1982.

Dickinson, Peter. "A defence of rubbish." (1970.) 73–6 in *Writers, Critics and Children: articles from 'Children's Literature in Education'*, edited by Geoff Fox et al. New York and London: Agathon Press/Heinemann, 1976.

Egoff, Sheila, G. T. Stubbs and L. F. Ashley, eds. *Only Connect: readings on children's literature*. Toronto and New York: Oxford University Press, 1969.

Fisher, Margery. *Intent upon Reading: a critical appraisal of modern fiction for children*. (Revised edition.) Leicester: Brockhampton Press, 1964.

Hazard, Paul. *Books, Children, and Men*. 1932. Translated by Marguerite Mitchell. Boston: The Horn Book, 1944. [Originally published as *Les Livres, les enfants et les hommes*.]

Hilton, Mary, Morag Styles and Victor Watson. *Opening the Nursery Door: reading, writing and childhood, 1600–1900*. London: Routledge, 1997.

Hollindale, Peter. *Ideology and the Children's Book*. Stroud: Thimble Press, 1988.

———. *Signs of Childness in Children's Books*. Stroud: Thimble Press, 1997.

Hunt, Peter. *Criticism, Theory and Children's Literature*. Oxford: Blackwell, 1991.

———. *An Introduction to Children's Literature*. Oxford: Oxford University Press, 1994.

———. "How not to read a children's book." *Children's Literature in Education* 26.4 (1995):231–40.

Inglis, Fred. *The Promise of Happiness: value and meaning in children's fiction*. Cambridge: Cambridge University Press, 1981.

Kuznets, Lois R. *When Toys Come Alive: narratives of animation, metamorphosis, and development*. New Haven and London: Yale University Press, 1994.

Lesnik-Oberstein, Karín. *Children's Literature: criticism and the fictional child*. Oxford University Press, 1994.

Lurie, Alison. *Not in Front of the Grown-Ups: the subversive power of children's literature*. London: Bloomsbury, 1990. [US title: *Don't Tell the Grown-Ups*.]

Meek, Margaret, Griselda Barton and Aidan Warlow, eds. *The Cool Web: the pattern of children's reading*. London: Bodley Head, 1977.

McGavran, J. ed. *Romanticism and Children's Literature in the 19th Century*. Athens, GA and London: University of Georgia Press, 1991.

McGillis, Roderick. *The Nimble Reader: literary theory and children's literature*. New York: Twayne, 1996.

Moebius, William. "Introduction to picturebook codes." *Word & Image: A Journal of Verbal/Visual Enquiry* 2.2 (1986 Apr.–June):141–58.

Nikolajeva, Maria. *Children's Literature Comes of Age: toward a new aesthetic*. New York and London: Garland Publishing, 1996.

Nodelman, Perry. *Words About Pictures: the narrative art of children's picture books*. Athens, GA and London: University of Georgia Press, 1988.

———. "The Other: orientalism, colonialism, and children's literature." *Children's Literature Association Quarterly* 17 (1992):29–35.

Perrot, Jean. *Art Baroque, Art D'Enfance*. Nancy: Presses Universitaires de Nancy, 1991.

Rahn, Suzanne. *Rediscoveries in Children's Literature*. New York and London: Garland Publishing, 1995.

Rose, Jacqueline. *The Case of Peter Pan, or the impossibility of children's literature*. London: Macmillan—now Palgrave Macmillan, 1984.

Rustin, Margaret and Michael Rustin. *Narratives of Love and Loss: studies in modern children's fiction*. London: Verso, 1987.

Sale, Roger. *Fairy Tales and After: from Snow White to E. B. White*. Cambridge, MA and London: Harvard University Press, 1978.

Shavit, Zohar. *Poetics of Children's Literature*. Athens, GA: University of Georgia Press, 1986.

Smith, Lillian H. *The Unreluctant Years: a critical approach to children's literature*. Chicago: American Library Association, 1953.

Stephens, John. *Language and Ideology in Children's Fiction*. London: Longman, 1992.

Styles, Morag. *From the Garden to the Street: three hundred years of poetry for children*. London: Cassell, 1998.

Tatar, Maria. *Off with Their Heads! Fairy Tales and the Culture of Childhood*. Princeton, NJ and Oxford: Princeton University Press, 1992.

Thacker, Deborah Cogan and Jean Webb. *Introducing Children's Literature: from Romanticism to Postmodernism*. London: Routledge, 2002.

Townsend, John Rowe. *Written for Children: an outline of English children's literature*. London: Garnet Miller, 1965. [Revised editions issued in 1974, 1983,

1987, 1990 and 1995: from 1983 the book's subtitle was altered to *An outline of English-language children's literature*.]

Tucker, Nicholas. *The Child and the Book: a psychological and literary exploration*. Cambridge: Cambridge University Press, 1981.

Wall, Barbara. *The Narrator's Voice: the dilemma of children's fiction*. London: Macmillan—now Palgrave Macmillan, 1990.

Zipes, Jack. *Breaking the Magic Spell: radical theories of folk and fairy tales*. London: Heinemann, 1979.

Appendix 4
Teaching Children's Literature in Higher Education: a Select Bibliography

Charles Butler

Brown, Penny. "Teaching children's literature as a comparative literary subject in a British university." *Signal* 99 (September 2002):189–99.

Describes a course entitled "Instruction and Amusement in Early European Children's Literature," devised by the author and David Blamires, and run at the University of Manchester. The course used classic texts in English, French, German, and Italian.

Clark, Beverly Lyon. "Kiddie lit in academe." *Profession 1996*. New York: Modern Language Association, 1996:149–57.

Discusses the changing status of children's literature within the academy, drawing on the author's own experience as a graduate student and teacher.

Cochrane, Kirsty. "Children's literature in New Zealand: new initiatives in higher education." *Signal* 64 (January 1991):25–32.

Describes the creation and content of a graduate course in children's literature at the University of Waikato, Hamilton—the first such course in New Zealand. The course is "an uncompromisingly literary" one, reflecting the author's belief that children's literature has not been taken sufficiently seriously, and that its literary qualities have tended to be subordinated to other (e.g. pedagogic) ends by those who have used it higher education.

DeCandido, Graceanne A. "A particular intensity: teaching children's literature online." *The Horn Book* 78.3 (May/June 2002):293–8.

An account of two courses in children's literature taught for the Rutgers School of Communication, Information, and Library Studies using a Virtual Learning Environment (eCollege).

Denham, Debbie. "Children's literature: a reflective approach to learning." *The International Review of Children's Literature and Librarianship* 9.2 (1994):88–103.

"This article considers the importance of providing future professionals with the skills to equip them to introduce books to children in an effective way . . . [It] looks at the module on Children's Literature offered as part of the BA(Hons) Information and Literary Studies course at the University of Central England, Birmingham. It examines this experimental module, which is based on Kolb's theory of experiential learning, and analyses lessons which might be learnt from this approach based on the assessment method for the module and on students' learning outcomes."

Hollindale Peter, with Rhianon Howells and Jacqui Newby. "Re-reading the self: children's books and undergraduate readers." *Signal* 79 (January 1996):62–74.

Uses the experience of two undergraduate students of children's literature to explore the distinctive challenges of studying in this area, particularly the relationship between the remembered experience of reading as a child and the contemporary experience of reading as a critic.

Joseph, Michael. *Teaching With* The Norton Anthology of Children's Literature: *A Guide for Instructors*. New York: W. W. Norton, 2005.

The guide has two sections. The first describes a number of courses that can be taught using the *Norton Anthology*, each of which comes with a sample syllabus. The second section provides introductions to the various genres into which the *Anthology* is divided, each with a set of possible teaching questions. The guide is connected to a general web site on children's literature, and a teachers-only web site to address the needs of instructors.

Lundin, Anne H. and Carol W. Cubberley. *Teaching Children's Literature: a resource guide, with a directory of courses*. Jefferson, NC and London: McFarland, 1995.

A useful reference work including a bibliography, a comprehensive list of courses in children's literature in the USA in the early 1990s, and a number of sample syllabi.

May, Jill. "What content should be taught in children's literature?" *Children's Literature Association Quarterly* 15.1 (1991–2):275–77.

Argues that elementary education students need courses in children's literature taught as literature rather simply than as a potential tool for introducing children to language skills.

McGillis, Roderick. "Learning to read, reading to learn; or engaging in critical pedagogy." *Children's Literature Association Quarterly* 22.3 (1997):126–32.

Argues for teaching the value of critical self-awareness in reading, inculcating a practice that resists the pressure of those ideological and cultural forces that seek to "pleasure us into quiescence."

Moon, Cliff. "Three ways to foster awareness of, and interest in, children's literature with PGCE primary students" *English in Education* 24.3 (Autumn 1990):27–34.

The three methods discussed are: a) the use of precourse reading lists comprising recently-published paperbacks; b) the scheduling of a "celebration" of children's books as part of orientation week; c) weekly bookshare sessions resulting in an indexed anthology.

Neumeyer, Peter. "Children's literature in the English department." *Children's Literature Association Quarterly* 12.3 (1987):146–50.

Classifies and discusses three objectives of a course in Children's Literature within an English department: "to provide general cultural enrichments; to develop students' ability to make substantial, confident, and independent critical judgements about books (not only children's books); and to give pleasure."

Nodelman, Perry and Mavis Reimer. *The Pleasures of Children's Literature* [3rd edition]. Boston: Allyn and Bacon, 2003.

This is not primarily a book about the teaching of children's literature but a general introduction to the discipline aimed at undergraduate students. It is however included here because it is deliberately organized in such a way as to make it serve as a convenient template for a teaching course.

Paul, Lissa. "Teaching Children's Literature in Canada." *Signal* 58 (January 1989):39–50.

A wide-ranging article on the state of children's literature studies within Canadian higher education, focusing particularly on its use with and by education students.

———. *Reading Otherways*. Stroud: Thimble Press, 1998.

Uses a workshop approach to explore different texts, including *Little Women* and *Carrie's War*; encourages a multiplicity of readings and reading styles.

Sadler, Glenn E., ed. *Teaching Children's Literature: issues, pedagogy, resources* (Options for Teaching 11). New York: Modern Language Association, 1992.

One of the MLA's "Options for Teaching" series. Like Vandergrift's (see below) it combines general theoretical discussion with a description of existing courses, and also provides bibliographical and other information (such as a list of book collections) that might prove helpful to researchers in children's literature.

Sutcliffe, Mary. "Children's books in teacher education at Westminster College, Oxford." *Signal* 77 (May 1995):134–50.

Annotated journal of nine months spent teaching a variety of children's literature courses to B.Ed., students at Westminster College, where the author's colleagues were Lesley Ashforth, Stephanie Lacey, and Philip Pullman.

Vallone, Lynne. "Children's literature within and without the profession." *College Literature* 25.2 (1998):137–45.

Assesses the current state and immediate propects of children's literature and its teaching within the academy.

Vandergrift, Kay E. *Children's Literature: Theory, Research, and Teaching.* Englewood, CO: Libraries Unlimited, 1990.

An impressive book by one of the most eminent and experienced scholars in the field. She discusses the merits and limitations of a large number of different teaching approaches, and provides a detailed account of the development of a sample course, a selection of syllabi and worksheets, and a comprehensive bibliography.

For more information/resources on teaching English (both print and web-based) please go to the following link on the English Subject Centre web site: http://www.english.heacademy.ac.uk/explore/resources/teachlib/index.php.

Index